XXXII - 7 basic doctrines of Del sentimiento trágico

TREATISE ON LOVE OF GOD

HISPANISMS

Series Editor
Anne J. Cruz

MIGUEL DE UNAMUNO

Treatise on
Love of God

EDITED AND TRANSLATED
FROM THE MANUSCRIPTS
WITH TEXTUAL NOTES BY
Nelson R. Orringer

UNIVERSITY OF ILLINOIS PRESS

URBANA AND CHICAGO

This book was negotiated through Ute Körner Literary Agent,
S.L., Barcelno—www.uklitag.com.
Manufactured in the United States of America
c 5 4 3 2 1

⊗ This book is printed on acid-free paper.

Library of Congress Cataloging-in-Publication Data

Unamuno, Miguel de, 1864–1936.
    (Tratado del amor de Dios. English)
    Treatise on love of God / Miguel de Unamuno; edited and translated
from the manuscripts with textual notes by Nelson R. Orringer.
    p. cm. – (Hispanisms)
Includes bibliographical references (p.) and index.
ISBN-13: 978-0-252-03124-3 (cloth: alk. paper)
ISBN-10: 0-252-03124-5 (cloth: alk. paper)
    1. God (Christianity)—Worship and love. 2. Spirituality. I. Orringer, Nelson R.
II. Title.
BV4817.U5318 2007
231'.6—dc22   2006029223

To the translator's grandsons

Ian James Orringer and Colin Joseph Orringer:

God love them!

Contents

Acknowledgments

To Dr. Miguel de Unamuno Adárraga, I owe deep thanks for permission to publish the English version of this work. Dña. Ana Chaguaceda Toledano, Director of the Casa-Museo Unamuno, deserves my warmest gratitude for making Unamuno's personal library available to me and for taking charge of putting in my possession the clearest possible photocopies of the manuscripts bearing the *Tratado* and Unamuno's notes on the work. To Lynn Sweet, Coordinator of Interlibrary Loans at the University of Connecticut, and to Interlibrary Loan Librarian Lana Babij, I am indebted for speedily placing in my hands the precise editions I needed to consult of the books read by Unamuno. I am grateful to Dr. Willis G. Regier, Director of the University of Illinois Press, for supporting and promoting publication of this masterwork. Finally, to Professor Thomas Franz of the University of Ohio, who carefully read and critiqued my translation, I express my deepest appreciation.

—N. R. O.
Storrs, Connecticut

Translator's Introduction

Problems posed by the unpublished manuscript

Tratado del amor de Dios (Treatise on Love of God) has remained unpublished for nearly a century. Yet the stature of the author, the circumstances of its composition, and its intrinsic value should have justified its printing. The philosopher of religion, educator, novelist, and poet Miguel de Unamuno (1864–1936) is a widely read and translated author of contemporary Spain. The present translation stems from a manuscript in Unamuno's hand, written in a script as clear as possible to be read without difficulty by José Ortega y Gasset (1883–1955), significant academic philosopher in Spain of the early twentieth century.[1] The writing, composed between 1905 and 1908,[2] has the following intention, revealed by Unamuno in an unfinished, discarded introduction, whose sentence fragments convey a transparent meaning: "Treatise on love of God and not on knowledge; not on the objective existence of God, but on His subjective existence. And not a guide nor an exercise of love, but a treatise, that is, disquisition on the subjective value of God. In order to love, it is necessary to personalize."[3]

Unamuno proposes to analyze how God is found within him as a beloved and loving Person. The writing is a confession in Saint Augustine's sense,[4] while at the same time pinpointing—and defending—the form of Unamuno's religious inwardness, much as Søren Kierkegaard does his own in his works.[5] Why a new treatment of an old theme, with title, form, and content modernizing a Christian tradition of confessional, apologetic, mystic, and ascetic treatises? Since Unamuno was a classicist, occupying a Chair in Greek at the Universidad de Salamanca, Church fathers like Athanasius, Origen—even the Latin-writing Tertullian—coexist in his pages with more modern religious treatise-writers like Albrecht Ritschl, Auguste Sabatier, and Ernest Renan.[6] Unamuno was writing, apart from intimate reasons, to stimulate Ortega, then a philosopher of culture, to reflect on religion. Yet we still have to wonder why: Unamuno, then serving as rector of Spain's oldest university, was approaching the height of his creative powers; Ortega, nineteen years his junior, was a fledgling philosopher at the time, living in Madrid when not studying in Germany, without a single major publication to his credit.[7]

Correspondence between Unamuno and Ortega shows that Unamuno at one point intended to send the *Tratado* by express mail to Ortega.[8] But no record is found that it ever reached Ortega or that Unamuno even mailed it. He severely revised it, abandoning some of its ideas, modifying others, while reorganizing and incorporating the whole into a different work, his main philosophical writing, *Del sentimiento trágico de la vida en los hombres y en los pueblos* (The Tragic Sense of Life in Men and Nations). This study came out as an article series in 1911 and 1912 in the cultural review *La España Moderna*, and appeared as a full book in 1912.[9] Why, if Unamuno once felt the *Tratado* worthy of Ortega's eyes, did he leave it unpublished in his personal archives, along with notes on which it was based? Answers to all these questions lie in Unamuno's biography, between early adolescence and 1911, as well as in his notes, identifying thematic concerns and influences on his thinking.

Unamuno's Spiritual Biography from 1864 to 1897

Unamuno's copious production, overflowing the nine-volume Escelicer collection of his misnamed *Obras Completas*, tells in essays, novels, lyric poetry, dramas, and newspaper articles of his lifelong struggle to reconcile reason and religious faith. The inner conflict began in early adolescence, in his native Bilbao. The product of a Basque family, with a liberal father who died early, and a conservative, devoutly Catholic mother, Unamuno soon learned to question his faith with his reason. Even during his most pious period, as a preadolescent and a member of the Congregation of Saint Louis Gonzaga, he mistrusted the apparent overzealousness of that saint, whose mischief-making at age four was to cause him bitter remorse to the end of his days.[10] Further, as a teenager, Unamuno lost his fear of hell and with it his orthodox Catholic faith.[11] Instead, he found the possibility of falling into the nothingness after death a far more frightful prospect,[12] a dread he would carry with him to the grave.

Whether he reasoned his faith to the point of destroying it and became an atheist for a brief period, or throughout his life, has long remained a subject of controversy among critics.[13] He tended to see himself as intellectually a skeptic, while subconsciously, emotionally, a believer. Certainly his attempts to reconcile reason and faith in his significant philosophical writings up to the *Tratado* evince failure, either at the time of composition, or afterwards, when he reflected on them. Between 1880 and 1884, while studying philosophy and letters in Madrid, he abandoned traditional Catholicism forever.[14] He rejected the thought of Spanish Catholic apologists Jaime Balmes and Donoso Cortés, along with that of Zeferino González, Bishop of Cordova, whose neo-Scholastic primers of philosophy confused and embarrassed him for their obscure style.[15] Rationalizing his faith as a sixteen-year-old, amidst the welter of intellectual currents in Madrid at the end of the nineteenth century, generated his skepticism.

A chaotic panorama of intellectual currents dominated the Spanish capital at the time: the Krausism of Julián Sanz del Río[16] and the propensity to reconcile that neo-Kantian idealism with five kinds of positivisms then exported into Spain;[17] in particular, the prestigious positivism of Herbert Spencer with its consequence of agnosticism;[18] ideas for national regeneration in accordance with Krausist ideologues like Joaquín Costa;[19] higher biblical criticism practiced in neighboring France by Ernest Renan and his followers[20] and in Germany by post-Hegelian and neo-Kantian theologians;[21] political radicalism of Marxists and anarchists; and more traditional Catholic voices like those of Marcelino Menéndez Pelayo.[22]

To harmonize reason and faith, young Unamuno tried to graft the thought of German rationalist G. W. F. Hegel onto that of the English positivist Spencer.[23] Balmes had given him, as a boy, a first confused glimpse of Hegel's dialectic, with its puzzling identification of being and nothingness.[24] In all likelihood, Unamuno had carried that memory of Hegel with him from Bilbao to Madrid. The recollection revived when his faith began to waiver and he started fearing the nothingness for the first time. Enrique Rivera de Ventosa has perceived that Unamuno always translated problems of ontology into problems of anthropology, questions of being into issues about being human.[25] This may have happened upon his first direct reading of Hegel, and it may help to explain his Hegelian reading of Spencer to supply the metaphysics he missed in the British positivist.

To be specific, Unamuno learned to read German by translating Hegel's *Wissenschaft der Logik* (Science of Logic).[26] This work rests on an ontic assumption: what is immediately given is being (the thesis). But this being is undetermined.[27] Its lack of determination implies non-being (the antithesis).[28] In Hegel's dialectic or reasoning process, thesis and antithesis rise to a new level of discourse by virtue of a new principle, the synthesis. This proposition denies part of the thesis and part of the antithesis while producing a contradiction between what it saves from each of them.[29] Yet being and non-being (or nothingness) become partially identical in the higher synthesis. The synthesis receives the name of the becoming (*das Werden*) in Hegel.[30] It is a proposition which, in turn, serves as a new thesis and renews the dialectical process.[31]

Unamuno's personal copy of the *Wissenschaft der Logik* bears suggestive annotations. He has marked Hegel's admission that it is paradoxical to identify being and non-being in the higher synthesis, but that logic goes beyond the mental powers of the common individual.[32] In fact, Hegel defines the human being as thinking, and human existence itself as thinking being.[33] Unamuno responds to this opinion with the word "intellectualism." It is impossible to date these annotations neatly written inside the back cover, but undoubtedly common sense is often associated in Unamuno's mind with Herbert Spencer, who reveres such knowledge.[34] According to Rivera de Ventosa, the combination of Hegel and Spencer robs Unamuno of religious faith.[35]

How and where does this happen? The answer may lie in an incomplete "Filosofía lógica" (Philosophy of Logic), written by Unamuno in 1886, at age twenty-two. The manuscript, discovered by Armando F. Zubizarreta,[36] contains a partial reaction against Spencer. In his book *First Principles*, Spencer asserts the relativism of all subject-object relationships while stressing the importance of the individual for knowledge: "The existence of each individual as known to himself, has always been held by mankind at large, the most incontrovertible of truths."[37] Spencer adds, "The fact of personal existence . . . has been made the basis of sundry philosophies."[38] Indeed, this truth of all truths will one day resurface in the first chapter of *Del sentimiento trágico*. Meanwhile, in the "Filosofía lógica," Unamuno apparently follows Spencer in affirming the relativity of every subject-object relationship, including the mental image of God and that of the soul. These mental images are equivalent for Unamuno to mere "Ideas" in Hegel's acceptance of a form or proposition lying beyond common sense.[39] However, Unamuno interrupts his "Filosofía lógica" right at this point. The interruption signals failure in his first formal attempt to reconcile reason

(Hegel's dialectic) with faith (the Idea of God, raised by Spencer). We may derive a biographical allegory from this failure in view of Unamuno's documented propensity to personalize ontology, relating it to himself. Unamuno's thinking being, springing from a will to live (which we may call a Hegelian thesis), clashes with the annihilating force of reasoned religious doubt (conceivable as an antithesis), and the contradiction gets internalized as the crux of his existence—his *Werden*, his becoming, his maturing (synthesis), his ever-renewed attempt to harmonize faith and reason on higher levels of reflection. In Unamuno, ontology, the science of being, is made to coincide with philosophical anthropology, the science of *human* being.[40]

In maturing, Unamuno seems to have undergone the impact of Spanish Krausism, that strange mystical neo-Kantianism, once mercilessly ridiculed in the Germany of Goethe,[41] yet coming to pervade many liberal educational institutions in Spain from about 1868 to 1936.[42] This philosophy rests on the doctrine of *pan-en-theism*, teaching that everything is in God and God in everything, like an ocean surrounding and permeating a sea-creature, or like the air around and within our bodies.[43] Defining itself as pan-harmonic realism, Krausism in Spain endeavors to reconcile religious faith with the material sciences. Around 1875, the more progressive Spanish Krausists, with Francisco Giner de los Ríos in the lead,[44] temper their idealistic speculation by absorbing empirical methods from positivistic philosophers like Spencer. This trend is what Antonio Jiménez García calls "Krauso-positivism."[45] In Unamuno's personal library, many books by positivists coexist with eight volumes by the Krauso-positivist Giner de los Ríos, revered by Unamuno as a great educator in Spain.[46] Unamuno's first major book of essays, *En torno al casticismo* (On Authentic Tradition, 1895), typifies Krauso-positivism. This five-chapter work was decisively influential on the group of writers who, along with Unamuno, were poetically known in their own times as the "Generation of 1898"— "Azorín" (José Martínez Ruiz), Pío Baroja, Ángel Ganivet, Antonio Machado, Ramiro de Maeztu, Ramón del Valle-Inclán, and initially José Ortega y Gasset, among others.[47] The major speculative ideas of the book derive from the Krausist Julián Sanz del Río and from the Krauso-positivist Francisco Giner de los Ríos, while Unamuno buttresses all this speculation on scientific data drawn from the positivist Herbert Spencer.[48]

A major idea passes from here into the *Tratado del amor de Dios*, begun only a decade afterwards. This is the doctrine that each being has a double obligation to be itself and, at the same time, without losing its own identity, to be all other beings. *Panentheism*—the notion of the dwelling of God in everything and of everything in God—lies at the root of this imperative and serves as a paradigm in all spheres of life. Sanz del Río, the founder of Spanish Krausism, holds with Krause that "the most civilized European peoples aspire . . . to unity and totality, to an equal and harmonic culture."[49] In *En torno al casticismo*, probably following Giner, who favors strengthening indigenous Spanish culture while opening it to culture beyond the Pyrenees,[50] Unamuno urges delving into popular Spanish usages while Europeanizing Spain.[51] Therefore Unamuno criticizes the Castilian tradition tending toward exclusivity and divisiveness, as distinguished from provincial usages, more open to universal currents. His analysis of Spanish culture as a whole leads him to differentiate two types of mystics: a closed Castilian variety like that of Saint John of the Cross and Saint Teresa of Avila, introspective and exclusivist;[52] and a more open, cosmopolitan kind, like that of the Salamancan theologian Fray Luis de León,[53] who, like Saint Francis of Assisi, reaches out to nature to attain God.

Unamuno garners from Fray Luis's main philosophical work, *De los nombres de Cristo* (Names of Christ), an ontological principle that comes to underlie all he writes in the *Tratado del amor de Dios:* "Consiste . . . la perfección de las cosas en que cada uno de nosotros sea un mundo perfecto, para que por esta manera, estando todos en mí y yo en todos los otros, y teniendo yo su ser de todos ellos, y todos y cada uno de ellos teniendo el ser mío, se abrace y eslabone toda esta máquina del universo"[54] (The perfection of all things is that each of us strive to be a perfect world so that in this way, I being in everything and everything being in me, and I having being from all things and things having my being, we all embrace and link this whole universal mechanism).[55] In this fashion, each individual approaches God, Who contains everything in Himself. The more the entity increases, absorbing all others while remaining itself, the more it assumes the image and likeness of God. Such a likeness Fray Luis defines as the general desire (*pío absoluto*) of all things and the end of all creatural yearnings.[56]

The self-affirmation of a being as such is what Unamuno terms its individuality. Its harmonious absorption of diverse contents into itself is what Unamuno calls its personality.[57] God, the Being toward Whom all others aspire, is definable as the maximum of individuality with the maximum of personality. In Fray Luis's words, God is an infinite number of incomprehensible excellences within one perfect, simple excellence.[58] Both in Fray Luis and in the Unamuno of *En torno al casticismo*, the striving of creatures toward the Creator and the tending of the Creator toward all creatures describe the love of every being. All creatures want to be all in Him and with Him in all. This notion will become seminal in the *Tratado del amor de Dios*.

The Crisis of 1897 and the Exposure to Modernist Theology

However, between the composition of *En torno al casticismo* and the elaboration of the *Tratado*, Unamuno suffers the most traumatic experience of his life, thereafter tingeing all he writes.[59] In March of 1897, affected by the hydrocephalia of his third child, Raimundo Genaro, he undergoes a spiritual crisis,[60] dissolving all intellectual syntheses of his previous periods. Obsessed with death, fearing for his life, he dreads the nothingness more than ever.[61] He blames his turmoil, perhaps sent by God, on his excessive intellectualism.[62] He resolves (albeit in vain) to recapture his childhood innocence and Catholic faith.[63] His *Diario íntimo* (Intimate Diary), written between 1897 and 1902, displays his rejection of authors that he continues to rebuff in the *Tratado del amor de Dios*, while approving others that keep on guiding him in the *Tratado*. In both works, he writes that with his reason he previously sought a rational God that vanished as a mere Idea.[64] He failed to feel the living God, inhabiting within and revealed through charitable acts. He shuns as false Spinoza's proposition 67 from the *Ethics*, which states that a free man thinks of nothing less than of death.[65] He senses that to become free in spirit he needs to undergo a kind of servitude and await liberation from the Lord to meditate on Jesus as the source of eternal life.[66] He denies as sterile aestheticism the Homeric reverence for fame, the notion from the *Odyssey* that the gods wreak the undoing of human beings to give posterity something to sing about.[67] Now Unamuno sees a clear distinction between reason and truth.[68] Eventually, in his *Tratado*, he will prioritize moral truth over cognitive truth.[69] Reaching the despair of realizing the infinite variety of all worldly goods, as expressed by the author of *Ecclesiastes* and by Unamuno's favorite poet Giacomo Leopardi, Don Miguel glimpses the abyss yawning before him, and he affirms that while discursive reason combines, analyzes, and destroys, faith creates.[70]

The creativity of faith becomes a way of life and a leitmotif of his writing. Once resigned to the impossibility of recapturing his childhood piety, he undertakes many spiritual exercises, all of which point to his cultivation of "faith for its own sake" (*la fe por la fe misma*),[71] to employ his formula of 1900. Having learned open-mindedness and tolerance from his Krausist elders, Unamuno exposes himself to the latest developments in spiritual culture. In a word, he imbibes modernism, a cultural posture begun in mid-nineteenth-century German Protestant theology and rapidly spreading to all spheres of culture on five continents. In fact, Unamuno is to become a major religious modernist of contemporary Spain despite the opposition of the Catholic Church of those times to theological modernism in the more industrialized European countries. "That modernist rascal!"[72] traditional Spaniards used to snap about the outspoken Unamuno in his lifetime. Like his contemporary, the vitalist philosopher Henri Bergson in neighboring France, the owlish Unamuno cut a unique figure, dressing like a Protestant pastor with tieless, buttoned white collars under a dark suit.[73]

A working definition of modernism can orient us to the kind of modernism practiced by Unamuno and his main influences with regard to religious faith. Guided, in the main, by Lawrence B. Gamache,[74] we may tentatively define modernism with the following characteristics, compatible with the conception held by the *modernistes* of Barcelona, the first to define themselves as modernists on the Iberian Peninsula and well-known to Unamuno:[75] it is (1) an attitude towards cultural creativity in all major spheres of culture, including religion, theology, philosophy, science, medicine, fine arts, literature, and architecture; (2) that attitude is grounded on an attraction to novelty at the moment, usually "urban and technical" instead of "rural and agricultural";[76] (3) without making a full-scale rejection of tradition in the various cultural fields, modernism places revered ideas and beliefs at the service of innovation as such; (4) this revisionist attitude towards tradition can trace its roots to the crisis in cognition and faith occurring around 1860, when Charles Darwin, Thomas Henry Huxley, Herbert Spencer,[77] and other positivist scientists and philosophers challenged Judeo-Christian beliefs on the origin and end of humankind; (5) as a consequence of cognitive and religious crisis, aided as well by mid-nineteenth-century economic troubles, there arises, on the one hand, a tendency to liberalize religion, starting with German and French Protestantism and continuing to Judaism, Catholicism, Islam, and other major faiths around the globe; and, on the other hand, there comes about an accelerating instability in the mathematical, material, and human sciences; (6) with traditional piety questionable, a new religious zeal begins to attach to creative effort as such, whatever the vocation or field of cultural endeavor.

Unamuno discovers this enthusiasm in the German and French liberal Protestants he avidly starts reading at the turn of the twentieth century. A letter dated December 27, 1899 and written by Unamuno to the Krausist Giner de los Ríos reflects the contagion of modernist fervor: "I am going to immerse myself for some time in German religious philosophy, in the students of Bruno Bauer, Schleiermacher, Harnack, Ritschl, etc.; it is a world full of never exhausted visions. In it one comes up against Krause at every turn."[78] It is doubtful that the obscure, pietistic Krause made any kind of appearance in anti-mystical Ritschlianism. Yet no one can question both in Krause and Ritschl the desire to reconcile faith and scientific research, tolerance of world religions, and the impassioned devotion to theological exploration for its own sake. Ritschlians decry dogma and celebrate faith insofar as it is a sentiment of intimate rapprochement with God. Like thinking appears in liberal Francophone Calvinists like Auguste and Paul Sabatier, Alexandre-Rodolphe Vinet, and Paul Stapfer,[79] all read by Unamuno at the same time as he read the German theologians.[80]

When doctrines lose credibility, amicable dissensions arise. Ritschl's students, for all their praise of their teacher, delight in challenging him and one another. Unamuno too joins the fray from afar. He accepts the Ritschlian assessment of Church history, yet balks where Ritschlians strike out against popular Catholic piety for what they see as its excessive irrationalism, otherworldliness, and mysticism. Unamuno boldly embraces the Ritschlian vision of that Catholicism as his own because it coincides with his own personal religious feelings, and he models his mature philosophy after it.[81] His most universal and elaborated philosophical work, *Del sentimiento trágico de la vida*, constitutes a more or less systematic sketch of an original form of Catholic Ritschlianism.[82] His religious essays represent milestones on the way to that exposition. One of these essayistic works is the *Tratado del amor de Dios*. Deep understanding of it requires examination of three of Unamuno's early essays on religious faith, published between 1897 and 1900, and his commentary on Cervantes's greatest fiction in the 1905 *Vida de Don Quijote y Sancho* (*Life of Our Lord Don Quixote*) as exemplifying religious modernism.

THREE ESSAYS ON FAITH (1897–1900)

The three essays on faith, "¡Pistis y no gnosis!" (Pistis and not Gnosis!, 1897), "La fe" (Faith, 1900), and "¡Adentro!" (Inside!, 1900), reflect a modernist's sensitivity, displaying faith in creativity. The first two writings spring from the same contrast, found in Church historian Adolf von Harnack, between faith, creative in essence, and stagnant dogmatic knowledge.[83] For Unamuno, faith, or what the New Testament calls πίστις, denotes confidence in the person of Jesus, hope in the next coming of the Kingdom of God, and freedom from dogma. Such faith vitalized the first Christian communities shortly after the life of Christ. On the other hand, γνῶσις signifies knowledge, adherence of the intellect to dogma, not faith properly speaking, in Unamuno's opinion.[84] Over time, dogma arose with the impact of Greco-Roman culture on Christian faith.[85] In becoming dogmatic, Christianity, for Unamuno and the Ritschlians, undergoes falsification, degenerating into revealed metaphysics. Whereas faith, they hold, is creative, flexible, sincere, and tolerant, dogma is rigid, insincere, and divisive. To employ Unamuno's image,[86] a crust forms over the burning volcanic mass of faith and separates it from the outside. Beyond Spain, Unamuno glimpses groups of religious youths organizing, comparable to the primitive Christian communities for their πίστις, their confidence in Christ and his second coming. In Spain, he discerns merely γνῶσις, formulaic credos.

Spanish youth, he thinks, finds itself falsified by not facing the future, but by being enslaved to the past.[87] To remedy this falsification, Unamuno recommends sincerity, tolerance, and mercy: sincerity in telling the truth always, giving air and life to the individual spirit; tolerance to understand the relativity of every doctrine or γνῶσις, to allow free development of individual religious sentiments, and to promote a unity of faith with a rich variety of beliefs; and mercy or compassion towards the sinner, the delinquent, and the criminal.[88] The truly faithful, wrote the Ritschlian Wilhelm Hermann, harbor thoughts of "faith in faith itself" (*Glaube in dem Glauben selbst*), a kind of confidence in the power of believing, an assuredness that brings about the inner revelation of God and thereby gives origin and certainty to religious faith.[89] For Unamuno, faith in faith itself ("fe en la fe misma") amounts to trust in the power of confidence in divinity.[90]

Faith also implies introspection and a lofty way of existence, focused on the universe as a whole. In the essay "¡Adentro!" Unamuno responds to a letter from an unnamed depressed correspondent, whose depression he attempts to convert into hope for the future. He draws a lesson from an unnamed writer, the Spanish ascetic Fray Juan de los Ángeles, whom he will misquote in one of the two epigraphs of the *Tratado*: "No seas, y podrás más que todo lo que es" (Cease to be, and you will have more power than everything that is). In "¡Adentro!" Unamuno writes that his friend's despondency is merely a sign of his awareness of his own radical nothingness ("la propia nada radical"), a humility from which it is possible to gain new strength to tend to be everything ("para tender a serlo todo").[91]

Trusting in the return of the usual high aspirations of the individual whom he addresses, he finds such ambitions lacking in Spain, where spiritual greed prevails. Praise of ambitiousness and criticism of greed are to reappear in the same terms in the *Tratado*.[92] In "¡Adentro!" Unamuno cites the parable of the buried talent (*Matthew* 25:14–29): Spaniards resemble the fearful servant, who thinks that his master wishes to reap where he never sowed, and hence buries the single talent given him by his master for safekeeping instead of earning more with it as two other servants did. The master, displeased with the fearful servant for not having invested the single talent, gives it instead to the servant who has earned most. Although this parable counsels vigilance and diligence in the proper use of all God's gifts, Unamuno reinvents the narrative as a warning against small-minded greed that smothers lofty ambition. Refashioning the Spanish adage that a bird in the hand is worth one hundred in flight, Unamuno thinks it better to sprout wings to pursue the one hundred birds in flight than to remain on the ground with a single bird in the hand.[93] Since Unamuno's correspondent is a writer, he advises aiming for a universal public, not one comprised merely of Spaniards. Unquestionably Unamuno strives for such universality in "¡Adentro!" and in the *Tratado*.

In the 1900 essay, he tells his friend that, to become universal, he should leave Madrid and go off to the country, where he can converse with the "congregation of all things."[94] In the *Tratado*, Unamuno, like Henry David Thoreau at Walden Pond, confesses that in the open air, nature, like a vast society, lovingly communicates with him.[95] In his relationship with society at large, Unamuno's writer friend should aim to stay himself while at the same time endeavoring to be everyone else. Unamuno writes, "Aspire to receive everything from society without chaining yourself to it, and give yourself entirely to it."[96] Not in the progress of ideas, but in the growth of souls should effort be invested. Therefore, Unamuno recommends avoiding exclusivist dogmatism while espousing all ideas as a form of creative iconoclasm.[97] Reality, ever flexible, does not fit into dogmas.

In general, Unamuno needs flexibility for his faith to grow. In the *Tratado* and later again in *Del sentimiento trágico*, he will confess, "My idea of God is different every time I conceive Him."[98] Unamuno's faith varies over the years. After the stage of Hegelian positivism, followed by Krauso-positivism, the spiritual crisis of 1897 caused him to waver between orthodox Catholicism and Liberal Protestantism. He admittedly converted to Liberal Protestantism in 1901,[99] precisely the period of "La fe" and "¡Adentro!" Finally, in 1904, he reaches intellectual maturity with a compromise between Catholicism and Liberal Protestantism, which can be called a form of Catholic Ritschlianism. Ritschl and his student Harnack criticized Catholicism for failing (unlike Protestantism, they thought), to give believers certainty in salvation through forgiveness of sin. Harnack took pains to show that popular Catholic piety fosters such uncertainty and even encourages mysticism,[100] mistrusted by Ritschlians for threatening the individual personality with dissolution in deity. In a Spain that he found religiously indifferent when not slavishly credulous, Unamuno discovered that Harnack's description of Catholicism matched his own personal religion with its uncertainty and mystical leanings.[101] He resolved to interpret his own heterodoxy as popular Catholic piety, and to preach it to Spaniards as their own subconscious form of religious devotion, with the hope of rousing them from their spiritual slumber. He would also export it in his publications to other nations as something worthy of emulation. In doing all this, he conducted himself as a modernist. For he placed religious tradition at the service of his creativity; affected by the world crises of knowledge and of faith, he criticized scientific reason, scientism, and religious dogma of all kinds not specifically promoting the eternal life of the believer; and with religious fervor, he embraced his vocation of preaching an insecure but creative belief in immortality.

VIDA DE DON QUIJOTE Y SANCHO (1905)
AND PAUL STAPFER

Such an attitude appears in *Vida de Don Quijote y Sancho* (1905). A significant presence in this work, and shortly thereafter in the *Tratado del amor de Dios*, is Paul Stapfer (1840–1917), a historian of universal literature and a philosopher of religion from Paris, who occupied a Chair of French Letters in Grenoble and in Bordeaux.[102] His book *Des Réputations littéraires* (*About Literary Reputations*, 1893) received readings and re-readings by Unamuno because in it he found a kindred soul. The work seemed to Unamuno to describe a sickness from which he himself also was suffering—"Herostratism," an obsession with immortality in an age no longer believing in the traditional vision of life after death.[103] However, Stapfer also contributed more positive doctrines to Unamuno's philosophy of religion, helping to generate the *Vida de Don Quijote y Sancho*.

All literatures, Stapfer maintains,[104] begin with their "Bibles," books par excellence, sacred sources of all the arts. Every interpreter adds something personal to the immortal works under the stimulus of their contradictions. What is more, Stapfer distinguishes the fame of an author from that of his or her work, and he cites cases in which the work is remembered and the author forgotten.[105] Hence, Unamuno holds that *Don Quixote* should be the "national Bible of the patriotic religion of Spain";[106] and he feels free to offer a personal interpretation of the novel, praising the character Don Quixote at the expense of the author Cervantes. After all, Unamuno recognizes the superiority of some authors to their works as well as the superiority of some works to their authors.[107] For this reason, Unamuno regards the national religion of Spain as faith in immortality, not based on dogmas or on juridical precepts; and the novel of *Don Quixote* is the Gospel of that religion, recounting the passion of its Christ-like hero.[108] Unamuno rewrites Cervantes's classic chapter by chapter, making the zeal for glory and renown the essence of quixotism.[109] In the apotheosis of the knight from La Mancha, we glimpse Unamuno's attempt, already seen in his essay "¡Adentro!," to inspire his countrymen to universal spiritual deeds. Don Quixote's beloved Dulcinea symbolizes for Unamuno the glory to which the knight aspires.[110] Love of Dulcinea, or faith in the ideal of glory, like every form of religious faith known to Unamuno, costs effort to maintain.[111] Whatever is meant by glory—and both Stapfer and Unamuno understand by that word a variety of forms, including literary renown, fame in the plastic arts as artist or as model, scientific prestige, "Herostratism," and Christian salvation—Unamuno prefers an eternal approach, never an arrival at Supreme Bliss, lest the individual soul find itself absorbed in, or annihilated by, the divine Object of its striving.[112] This dynamic view of life after death returns in the *Tratado del amor de Dios*,[113] which we analyze forthwith.

Tratado del amor de Dios

EARLY HISTORY OF THE WORK

In May 1905, shortly after finishing and sending his *Vida de Don Quijote y Sancho* for publication, he begins writing his treatise. In a letter of January 1906 to A. V. González, he informs that he is working on "a work, perhaps mystical, on a religious conception, on a *Tratado del amor de Dios*, in which I started from the inanity—from the logical standpoint—of the proofs of God's existence and sought the solution through another route. And while meditating on love for God, which is compassion for God, for the universal Consciousness, while envisioning It imprisoned in matter, . . . I gradually felt overcome by the enormous affliction of existing in time, by the sadness of having consciousness."[114]

Nevertheless, six years afterwards, having undergone many spiritual vicissitudes, Unamuno reveals in other correspondence that the *Tratado del amor de Dios* is about to appear in fall of 1911 with the title *Del sentimiento trágico de la vida*.[115] Since he identifies the two writings, he invites us to see them as a single work. Yet comparison proves their difference and the self-sufficiency of each, even though many paragraphs of the treatise have become embedded in the text of the later writing, while other notions have undergone change. To account for the shifts, we need to take into account Unamuno's vacillating relations with Ortega y Gasset from 1905 to 1911, at a time of national defeatism.

At this point in its history, Unamuno's homeland was still smarting from humiliating defeat in the Spanish-American War of 1898, for Spain had acquired painful consciousness of being a cultural backwater of Europe. High illiteracy, coupled with a tiny intelligentsia in relation to the general population,[116] explained that Spanish thinkers knew one another well; their voices resonated in the national Press with an echo louder than is the case in nations with greater intellectual resources. Unamuno was the most eminent administrative official at the Universidad de Salamanca, and Ortega was the scion of two powerful families highly placed in journalism.[117] Unamuno, who early recognized Ortega's intellectual gifts, offered him what Victor Ouimette calls "spiritual leadership," which he accepted until 1909.[118] Just as Unamuno had given the young Ortega's name much-desired publicity in an article of 1904,[119] so Ortega helped members of the Generation of 1898 older than he to receive national recognition,[120] and often urged Unamuno to contribute articles to his own journals. Ortega shared Unamuno's concern with Spain's decadence.[121] He won a prestigious national post-doctoral fellowship to explore philosophical criticism in Germany in 1906.[122] By mail Unamuno asked him to send him books from Germany on philosophy and theology,[123] for Ortega began studying culture-philosophy in Berlin and in Marburg-an-Lahn.[124]

These facts would account for the tone of the letters between them concerning the *Tratado del amor de Dios*. The correspondence still preserved contains only four explicit references to the *Tratado*, dispersed throughout four letters written between May 1906 and May 1908. But in lost letters the work must also have received mention. In a letter of May 17, 1906, Unamuno writes to Ortega, "Now, besides my *Tratado del amor de Dios*, I am making verses."[125] In all likelihood, Unamuno had mentioned his painstakingly written treatise before in greater detail in a letter that has gone astray, or he would not have been so elliptical here. Nor would he have written to Ortega on December 2, 1906, with no further justification at all, "If you wish I will send you, certified, the manuscript of my *Tratado del amor de Dios*. You read it and you return it to me."[126] To such an offer Ortega responds in a letter dated December 30, 1906: "I hardly need to tell you that I would be very happy to have you send me the manuscript of your *Tratado*."[127] But the twenty-three-year-old thinker does not measure his words. In the same letter the self-possessed, sardonic Ortega jokes to the Rector of Salamanca, about whom rumors are circulating of his search for a high academic position in Madrid:[128] "Why don't you devote yourself more fully to Philosophy of Religion and we'll invent a new academic chair in your honor in Madrid at highest pay? I think that what you need, dear Don Miguel, is self-control, a mute for your guitar, a little hair-shirt; otherwise, we plunge head first into mysticism as if possessed by the devil, and through that fact alone we set ourselves outside Europe, flower of the universe."[129] Quite likely Unamuno interpreted this statement as a none-too-subtle expression of reluctance on Ortega's part to read his treatise.

In a letter dated January 3, 1907, only four days after the previous one, with no evidence of an intervening mailing from Unamuno, Ortega writes to him, "When will you be persuaded, my dearest Don Miguel, that what you are doing should be done by your students? When will you be persuaded that your mission consists of doing what your students cannot? And that only by doing what you should, can you *have* students one day?"[130] Unamuno does not respond to these reproaches. Twenty-four days later, Ortega writes to Unamuno, "My dear Don Miguel: I am very thirsty for a letter from you which is late in coming and which can enable me to enjoy the pleasant companionship of your soul."[131] The references to the treatise disappear, shunted aside by Ortega's request for Unamuno's collaboration in his new weekly journal, *El Faro* (The Beacon). The final allusion to the treatise emerging from Unamuno's pen appears in his letter to Ortega dated May 14, 1908. Here Unamuno refuses to go to Madrid from Salamanca: "No, I have more to do. I have gone back to my beloved *Tratado del amor de Dios*. I am redoing it, and I already have someone who has promised to translate it to Italian, which is how it will come out. The concept of immortality is a more lasting thing than any law for or against terrorism" (a theme on which it had been falsely assumed that Unamuno possessed information).[132]

THE SUBSTANCE OF THE *Tratado*

What would Ortega have read had he shown the patience to study and savor the *Tratado del amor de Dios*? He would have leafed through a ninety-two-page handwritten manuscript with occasional marginal notes, insertions of words or phrases, a list of endnotes containing additional paragraphs to be introduced into the body of the text, and some allusions to philosophical, theological, and literary sources with page numbers. Throughout the essay, Unamuno poses a series of questions on religious love, passing from the universal to the concrete and offering tentative solutions. First, the essayistic voice identifies itself as a previously disoriented soul and explains the causes. According to the first chapter of the work, the possibility exists of reaching God either through love or through knowledge. The essayist had chosen the second alternative, use of the head, while neglecting the heart, which hardened and turned his soul away from God.[133] Also, the route to God through intelligence led to an impasse. Relying on Ritschl,[134] Unamuno argues that the traditional proofs of God's existence, showing Him worthy of love, are rationally flawed. Needing guidance toward God, the essayist's soul now chooses the pathway through the heart.

The second chapter of the essay broaches the question, what is love? Grasping the essence of love in general will give knowledge of the love needed to reach God. Philosophers, mystics, and ascetic Catholic writers agree that love is the drive to undergo a virtual death within the self so as to be resurrected in the beloved.[135] Unamuno's basic philosophical intuition, derived from the Krausists and Fray Luis de León, resounds once more: the soul strives to persist in its own being while at the same time endeavoring to be the Other. A gamut of diverse forms of love unfolds, each one repeating the same pattern of self-love spilling over into love of another while conserving the self. At the base of every form of love lies sexual love, as Unamuno has learned from Schopenhauer;[136] but sympathy for the beloved can spiritualize love, thereby authenticating it. Self-love yields self-pity, which, when deep enough, originates compassion for one's neighbors, for the world as a whole, and eventually for the Consciousness of the world—God.[137]

However, Unamuno's essay deals not only with love for God, but also with God's love for the soul. Augustine knew that the more he sought God, the more God would come out to find him.[138] The mutual finding arises through faith, which the modernist Unamuno esteems as the creative faculty in the human being. The third chapter of the treatise concerns the progressive revelation of God within the soul: the worshipper creates Him within through faith, while God creates Himself within the worshipper continually through love. In the *Tratado*, Unamuno reveals for the first time that from German philosopher and sociologist Georg Simmel he has derived his major notion that to believe in God means wanting Him to exist.[139] In explaining *how* to believe, the essayist voices a fear that a rationalistic reader—undoubtedly Ortega—will proffer an ironic smile. In Ritschl, however, Unamuno has found a conception of personal Providence to confirm his own belief that God is watching over him;[140] and in the American pragmatist William James, he has read of the experiences of other believers that have felt the same way, with God to guide them out of their perplexity.[141]

Faced with the dilemma about whether a God created by faith really exists in truth, Unamuno focuses on Pontius Pilate's question, what is truth? In the fourth chapter of the essay, he maintains that knowledge stems from the need for self-preservation, as Schopenhauer and the British philosopher-politician Arthur James Balfour hold.[142] But love comes from the need for self-perpetuation. The instinct of self-preservation grounds the individual; the instinct of self-perpetuation, society. Society provides the individual with senses that would otherwise be lacking for survival, as Unamuno has learned from Simmel.[143] The same author has taught him that God is also a product of society![144] Unamuno, guided by Auguste Sabatier,[145] concludes that God is by definition the Being to Whom all pray, the Being resulting from the fusion of all religious imaginings, no matter how crude, no matter how sophisticated. Yet certain fantasies of God acquire preeminence in Unamuno's mind over others. The one preferred by him is William James's conception of God as Producer of immortality.[146] Faced with a reader as formidable as the young Ortega, Unamuno identifies with the apostle Paul, preaching the Resurrection before the refined Athenians, who can tolerate any doctrine but that one.[147] The treatise acquires the somber tones of a *memento mori* as the essayistic voice, imagining death, pleas for immortality. The complex section on truth not surprisingly ends on a note of uncertainty.

In chapter 5 of his treatise, Unamuno explores the mystery of mortality. Led by Stapfer, whose essay on the varieties of glory had contributed much to *Vida de Don Quijote y Sancho*, the essayist links figures as varied as Dante, Boccaccio, and the young Saint Francis of Assisi, all desiring eternal fame as a substitute for immortality.[148] Unamuno picks up where he left off in the 1900 essay "¡Adentro!," with its defense of high-minded pride and its attack on spiritual greed. But he adds something new: the longest direct quote in the treatise, one stemming from Rousseau's *Émile*.[149] It seems to be aimed at the novice in philosophy, Ortega. Rousseau criticizes philosophers' thirst for glory, eclipsing even their will for truth, as they eye rival philosophers. Yet Unamuno only half-veils his own confession of envy of other great writers who, by occupying a place in the Olympus of fame, rob space from luminaries that follow them in history. Unamuno's personal notes to his treatise reveal that he appears to have resented Shakespeare![150]

Besides contributing to Unamuno's treatise thoughts on how to achieve immortality in life, Stapfer provides a doctrine that stands out among the others: the vision of beauty as the essence, the element of eternity, possessed by every being.[151] The essayist Unamuno inquires into his own beauty, and arrives at an answer: that part of his biography which, captured in his works, will live forever.[152] The eternal part of things awakens our love for them. The path to the beautiful, though, begins with compassion for the beloved qua non-beautiful, suffering for his or her imperfections. This fellow-feeling grounds charity; and charity has for its ultimate object God, the infinite Sufferer.

In chapter 6 of the treatise, Unamuno defines charity as the impulse to free all beings, the ego and God included, from pain. To clarify charity, he exposes in depth the rôle of pain in the universe. In this undertaking, he is largely aided by Auguste Sabatier,[153] who conceives pain as consciousness-raising from birth to death; by Schopenhauer, who senses suffering in all beings, animal, vegetable, and mineral;[154] and by Fray Tomé de Jesus, who regards God as a suffering Self-Giver, motivated by supreme love.[155] That Portuguese priest has contributed to Unamuno's thought an invasive morality, a vision of Christ cramming into a few years as much tribulation as possible, helping others whether they wished aid or no.[156] This style of daily living enables each of us to remain ourselves and at the same time to identify with all others in the world.

While the fifth and sixth chapters of the treatise deal with kinds of immortality in this life, the seventh addresses the problem of the Afterlife. This chapter is only one of three to which Unamuno has given a title—the others are the eighth and ninth. He may owe the title of chapter 7, "Life in God," to the German historian of religion Otto Pfleiderer.[157] In all expressions of worshippers symbolically and mystically living in Christ, or experiencing Christ's or God's spirit dwelling within, Pfleiderer detects the supernatural condition of the redeemed human being, bonded to God, in much the same way pagans in orgiastic cults felt themselves being-in-God or filled with God. But the idea of mysticism as a foretaste of eternal life arouses in Unamuno Ritschl's concern that mystics lose their own personalities in divinity. Will such loss take place after death? Both the prospect of annihilation and that of statically enduring after death terrify Unamuno. He earnestly yearns for endless growing toward God without ever arriving,[158] as he revealed in the *Vida de Don Quijote y Sancho*. However, with anguish he considers the possibility of taking the Kierkegaardian leap of faith from finite existence to infinity and losing individual personality through absorption in God. This possibility Unamuno could accept, he allows, if assured that God would benefit from his sacrifice. God would thereby have to secure His own personality and His individuality, two traits defined by Unamuno with the help of Ritschl.[159]

Certain that all religion is a foretaste of the Afterlife, Unamuno devotes the eighth chapter of his essay to the question of what precisely constitutes religion. Relying mainly on Schleiermacher's and Sabatier's conception of religion as commerce with a superior being on whom we feel dependent,[160] Unamuno delves into its origins. He synthesizes three theories: that religion originates in dependence on a greater being; that it arises out of cosmic dread; and that it emerges from the cult of the dead: all point to the need to save human consciousness. Hence Unamuno rejects materialistic, scientific attitudes of all kinds towards religion, because he glimpses in antireligious scientism a new form of paganism, combating religion on its own turf.[161]

Scholastic philosophy, he finds, has scientific pretensions yet lacks the disinterestedness of pure science; while ethics, the science of doing good works, can never serve as a substitute for religion. Immortality cannot be awarded or denied on the basis of good or bad deeds; with Ritschl, Unamuno argues that religion is not a penal code.[162] Instead, he believes with Paul Stapfer in facultative immortality: whoever yearns for immortality, and acts accordingly, receives it, while whoever resigns himself to annihilation is nullified.[163] What, then, in the final analysis is religion? Like Kierkegaard, Unamuno finds it false to try to understand it without feeling it in a concrete form—for both, Christianity.

The final chapter of the *Tratado del amor de Dios* takes up the question of the essence of Christianity. Kierkegaard and Harnack are everywhere in evidence in the intense but unfinished ninth chapter: Kierkegaard, in stressing the concrete inwardness of Christian faith, and Harnack, in supplying data about Saint Athanasius, for whom God became human so that human beings could become gods. Favoring consciousness-raising about religion, Unamuno finds it necessary with Kierkegaard to form some idea about what Christianity is. Christianity worships the concrete human being, not abstract humanness the way paganism did. The concrete human seeks pain and suffers; an abstract idea of humankind does not.[164] To aggrandize the suffering individual insofar as he or she is human, Unamuno accepts Saint Athanasius's idea that God the Father and Christ the Son share the same substance. Therefore, the same deity that died on the cross created the universe.[165] Unamuno affirms the superiority in Christianity of eschatology, concern with the Afterlife, to ethics, the science of right conduct.[166] His treatise abruptly but suggestively closes with the example of a concrete believer in Christ's immortality: Saint Paul, unable to know Jesus in his lifetime, yet compensating by giving birth to Christian theology.[167]

In conclusion, Unamuno's treatise moves from the universal to the concrete. From the problem of selecting love or knowledge to reach God, it settles on love; defines love in general; passes to love of the human being for self, others, the world, and God; grounds human faith on God's love; reaches a comprehensive idea of God through the varieties of human beliefs; chooses among all others that of God as loving Producer of immortality; explores forms of immortality in this life and possible forms in the next; examines religions as prefigurements of the Afterlife; and finally settles on Christianity as the religion lovingly immortalizing human concreteness.

BIRTH OF *Del sentimiento trágico:*
IMPACT OF ORTEGA AND PIUS X

Many ideas pass from the *Tratado del amor de Dios* into *Del sentimiento trágico*, but the thoroughness of the editing negates Unamuno's identification of the two made in his correspondence. The discrepancy in length offers an initial idea of the difference: the *Tratado* consists of nine brief thematic divisions; *Del sentimiento trágico*, of twelve lengthy chapters. Unamuno is striving in the longer work to display rigorous scholarship. From this book he has withheld passages of an intimate nature embellishing the earlier book—and paragraphs of apocalyptic preaching, advocating adherence to his personal Christianity.[168] Whatever intimacies filter into the newer work don disguises—sometimes the use of the third-person singular or else first-person plural rather than the first singular.[169] Unamuno adds many new authorities and cites them more meticulously in the second treatise than he did in the first, as if to ward off possible criticisms of representing ideas of others as his own.[170] Perhaps to emulate his admired William James, he includes in *Del sentimiento trágico* nearly page-long quotes, never to be found in his other essayistic works.[171] He tones down his vision of faith as religious sentiment as opposed to knowledge, and now admits the need for doctrine, as traditional Christianity holds.[172] Most noticeably, he changes the order of ideas borrowed from the *Tratado* and re-employed for *Del sentimiento trágico*. The *Tratado* focuses with ever-greater concreteness on the faith of the individual Christian believer. However, *Del sentimiento trágico* displays an attempt to systematize a philosophy of religion with universal pretensions.

To clarify how much of the *Tratado* reappears in *Del sentimiento* and where, I list Unamuno's manuscript page numbers in the *Tratado* (denoted in the translation by numbers in square brackets), preceded by my chapter numbers, and across from those pages the corresponding chapter numbers and pagination of *Del sentimiento trágico* from the Escelicer edition of the *Obras Completas*, volume 7. The following list does not mention the frequent changes that Unamuno introduces into the passages borrowed from the earlier work, nor omissions:

Passages from *Tratado* manuscript	Equivalent passages from *Del sentimiento trágico*
Ch. 1, pages 2–5	Ch. 8, pages 204–5, 208–9
Ch. 2, pages 5–14	Ch. 7, pages 187–94, 196–98
Ch. 3, pages 14–20	Ch. 9, pages 219, 222–25
Ch. 4, pages 22–27	Ch. 2, pages 122–25
pages 28–30	Ch. 9, page 226 (tangential)
	Ch. 7, page 199
pages 31–32	Ch. 8, pages 214–15
pages 33–35	Ch. 9, pages 226–28
page 36	Ch. 3, page 137–38
pages 37–49	Ch. 3, pages 131–39
pages 49–51	Ch. 6, pages 179–80
page 51	Ch. 5, pages 162–63
Ch. 5, pages 52–58	Ch. 3, pages 139–43
pages 59–66	Ch. 9, pages 228–33
Ch. 6, pages 66–70	Ch. 9, pages 233–36
Ch. 7, page 78	Ch. 10, pages 238, 244
page 80	Ch. 6, page 182
page 81	Ch. 8, page 217
page 82	Ch. 10, page 243
page 83	Ch. 8, page 210
page 84	Ch. 10, page 251

Ch. 8 (thoroughly revised in *Del sentimiento*, ch. 4, 153, ch. 10, pages 237, 254)

Ch. 9 (all but abandoned except for isolated ideas in *Del sentimiento*, ch. 1, page 112; ch. 4, page 147)

(Few ideas flow from the *Tratado* into *Del sentimiento*, chapters 1, 11, and 12; *Del sentimiento*, chapters 4 and 8, are virtually independent of the *Tratado*.)

The main ideas of *Del sentimiento trágico de la vida* are reducible to the following, some only partially or not at all covered in the *Tratado:* [α.] The effort to persevere in being, to live forever, forms the point of departure of all endeavors, physical or mental, of the flesh-and-blood human being.[173] [β.] Yet discursive reason denies the perpetuation of that effort while religious faith affirms it, and the clash between the two yields the tragic sense of life.[174] [γ.] Nonetheless, faith, overcoming reason, allows access to universal Truth.[175] [δ.] This process can reveal a God consisting of Personality, Love, and Will to immortalize believers.[176] [ε.] He is inseparable from problematic faith in Him, from the questionable hope of salvation it offers, and from the suffering love on which it is grounded.[177] [ζ.] History aims toward universal salvation, the apocatastasis or restoration of all creatures to God, with all in Him and Him in all.[178] [η.] Therefore, right conduct consists of taking each day a step towards the apocatastasis, the spiritualization of matter through a morality of self-imposition on others; and if immortality does not lie ahead, daily conduct should make it an injustice to be annihilated.[179]

Now, the idea that every being strives to persevere in being stems from the *Tratado*, which sees this self-preservation as the purpose of all knowledge.[180] In *Del sentimiento trágico* (ch. 2), Unamuno calls this doctrine the point of departure of philosophy, and he in fact makes it the starting point of his philosophy of religion. He therefore displays a will to systematic thinking. The concept of the flesh and blood human being as the subject of philosophy does not come in the *Tratado*, but does bear a tangential relationship to its final chapter, accompanying Kierkegaard in viewing Christianity as the religion of the concrete, suffering human individual. The idea of the clash between reason and faith appears in both treatises; the label, the "tragic sense of life," shows up only in *Del sentimiento trágico* as a felicitous formula that occurs late to Unamuno. Both works contain the idea that the living God is attainable through faith, a dead one through reason. In both works appears the idea of God as Love, Personality, and Producer of immortality. Both writings hold the same ideas on hope and love, but the doctrines on faith, as indicated, display modifications.

In both essayistic studies, Unamuno downplays ethics as compared to religion. The *Tratado*, with its antiscientific bias, labels ethics a science and subordinates it to religion.[181] However, in *Del sentimiento trágico*, he treats this subordination in a deeper, more systematic fashion. In the *Tratado*, he has noted Origen's idea of the apocatastasis, the spiritualization and restoration of all beings to God.[182] Yet not until *Del sentimiento trágico* does Unamuno apply this doctrine to right conduct in daily living: here he maintains that individuals must impose their good behavior on their neighbors to promote the spiritualization of all beings. In the *Tratado*, the morality of mutual self-imposition has received only isolated remarks. Nor does it occur to Unamuno to adapt Luther's secularization of the concept of vocation to his own morality until writing *Del sentimiento trágico*. Here he holds that we should perform our callings so as to deserve immortality, making a daily prayer of whatever we do.[183] This inspiring idea, absent from the *Tratado*, rings true to the modernist propensity to make a religion out of cultural creativity. Finally, the notion to live in such a way as to make annihilation an injustice belongs to *Del sentimiento trágico*,[184] not to the *Tratado*.

The seven basic doctrines of *Del sentimiento trágico*, as here outlined, constitute the crux of the work; the *Tratado* has contributed five of these (though in different order and with considerable conceptual and substantive revisions), with the other two only tangential to the earlier work. Therefore, the two writings differ. Chapter 4 of *Del sentimiento trágico*, on the essence of Catholicism, reviews a great deal of Church history, with isolated ideas on Saint Athanasius and Scholasticism borrowed from the *Tratado*, though otherwise relying on much new doctrinal material. A polemic against Ortega occupies some of the penultimate chapter and much of the final one of *Del sentimiento trágico*; and, since it has to do with events unfolding after the writing of the *Tratado*, it has no bearing on its doctrinal content as philosophy of religion.

How can we account for the differences between the *Tratado* and *Del sentimiento*, so that Unamuno preferred the second and left the first unpublished? New developments took place between 1906 and 1911 in Unamuno's relationship with Ortega: they brought out in the Press their debate between philosophy of religion and philosophy of culture. This publicity evidently encouraged Unamuno to set his thoughts in order as never before.

In addition, an event occurred in the history of religion, one which Unamuno thought it necessary to address in his treatise—the declared opposition of the Vatican to modernist theology. The decree "Lamentabili" of the Holy Office, dated July 3–4, 1907, condemned sixty-five propositions attributed to modernist theologians.[185] On September 8, 1907, Pope Pius X published an encyclical, *Pascendi Dominici gregis* (Of Feeding the Lord's Flock), with the official title, *De Modernistarum doctrinis* (Concerning the Doctrines of the Modernists), attempting to synthesize, criticize, and anathematize the doctrines of modernist theologies.[186]

The antimodernism of the Vatican necessarily affected Unamuno's philosophy of religion. He had heavily relied on thinkers from liberal Protestantism whose influence on the new thinking in Catholicism was coming under fire. Unamuno therefore decided to incorporate the modernist controversy into *Del sentimiento trágico*. If the tragic sense of life, by definition, is the struggle between reason and faith, modernists newly anathematized by the Church would represent the side of reason; the anathematizing Church, the side of faith. Unamuno would seem impartial, compassionately encompassing both sides.[187] Interestingly enough, his work bears a long quote from the excommunicated modernist Alfred Loisy and praise for Loisy's ally E. Le Roy's book, *Dogme et Critique*, condemned by the Church,[188] without any quotations from the papal decree or the Encyclical. Pius X had condemned the modernist subordination of revealed faith in the form of dogma to the sentiment of faith.[189] Perhaps for this reason Unamuno softened his stance towards doctrine in *Del sentimiento trágico*. He seemingly rejected his unmitigated preference for *pistis*, faith free of dogmas. Instead, he admitted that faith "needs a [doctrinal] matter on which to be exercised."[190]

In conformity with the Encyclical, in *Del sentimiento* he underscored his preference for Christ revealed throughout history to the historical Jesus.[191] In addition, he eliminated from *Del sentimiento trágico* his definition of religion included in the *Tratado*, derived directly from Sabatier and bearing the unmistakable stamp of Schleiermacher—religion as intercourse between the individual and the superior spirit on which he feels dependent.[192] Authorities in the Vatican held that modernist theology had gotten its start with Schleiermacher, and regarded Sabatier as a radical modernist.[193] Unamuno also omitted the opinion, borrowed from Harnack, that Scholastic philosophy had deduced all its truths from a false god.[194] Given the omnipresence in both Unamuno's works of Albrecht Ritschl—deemed by the Church the father of a more "temperate modernism"[195]—there can be little question as to where Unamuno's sympathies lay. He still continued to believe in faith for its own sake, enabling him to change doctrines as the sentiment moved him from period to period and from work to work, long after the publication of *Del sentimiento*.

Another reason for the drastic revision and expansion of the *Tratado* is a brief rift with Ortega. This author, advocating, as we have seen, the Europeanization of Spain, insults Unamuno in the press with some of the reproaches visible in his earlier private correspondence with him. In a well-known article of 1909, "Unamuno y Europa, fábula" (Unamuno and Europe, a Myth), Ortega calls Unamuno an "energúmeno español" (a

Spaniard possessed by the evil spirits),[196] an epithet derived from the private letter to Unamuno dated December 30, 1906, already examined here. Ortega criticizes Unamuno for preferring the Spanish mystic Saint John of the Cross to René Descartes, father of philosophical idealism. With sarcasm, Ortega describes Saint John as "the pretty little friar with an incandescent heart, who weaves lacework of ecstatic rhetoric in his cell."[197] Ortega adds that, in reaction to Unamuno's heated defense of Spanish philology, represented by the revered Ramón Menéndez Pidal,[198] the Europeanist historian Américo Castro Quesada argued that Menéndez Pidal acquired his methodical discipline from European philologists.[199] "On this occasion," concludes Ortega, "Don Miguel de Unamuno, the Spaniard possessed by evil spirits, has fallen short of the truth. And it is not the first time we have thought whether the red, burning hue of the towers of Salamanca has come to them from the fact that those venerable stones blush when they hear what Unamuno says while walking among them in the evening."[200]

Ortega wounded Unamuno deeply as he was preparing his *Tratado* for publication. The proof lies in his notes to the *Tratado*, as well as in the final chapter of *Del sentimiento trágico*. Among those notes appears an epilogue to the *Tratado*, which Unamuno decided to omit. Yet the response to Ortega is clear: "The author of this book is not someone possessed of irrational force, of evil spirits. He well knows on what to rely. He does not lack critical faculties and is the first to recognize the flimsiness of his arguments from the rational, logical, scientific or objective viewpoint, but he *wishes* this to be so. And he especially execrates those that conform to reason."[201] If the *Tratado* is about Unamuno's religious inwardness, then it would defeat his purpose to limit himself to the use of abstract reason to the exclusion of intuition and imagination.

The humiliation suffered by Unamuno continues to affect him when he publishes the final chapter of *Del sentimiento trágico*, which is basically polemical and has little in common with the *Tratado*. That chapter 12, titled "Don Quixote in the Contemporary European Tragicomedy," compares Don Quixote to the suffering Jesus, a martyr to glory yet victim of scorn (like Unamuno himself). Complaining of Ortega's exaggerated Europeanism without mentioning him by name, Unamuno remarks that the geographical notion of Europe has changed as if by magic into "an almost metaphysical category," perhaps without sufficient knowledge of what Europe stands for. To conceive it merely as the combination of France and Germany (as Ortega presumably does) is simplistic. Having held with Ritschl that a single soul is worth more than the world, Unamuno insists on the superiority of a single soul to all philosophies: "Saint

Teresa is worth . . . any *Critique of Pure Reason.*"[202] Don Miguel gently jabs at Ortega for his sarcasm of 1909. He writes that saints have concerned themselves little with cultural progress and much, on the other hand, with the salvation of souls of individuals with whom they have lived. "What meaning, for example, in the history of human culture does our Saint John of the Cross hold, that incandescent little friar, as he has been called in a highly cultural fashion—though I do not know if in a very cultivated one—in comparison to Descartes?"[203] Let Spain therefore preach the religion of personal immortality to Europe, Unamuno affirms, even at the risk of suffering withering humiliation by European culture-lovers (like Ortega).[204]

If Ortega had contributed to *Del sentimiento trágico* merely the inspiration for its polemical finale, not strictly necessary to the work, the final version would have remained more faithful to the *Tratado del amor de Dios.* Instead, Ortega exercised as well a positive influence on Unamuno's expository style. While first-person confessions gave way to third-person generalizations about faith, what Unamuno's writing lost in intimacy, it gained in breadth. Instead of concentrating on his own intuitions of the God-relationship and of life after death, he amassed many testimonies of others, all missing from the *Tratado.* The visions of mystics from Meister Eckhart to Saint Teresa of Avila, from Jakob Boehme to Emanuel Swedenborg, imparted new richness to Unamuno's text.[205] He invented a philosophical language that Ortega himself would borrow, especially in philosophizing from 1914 onward, about the relationships between reason and life.[206] Finally, perhaps out of admiration for the systematic Ortega, he ordered his thinking into what, despite appearances, approaches a system of ideas, modeled after Ritschl's, though Catholicized in his own heterodox way.[207] For any reader who reflects on religious themes, however, the *Tratado del amor de Dios* has something somber to convey, though expressed with vigor and depth. The reading of it energizes more than does that of *Del sentimiento trágico,* which often enervates. The *Tratado* has a suppleness and directness often lacking in the longer work. Above all, it sheds light on the most fecund period of Unamuno's intellectual production.

Criteria Employed for the Preparation of the Manuscript

In the Unamuno archives, the folder bearing the *Tratado* holds three different series of documents, which I will here label A, B, and C. By far the most significant is series A, headed by the two epigraphs of Plato and Fray Juan de los Ángeles respectively that Unamuno had intended for his *Tratado*, followed by ninety-two handwritten pages, each one assigned page numbers by the author. This is the *Tratado* proper, and I include the author's page numbers in square brackets in the text. Each square bracketed number precedes the words that form the first line of the manuscript page on which Unamuno had penned them. Where Unamuno mentions names of authors of his ideas and page numbers of their works, I identify the works by title in footnotes using Mario and María Elena Valdés's *Source Book*, a list of all but a few of the books found in Unamuno's personal library at the Casa-Museo Unamuno. In addition, I try to supply in my endnotes pertinent clarifying annotations made by Unamuno of given passages in the very volumes he consulted while elaborating his *Tratado*.

The *Tratado* not only bears page numbers on each page, but also parenthesized numbers in the text itself. These numbers correspond to numbered paragraphs on a different sheaf of pages, series B, comprised of fourteen handwritten pages, each one also bearing its own page numbers. The numbered paragraphs of series B may give the appearance of being endnotes, but careful examination reveals that they are not. Instead, they contain ideas probably intended to be integrated into the main text of the *Tratado*. Not only do they invariably clarify the notions they follow in the *Tratado*, but wherever the numbered paragraphs of series B pass into published versions of *Del sentimiento trágico*, they always appear as part of the text. Obviously, Unamuno made his purpose for them clear to his editors. Therefore, I integrate them into my text of the *Tratado*. Also, I indicate with an endnote wherever a sentence in my text stems from one of the numbered paragraphs of series B. This precaution will enable future editors of the *Tratado* to correct me if I have erred by inserting those paragraphs into the work itself. A further liberty I take with the text of the *Tratado* is that of dividing it into chapters for ease of reading. Unamuno himself divided the last three segments of his treatise into chapters with the titles "Life in God," "Religion," and "Christianity." Why, then, should the other divisions of his treatise not bear clarifying titles as well? I cull my titles from questions posed in the text itself at the end of each division of subject matter, questions answered by the following textual segment that my titles head.

The third series of archived documents, which I label C, consists of a packet of twenty handwritten papers labeled "Mi confesión" (My Confession), and seems to form the beginning of a book, addressed to youth in Spain and Spanish America, on the theme of "Herostratism." This rambling essay with an unsure style, filled with pairs of synonyms from which Unamuno never selects his preference, contains some of the primitive versions of thoughts that afterwards pass to the *Tratado* and from there to *Del sentimiento*. However, the fact that Unamuno has kept series C apart from series A and B seems to indicate his reluctance to have C published along with the other two. At times, consultation of C aids in determining the correct version of Unamuno's wording in A and B; but, in general, what sparse information C contains to illumine the *Tratado* appears documented in my endnotes.

On the other hand, Unamuno has categorically indicated his desire, in the manuscript of the *Tratado*, to publish his essay "¿Qué es verdad?" (What Is Truth?) in conjunction with chapter 4 of the *Tratado*. Consequently, I translate that essay in the Appendix, placed at the end of the basic text. The essay first appeared in the journal *La España Moderna* (March 1906), pp. 5–20, and reappears in the Escelicer edition of the *Obras Completas*, vol. 3, pp. 854–64. Filled with circumstantial trivia and anticlerical bias, this writing does not form part of the *Tratado* itself, which is more elevated in tone. However, in deference to the author, I have endeavored to annotate it with the same care I tried to bring to the remainder of the *Tratado*.

Often of more use than either series C or the article "¿Qué es verdad?" is yet a fourth series of manuscripts appearing apart in the Unamuno archives. This series, which I denote D, contains scraps of notes, jottings of ideas, and names of influences, some of which disappear before reaching the manuscript of the *Tratado* (series A) or *Del sentimiento*. These jottings provide much clarification. The only difficulty they present lies in the lack of pagination. Hence in my endnotes I must refer to them by distinguishing features on the page (for instance, a title if any), together with a reference to series D.

TREATISE ON LOVE OF GOD

καὶ γὰρ ἴσως καὶ μάλιστα πρέπει μέλλοντα ἐκεῖσε ἀποδημεῖν διασκοπεῖν τε
καὶ μυθολογεῖν περὶ τῆς ἀποδημίας τῆς ἐκεῖ, ποίαν τινὰ αὐτὴν οἰόμεθα εἶναι·
—*Phaedo*

(And indeed it is perhaps especially fitting, as I am going to the
other world, to tell stories about the life there and consider what we
think about it; for what else could one do in the time between now and
sunset?—Plato, *Phaedo* 61 d-e. Tr. Harold North Fowler, 215)

"No seas, y podrás más que todo lo que es."
Fr. Juan de los Ángeles, *Diálogos de la conquista del reino de Dios.*
Diál. 3:8

(Cease to be, and you will have more power than everything that is.)
—Unamuno's modification of Fray Juan de los Ángeles, *Dialogues on
the Conquest of the Kingdom of God*, 3:8

1   Love of God and Knowledge of God

Love is one thing, and knowledge of God another; although, in reality, it may not be possible to love without knowing nor to know without loving.[1] The old aphorism that nothing can be desired without having been known beforehand should be completed by saying that it cannot be known without having been desired before, before it is known.[2] And the fact is that love and knowledge engender one another. One must love in order to know, and one must know in order to love.

And which is the better route: to begin with knowledge so as to go on to love, or to begin with love in order to go on to knowledge?[3] The first route, for what it does to God, has led human beings to the hard-headedness of despair.

The first route, the intellectual route, led me, my God, to deny You, to blaspheme You, to quash my inner anxieties in the acceptance of the "no."[4] And since You enshrouded my intelligence in shadows to separate me from You, light up my heart so that I may return to You.[5]

For many years I sought God by the logical route, and God vanished from me into the idea of Himself. With rationales and theological proofs, He veiled Himself from me behind the idea I attained of Him, and I remained without God.[6]

That idea of God is only the Aristotelian idea of a Supreme Being, Immovable Prime Mover of all that exists, a God by removal.[7] With the removal of everything human, everything finite, everything transitory from that idea of God,[8] the idea was becoming idealized to the point of losing all reality.[9]

That God of Whose existence we are given proofs and arguments is nothing more than a hypothesis, a concept [2] that we have devised to explain to ourselves the why and wherefore of existence and the essence of things: why they exist, and exist as they exist, and not any other way.[10] And that explanation explains nothing because it needs in turn to be explained. The basis of the whole sophism is this: there has to be an ultimate explanation of the universe, and that explanation has to be known by us.[11] Poor mortals say to themselves, "So it is that I do not explain to myself the Universe without God; therefore God exists. No, or afterwards I will be left without explaining the Universe."[12]

Let us first consider the existence of what exists. From our existence, and that of the Universe, we induce that a God exists, Who creates us; and therefore we say that the universe exists and that I exist because God has created it, because God exists. It is clear to see that this is a vicious circle, a dreadful circle. From the fact, necessary qua fact, that from the existence of the universe and of myself I deduce the existence of God, and from the need that God exist, I deduce my own existence and that of the Universe. But what inner necessity is there for me or for the Universe or for God to exist? Can I not conceive that there would be nothing, absolutely nothing, neither Creator nor creation? Necessity is nothing more than a mode of being. And if on the one hand we deduce the fact that a thing exists from the need for it to exist, what is certain, on the other hand, is that we have induced the need for it to exist before the fact that it exists.[13]

And if from the existence of things we pass to their essence, to their mode of being, to their being as they are and not otherwise, here too God is a hypothesis that does not sufficiently explain what is attempting to be explained with it. To say that [3] things are as they are and not otherwise because God has made them so, is to say nothing. For it is possible to ask why God has made them so. If they tell us the reason for his having made them as they are and not otherwise, that reason is enough and God superfluous; and if they do not give us that reason, God is an explanation that explains nothing, because he demands in turn to be explained.

One wonders if a thing is impossible because God does not will it, or if he does not will it because it is impossible. God has to submit to the logical law of contradiction and, according to the confession of theologians, cannot make two and two equal three or five; the law of necessity is over Him. And in the moral order, one asks if lying or murdering is bad because God has established it this way, or whether He has established it because it is bad. If the first, God is a capricious and absurd God that establishes one law when He could have established another, and if we admit the correctness of the preexisting law, God is superfluous; and if the second, if He has established it thus because it is evil in itself, there is a law over God, and God is again superfluous.[14]

Years ago, when I was little more than a boy, I read this judgment of a physiologist in a book: God is a barrier situated at the ultimate limits of human knowledge and accompanied by a great X; in the measure intelligence advances, the barrier recedes. And I wrote in the margin with a pencil, "From the barrier to here, everything is explained without Him; from the barrier to there, neither with Him nor without Him; God, as a result, is superfluous." And the idea of God is superfluous, in fact, as a rational explanation of the Universe.

Human beings understand the Universe and explain it to themselves, better or worse, by reducing it to science in their minds. They afterwards project their intelligence to the infinite and cause that science, those ideas with which they explain the Universe, to be the creators of the Universe itself. This is the idea of God. It is the mechanics producing and governing movement, it is the projected law.

We speak of order. Order is what there is, it is the way things happen. If things happened otherwise, the order would be another. The way things happen has made our way of conceiving their occurrence; and since we conceive it in accordance with the way it is, and it happens in accordance with the way we conceive it, we say there is order.[15]

On any side that God is viewed, He is [4] resolved and dissolved in a pure logical abstraction. Out of wanting to view Him everywhere, we end up by not seeing him anywhere; He evaporates.[16] "Deus propter excellentiam non immerito Nihil vocatur" [God, on account of excellence, not undeservedly is called Nothing] (Scotus Erigena).[17] The ideal construction of the logical or Aristotelian God recalls the well-worn joke about that artillery sergeant that explained to a soldier how cannons are made, and said to him that it was only necessary to grab a big hole and cover it with iron. One grasps the concept of the pure, Supreme Being, which is nothing but a logical hole, a vacuum, and one covers it over with anthropomorphic attributes that disfigure it.

And the fact is that we have searched by using reason, and by using reason, only the *idea* of God is reached, *not* God Himself.

The idea of God is a hypothesis, as is the idea of the ether. The ether is a supposed entity that only has value insofar as it explains what it tries to explain: light, whenever otherwise unexplained.[18] And thus the idea of the God is a hypothesis also, that only has value insofar as with it is explained what it is a question of explaining: the existence and essence of the Universe, whenever otherwise unexplained. And since it does not explain it, because it is a pure begging of the question, the idea of God misses the mark. But if the ether is only a hypothesis to explain light, air, on the other hand, is an immediately sensed reality, and even though sound may not be explained with it, we would have the direct sensation of the air, especially in moments of shortness of breath. And in the same way God Himself, as opposed to the idea of God, can come to be an immediately sensed reality. Even though neither the existence nor the essence of the Universe may be explained with Him, we have at times the direct sensation of God, especially in moments of affliction.

My studies and meditations on philosophy and theology were leading me little by little to the most radical phenomenalism,[19] and with my reason I came to be completely atheistic. And then, when my soul was roaming through the dreadful high and cold regions of intellectualism, I used to say that we should seek no more consolation than [5] truth, while I called reason the truth. But I was sinking little by little into intimate despair in the rational abyss, into the sense of the emptiness of everything existing, and from the very depth of misery rose the truth, consolation. For God has caused the human being not to begin to rise until finishing the descent. To begin to achieve consolation it is necessary to reach ultimate disconsolateness, supreme anguish, the awareness of our own nothingness. Only when the human being has come to the self-conception and sentiment of not existing, like the "shadow of a dream" according to Pindar's energetic phrase,[20] is the road to consolation reached. And this dreadful consolation is a consolation that springs from despair and gathers nourishment from it, a consolation that is at base despair itself struggling to acquire hope. To believe in God is, properly speaking, to want God to exist. And God does not exist but "super-exists" ("sobrexiste"), a mode of being that lies outside our grasp.[21]

How does one reach God? Through love. And what is love?

2 *What Is Love?*

Love is what is most terrible and tragic in the world. Love is the child of deceit and the parent of disenchantment;[1] love is the consolation in disconsolateness. Love furiously seeks through its object something that lies beyond it and, not finding it, despairs.[2]

Whenever we speak of love we have sexual love in mind, love between man and woman, love that perpetuates the human lineage upon earth. It is the type of love that generates all other types.[3] [6] In love we seek to perpetuate ourselves, and we perpetuate ourselves on earth only on condition that we die, that we surrender our lives to others.[4] The humblest little animals, the lowest living beings, multiply by dividing, splitting in two, ceasing to be the singles they once were. And every act of engendering is a ceasing to be what one was, a splitting, a partial death.[5] Perhaps the supreme delight of engendering is nothing but a taste of death in advance, the rending of one's own vital essence. We unite to someone else, but only to split apart; the most intimate embrace is only the most intimate rending. At base, sensual, amorous delight, the spasm of genesis, is a sensation of resurrection, of coming to life again in someone else, because only in others can we become eternal.[6]

There is, without a doubt, something tragically corrosive in the depth of love in its primitive, animal form, in the unconquerable instinct that impels a man and a woman to mix their bodies in a furious embrace. The same that unites their bodies separates their souls; when they embrace one another, they hate one another as much as they love one another,[7] and above all they struggle, they struggle for a third being still without life.[8] Love is a struggle. There are animals whose male, when united with the female, mistreats her, and there are females that devour the males as soon as the males have fertilized them.[9]

It has been said of love that it is a mutual egoism. Each of the lovers seeks to possess the other; and while seeking by means of that other, even without knowing it, their own self-perpetuation, each seeks self-gratification. Each of the animals is an instrument of immediate gratification, of mediate self-perpetuation, for the other. And thus they are tyrants and slaves—each one of them at the same time a tyrant and a slave of the other.[10]

And at base what animals perpetuate on the earth is flesh, the flesh of pain; it is [7] pain, it is death.[11] Love is child and parent of death at the same time, death its parent and child.[12] There is in the depth of love an eternal despairing. And from the depth of this despair arise hope and consolation.[13] From this love of which I am speaking, from this love of the whole body with its senses, from this falling in love, there arises spiritual, painful love.

This other form of love, this spiritual love, is born of pain, is born of the death of carnal love. The lovers do not come to love one another while giving up themselves, fusing their souls, unless they have suffered together, when the powerful hammer of sorrow has pummeled their hearts, mixing them together in the same clay mortar.[14] Sensual love mingled their bodies and separated their souls, and from that love they bore fruit, a child of the flesh. And this child, engendered in death, fell ill and died. And over the deathbed of the fruit of their carnal union and spiritual separation, with bodies separated, cold with pain, and souls mingled in sorrow, the lovers, the parents, hugged one another in despair, and right there was born spiritual love from the death of the child of the flesh. Human beings love one another with this love only when they have suffered together, when at some time they plowed the rocky ground, bound to the same yoke of a common sorrow. At that time they knew one another and felt one another in their common misery, they had compassion for one another, they loved one another. To love is to feel compassion.[15]

And this is felt more clearly and strongly even when there sprouts, takes root, and grows one of those loves that have to fight against the fearful laws of Destiny: one of those loves that are born tragically, inopportunely, before or after the moment in which the world, which is custom, would have received them. The more walls placed by Destiny and the world and its law between the lovers, the more strongly they feel impelled toward one another. And the bliss of loving one another is suffocated for them and grows within their pain of not being able to love one another, and from the roots of their hearts they feel compassion towards one another; and this common compassion which is their common misery and common happiness, kindles and at the same time nurtures their love. And they suffer and rejoice while suffering their joy and rejoicing in their suffering. And they place their love outside the world, and the strength of that poor suffering love under the yoke of Destiny causes them to intuit another world in which there is no other law than that of freedom to love, another world in which there are no barriers because in it there is no flesh. For nothing strikes us more about hope and faith than the impossibility that a love of ours may bear fruit in this world of flesh and appearances.[16]

To love is to feel compassion. And whoever feels more compassion loves more. Human beings are kindled in burning charity towards their neighbors because they reached the depths of their own misery, of their own quality of being mere appearance, of their nothingness, [8] of their non-being; and turning their eyes afterwards to their fellow creatures, they saw them as wretched, made of mere appearances, without being, and they felt compassion for them and loved them.[17]

Human beings yearn to be loved, yearn to receive compassion. Human beings want their pains and sorrows to be felt and regretted. There is something more than a trick to obtain alms in the matter of the wayside beggar's showing the traveler his sores or his gangrenous stump. The alms are not aid to endure the troubles of life; alms are compassion. The mendicant is not grateful for the alms to the one who gives them while averting the face to avoid seeing him and to remove him from the giver's presence. He tenders more gratitude if given compassion and not aid, rather than if while given aid he gets no compassion, even though he may prefer this. Observe with what satisfaction he tells his hardships to the one who becomes moved while hearing them. He wants to receive compassion; he wants to be loved.[18]

Woman's love especially is always, at base, compassion. Every woman's love is by essence motherly love, compassionate love.[19] A woman surrenders to her lover because she feels him suffering. Isabel pitied Lorenzo, Juliet Romeo, Desdemona Othello, Francesca Paolo.[20] Woman seems to say, "Come here, poor little thing, and do not suffer so much for my cause!" And therefore her love is more amorous and purer than the man's, and braver and longer.

Compassion is the essence of conscious love, of human love in the proper sense, not mere animal love. Love is compassionate, and even more so the more it loves.

I said that it is necessary to love in order to know, and this means, that to know something, it is necessary to feel compassion towards it; it is necessary, in some way or other, to suffer along with it.

When love, with the growth of this burning eagerness for the beyond and for the within,[21] goes on extending to everything it sees, it continues feeling compassion for everything. In the measure you enter and go deeper into yourself, you are discovering your own emptiness, the fact that you are not everything that you are, [9] that you are not what you would like to be, that you are nothing at all.[22] And when touching your own nothingness, when feeling you have no permanent base, when failing to arrive either at your own infinity or at your own eternity, you give compassion with all your heart to yourself; and you start burning with painful love of yourself, while killing what is called self-love but is only a kind of sensual delectation of yourself, a self-enjoyment of the flesh of your soul.[23]

And from this painful love of yourself, from this intimate despair because you were nothing before birth and will be nothing after death,[24] from this compassion, you come to feel sympathy, to love, all your fellow creatures, wretched shadows that march from the nothingness to the nothingness, sparks of consciousness that shine an instant in the infinite, eternal darkness.[25] And from the other human beings, your fellow creatures, passing amidst those who are most like you, amidst your brothers and sisters, you go on to feel compassion for all poor living beings and even beings that do not live, to all that exists. That faraway star, shining there above during the night, will one day be snuffed out and will become dust and will stop shining and existing. And like it, the entire starry sky. Poor sky![26]

And while it is painful to have to cease to be one day, perhaps it would be even more painful to continue always being oneself and nothing more than oneself, without being able to be someone else at the same time, without being able to be at the same time all other beings, without being able to be everything.[27]

When someone expresses the wish to be someone else, I always answer that that is something absurd. To wish to be someone else is to wish to cease being oneself; and since the other already has being and is not the creation of someone ceasing to be, that wish for otherness is nothing more than a wish for ceasing to be.[28] What is desired is to be someone else and at the same time [10] oneself, to receive another's consciousness into one's own. One does not wish to be another, but to have something that that other has, or to represent something represented by that other. And the human being is consumed by the yearning to have everything that others have and to represent all that the rest do. This would be to suffer what everybody suffers.

If you look at the universe the closest you can, within yourself—if you contemplate all things in your consciousness, where they all have left their painful trace—you will reach the base of the tedium not of life alone, but of something further, the tedium of existence, the base of the vanity of vanities[29]—how fearful!—you will come to feel compassion for everything, universal love.

To love everything, to feel compassion for everything, it is necessary that you feel it all within yourself, that you personalize everything. Love personalizes all that it loves, all that it pities. We only pity what is similar to us; and insofar as it is, and our compassion grows, and with it our love, in the measure that we discover the similarities things have with us.[30] If I pity and love the poor star that will disappear one day from the sky, it is because compassion, love, makes me discover in it a consciousness, more or less obscure, that makes it suffer because it is nothing more than a star, because it cannot be anything else without ceasing to be what it is, because it has to cease to be it one day. Every consciousness is consciousness of death.[31]

Love personalizes all that it loves, and when love is great and alive and loves everything, it personalizes everything, it personalizes the all, it discovers that the total All, the Universe, is a Person,[32] [11] is a Consciousness that suffers; and it pities the conscious Universe, loves it and discovers God. It pities God and feels pitied by God, loves Him and feels loved by Him. It harbors its misery in the bosom of eternal and infinite Misery.[33]

———————

God is the personalization of the All. He is the eternal and infinite Consciousness of the Universe, Consciousness imprisoned in matter and struggling to disengage Himself from it.[34] We personalize the All to save ourselves from the nothingness.

The only truly mysterious mystery is the mystery of pain.

Pain is the route of consciousness; through pain beings reach self-consciousness. To have consciousness is to know that one is different from other beings, and one comes to feel this distinction only through a clash, through pain.[35] Self-consciousness is nothing but consciousness of one's own limitation. I feel myself when I feel I am not the others; to know up to where I have being is to know where I end, and from which point I am not.[36]

We pity what is similar to us, and we pity it all the more the more and better we feel its similarity to us. And if this similarity can be said by us to call forth our compassion, it can also be maintained that it is our supply of compassion, quick to shed itself upon everything,[37] that makes us discover the similarity of things to us, and the common base that unites us with them in pain.

Our struggle to acquire, keep, and increase our own consciousness makes us discover in the excitations and movements of all things a struggle to acquire, keep, and increase consciousness. [12] Beneath the acts of my closest fellow creatures, other human beings, I sense—rather I con-sense ("con-siento")[38]—a state of consciousness as mine beneath my own acts. When I hear my brother scream in pain, my own pain is aroused and screams in the depths of my consciousness. And in the same way I feel the pain of animals, and feel the pain of a tree from which they pull off a branch, especially when I have a lively fantasy, which is the faculty of intuition, of inner vision.

Descending from the human species, we suppose that all living beings have some more or less obscure consciousness, and rocks too, which also live. The monera, on splitting in two, should feel some painful delight, a sensation of love and death at the same time, of death and resurrection. And the evolution of organic beings is nothing but a struggle for the plenitude of consciousness by means of pain, a constant aspiration to be others without ceasing to be what they are, to break their limits by limiting themselves. What a fearful contradiction of life!

In as many evolutionist theories as have been proposed, there always remained outside of doctrines the inner resource, the essential motive. What is the hidden force that produces the self-perpetuating of organisms and the fighting to persist and propagate? Selection, adaptation, everything, these are outer conditions. This inner, essential form has been called will.[39] It is what we feel as will in ourselves; it is the impulse to be everything, to be all else without ceasing to be ourselves.[40] That force is the divine in us, God Who acts in us, because He suffers in us.

And that force, that aspiration to consciousness, [13] we find in everything. It moves and excites the most minute living beings, moves and excites the cells of our bodies, the globules of our blood. Our cells, our globules, have their rudimentary cellular or globular consciousnesses.[41] And if these cells communicate among themselves—or if in fact they communicate in some way—and if some of them expressed their belief that they formed part of a superior organism endowed with collective and personal consciousness, the thing would be as if I expressed my belief that we human beings are after the fashion of globules of blood of a Superior Being, of a Supreme Being, that has His collective and personal consciousness.

Perhaps the immense Milky Way that we contemplate at night, that enormous ring of which our whole planetary system is nothing but a molecule, is a cell of the Universe,[42] Body of God.[43] The cells of our body work together with their activity to maintain and fire up our consciousnesses, and if the consciousnesses of all of them entered wholly into ours, if I had consciousness of all that happens in my bodily organism, I would feel the whole Universe pass through me, and the painful sensation of my limits would be erased. And if all the consciousnesses of all beings wholly enter into Universal Consciousness, then God is perfect and complete.

Within us consciousnesses are born and die at every instant, and this being born and dying that they undergo constitutes our life.[44] And when they die abruptly, in a collision, they produce our pain. Likewise, in the bosom of God, consciousnesses are born and die, with their births and deaths constituting His life.

When compassion reveals to us the whole Universe [14] struggling to acquire, preserve, and increase its consciousness, while feeling the pain of the disharmonies produced within it, compassion reveals to us the similarity of the whole Universe to us. It makes us see in it our Father, of whose flesh we are flesh.[45] Love makes us personalize the all of which we form a part, and it discloses God to us. All things are eternally producing God. Why should it not be so?

And the reasoners come, the logicians, and say to us, "Why should it be so? All that is nothing more than a daydream of fantasy, not a teaching of reason. Who proves that?"

This is proved by faith, faith in God, born from our love of God and from love of God for us. As far as reason is concerned, it is sufficient that the opposite is impossible to prove. Reason does not prove to us that God exists, it is certain; but it is no less certain that neither does it prove to us that He does not exist, much less than He cannot exist.[46] Reason is nothing but a negative, limiting faculty; the affirmative, liberating faculty is something else.

What is faith in God, and what does that faith prove?

3 What Is Faith?

"What thing is faith?" asks the catechism of the Christian doctrine that they taught us as children, and it answers, "To believe what we did not see."[1] And thus is established the preconception that faith is something of the intellectual order, that is, something alien to will. In our language, to believe means to give credence to something, and it refers to a person; we believe the person that states something to us, rather than what that person states.[2] I say that I know that there is an animal called a dog or a horse because I have seen them, and that I believe in the existence of [15] one called a giraffe or a duck-bill platypus, and that it has this or the other shape, because I believe those who assure me that it exists.[3] And thus it turns out that that belief usually means for us something inferior to science, since we say, "I am not sure of it, but I believe it is so. . . ."[4] On one hand, faith is for us the highest degree of certainty, leading human beings to sacrifice and death,[5] and on the other hand, faith, belief, believing, means something less than knowing something and being sure of it. How is this contradiction resolved?

It is resolved by removing faith from the domain of intelligence and carrying it to that of will.

All of us are sure that two and two make four, that the three angles of a triangle are worth two straight lines, and that other scientific statements are true. And yet we would not sacrifice our lives to preserve them. We know that they are self-sufficient and do not need the sacrifice of our lives, and useless, vain sacrifice repels us. But, in exchange, many are willing to lose their lives to keep their religious faith, and thus martyrs have made the faith even more than the faith has made martyrs.[6]

And it is a fact that faith is not the mere adhesion of the intellect to an abstract principle, it is not the recognition of a theoretical truth (Ritschl III 87)[7] in which will does nothing but move us to pay attention; faith is a thing of will, it is movement of the soul toward a practical truth, toward something that makes us live and not merely comprehend life (Thomas, *Secunda Secundae* q. 4, art. 2).[8]

Although we say that faith is a thing of the will, perhaps it would be better to say that faith is another psychic potency,[9] different from intelligence, will, and sentiment. We would therefore have knowing, feeling, willing, and believing, that is, creating. For neither intelligence, nor sentiment, nor will creates, but operates upon already given matter, matter given by faith. Faith is the creative power of the human being. But as it has a more intimate relationship to will than to any other of the three potencies, we present it in volitive form. Let it be noted, however, that to want to believe—that is, to want to create—is not precisely believing or creating, although certainly the initiation of it.[10]

Faith is the flower of will and it is the business of faith to create. Faith creates its object. And faith in God consists of creating God, and since it is God Who gives us faith in Him, it is God Who is creating Himself continuously in us. The power to create a God in our image and [16] likeness does not mean, in a word, anything unless we carry God within, and God is continually creating us in His image and likeness.[11]

And one creates God—that is to say, God creates Himself in us—through love. To believe in God is to love Him or to fear Him. One begins by loving Him even before knowing Him, and loving Him is how one begins by seeing him and discovering Him in everything.

The gentiles that say they believe in God and neither love Him nor fear Him, do not believe in God but in those that have taught them that God exists, and these teachers all too often do not believe in Him either. Those without passion in their soul, without anguish, without uncertainty, without doubt, with despair in consolation, think they believe in God; they believe only in the idea of God, but not in God Himself.

And just as one believes in God out of love, one can also believe out of fear and even out of hate, as that thief [Vanni Fucci] whom Dante causes to make obscene gestures from hell (*Inferno* 25.1–3).[12]

Devils also believe in God.[13]

And do you not think that a manner of believing in Him is that fury with which those who want to believe in Him, but cannot achieve as much, deny Him and even insult Him? They want Him to exist as we believers do, but they are weak and passive human beings in whom intelligence, which is our weakness, overpowers will, our strength, and drags it along instead of being led by it, and the head nay-says what the heart yea-says, and [17] they despair and deny out of despair, and upon denying affirm and create what they deny, and God reveals Himself to them by affirming Himself through negations of Himself.[14] There are those who, envious of simple faith and not succeeding in attaining it, attack the simple believers, the loving believers, and call them simple or even stupid, if not hypocritical and deceiving.[15]

But with all this it will be said to me that to teach that faith creates its object is to teach that such an object lacks objective reality outside faith itself, just as to maintain that faith is needed to contain or console the people is to affirm that the object of faith is illusory. What is certain is that to believe in God is today, before and above everything, for intellectual believers, to want God to exist (see Simmel 1.404 *et seq.*).[16]

To believe in God is, in the first instance, to want God to exist and to act as if He existed. And through this route of willing His existence, and acting in accordance with such a desire, is how we create God—that is, how God creates Himself in us, how God manifests Himself to us, opens and reveals Himself to us. For God comes out to meet those who seek Him with love, and out of love removes Himself from the one who seeks Him with cold, unloving reason.[17] God wants the heart to rest, but not the head to rest, since in physical life the head sleeps and rests, and the heart ceaselessly keeps watch and labors. Hence science without love separates us from God; and love, without science, leads us to God and through God to wisdom.[18] Blessed are the pure of heart, for they shall see God![19]

And if you asked me how I believe (*creo*) in God, that is, how I create (*creo*) God,[20] or rather how God creates Himself in me myself and reveals Himself to me, I will have to [18] enter into a field that, if it does not scandalize those that only believe in Reason, will make them laugh or smile.

I believe in God as I believe in my friends because I interact with Him, and I feel the breath of His affection and His invisible and intangible hand that leads me hither and yon, because I have intimate awareness of a private providence and of a Universal Mind that traces out my own destiny for me. And the concept of law neither says nor teaches anything to me.[21]

Time and again during my life I have seen myself in peril, suspended over the abyss; time and again I have found myself at crossroads where a cluster of roads opened up to me where, by taking one, I renounced the rest, since the roads of life are unrevertible; and time and again at such solemn moments I have felt the pressure of a sovereign force, intelligent and loving. And afterwards the pathways of the Lord have opened to me.[22]

I feel the Universe calling me and guiding me like a person; I hear within me its wordless voice, telling me, "Go and preach to all the peoples!"[23] How do you know that a human being that you have in front of you has a consciousness like you and an animal has a more or less obscure one, and a stone does not? By the way the human being, after the fashion of a human, your like, behaves with you, and the way a stone does not with you, but passively undergoes your conduct. For thus it is that I know that the Universe has a consciousness like me, by the way the Universe behaves with me humanly, after the fashion of a human being. I sense the conscious personality of everything that surrounds me.[24]

There sits a formless mass; it seems to be a [19] kind of animal; limbs are not discerned on it; I only see two eyes, two eyes that look at me with a human gaze, with the look of a fellow creature, with a look that asks compassion of me, and I hear breathing. And I conclude that in that shapeless mass there is a human being and a consciousness there like my own. And in this way, no other, the starry sky looks at me, with a superhuman look, with a divine look, with a look that begs supreme compassion of me and supreme love; and I hear in the serene night the breathing of God, and He touches the apex of my heart and He reveals Himself to me. The Universe lives, the Universe suffers, the Universe loves, and it asks us for love.

From loving these important little things that leave us just as they came to us without attachment of any kind to us, we pass onward to love more permanent things, incapable of being grasped with our hands. From loving goods we pass onward to love the Good, from loving beautiful things to loving Beauty, from loving true things to loving Truth, from loving enjoyments to loving happiness, and finally to loving Love.[25] And the Good and Beauty and Truth and Happiness love you in turn, and make you good and beautiful and true and happy, and Love makes you amorous, loving, and lovable.[26] I go out of myself to enter more into my supreme Ego; my consciousness goes out of itself to submerge itself into the total Consciousness of which it forms part and which it is ceaselessly constituting (*Theologia deutsch* 169 et seq. Suso 355).[27] And God is nothing but Love,[28] the Love that arises from universal pain and becomes consciousness, since consciousness is a form of pain.[29]

And they will even tell me that this is tantamount to moving in [20] a ring of iron, and that such a God has no objective reality, does not exist. And here it is fitting, so as to be fair to reason, to examine what that matter of existing may be, and what it means that a thing exists.

What is it, in fact, for a thing to exist when we say that a thing exists? To exist is for something to be placed outside us in such a way that it would precede our perception of it, and may or can subsist outside us even though we may disappear. And am I really sure that something might precede me or that something will survive me? Can my consciousness know that there is something outside itself? As much as I know and can know—that is to say, all that of which I have or can have consciousness—is in my consciousness or can be in it.[30]

Let us not get snarled up, then, in the insoluble problem of the objectivity of our perceptions, and let us simply hold fast to the notion that to exist is to act and that all that acts exists.[31] And since God acts, God exists.[32]

And here we backslide, and they will tell me that it is not God, but the idea of God that acts in us. And I will say that it is God through His idea, and often without the idea, by Himself. And again will sound the retort asking me for proofs of the objective truth of the existence of God, since, like the Jews, we ask for signs.[33] The truth . . . the truth . . . and what is the truth?[34]

4   *What Is Truth?*

"What is truth?" asked Pilate,[1] and without waiting for an answer turned around to wash his hands to excuse himself from the death of Jesus, Our Lord.[2] And thus many ask what truth is without [21] a mind to receive the answer, only to turn around to wash their hands of the crime of having contributed to killing God in their own consciences or in the consciences of others.

What is truth? There are two kinds of truth: logical or objective truth, whose perversion is error; and moral or subjective truth, whose perversion is the lie. And I say that ordinarily error is the child of the lie.[3]

And this moral truth, the way to reach the other truth, which is also moral, teaches us to cultivate science. Science is before all and above all a school of sincerity and humility.[4] Science teaches us to submit our reason to truth and to know and judge things as they are, that is to say, as they wish to be and not as we wish them to be.[5] In a religiously scientific research project, it is the very data of reality, it is the perceptions we receive from the world that come to be formulated as a law in our minds, not we who formulate them as such. It is the numbers themselves that perform mathematics within us.

Science is the most devout school of resignation and humility, since it teaches us to bow before the most apparently insignificant fact, before the minuscule fact that passes by us least noticed.[6] Science is the portico of religion.

And the truth that science pursues is the truth of knowledge.

Human beings have much debated, and will keep on [22] debating a great deal, since the world was submitted to their debates, about the origin of knowledge, but leaving aside for later that part of it in the deep bosom of existence, what has been ascertained and is certain is that in the order of the appearances of things, in the lives of beings endowed with some knowing, whether this be more or less hazy, or whether their acts seem to be endowed with it, knowledge is shown to us to be linked to the need to live and to acquire sustenance to achieve it.

In terms concrete enough to border on grossness, it can be said that the brain has sprung from the stomach. In beings on the lowest rung of the scale of living species, acts that present characteristics of willfulness or spontaneity, those that seem linked to a more or less obscure consciousness, are acts addressed to obtaining the subsistence of the being performing them.[7]

Such is the origin of knowledge that we can call historical, whatever its origin in any other respect. Beings that seem endowed with knowledge know in order to be able to live; and only insofar as in order to live do they need to know it. It is certain that in the human being treasured cognitions, that began by being useful and ceased to be it, have come to constitute a wealth that exceeds by far that which is necessary for life; although, on the other hand, we may still need many cognitions to live better, and that treasure of inherited cognitions has produced the yearning to know for the satisfaction [23] of knowing, and for science, and all the wealth of intelligence. But this does not veil from us the fact that, at its origin, all knowledge sprang from the organic need for self-preservation.[8]

With very deep symbolic meaning, *Genesis* dates human progress from the original sin of our supposed first parents, when in disobedience to Yahweh they tasted of the fruit of the tree of the knowledge of good and evil to become like gods possessors of that knowledge.[9] And thus it is said that it was the curiosity of the woman, Eve, the one more subject to organic necessities and to the need for self-preservation, who brought the fall and with the fall redemption, the one who placed us on the road toward God, toward arriving at Him and being in Him. And it is generally also said that the origin of philosophy is curiosity or the innate wish to know that is found in the human being.[10]

But this curiosity, this innate desire to know, is only roused and acts after the satisfaction of the need to know in order to live;[11] and even though at some time it might not happen in this way in present conditions of our lives—but rather curiosity might surpass necessity and science surpass hunger—the fact is that curiosity sprang from need.

And this is the dead weight and the gross matter that science bears in its bosom; and the fact is that—while aspiring to be a knowing for its own sake, a knowing of the truth for the truth itself—the needs of life force and twist science to place itself at their service; and human beings, while they think they seek the truth for its own sake, seek in fact life in truth.[12] The variations of science depend [24] on the variations of human needs. Men and women of science, whether they want to or not, whether aware of it or not, labor at the service of the powerful or at the service of the people that ask of them confirmation of their yearnings.

Thus it is and perhaps thus it will always be, since it cannot be otherwise. And instead of aspiring to rebel against as necessary a need as any of the other laws that science may formulate, the sensible human being should accept it and plan and act accordingly.

Knowledge is at the service of the need to live and primarily at the service of the instinct of self-preservation. And this need and this instinct have created in man the organs of knowledge by giving them the range they have. The human being sees, hears, touches, tastes, and smells what is needed to see, hear, touch, taste, and smell to preserve that human's life. The decline or loss of any one of those senses increases the risks surrounding that life, and if it does not increase them as much in the state of society in which we live, it is because some see, hear, touch, taste or smell for the others. A blind person alone, without a guide, could not live very long. Society is another sense, the true common sense.

And the human being, in the natural state as an isolated individual, does not see, nor hear, nor touch, nor taste, nor smell any more or less than what he needs to live. If he does not perceive simple colors outside the rainbow, either beneath red or above violet, it is doubtlessly because he [25] has not needed to in order to preserve himself. And the senses themselves are an apparatus of simplification that eliminates from objective reality all that which is not necessary for us to know to be able to use objects to the end of preserving life.[13]

In complete darkness an animal, if it does not perish, ends up by becoming blind, and if not it, its offspring. Parasites in the entrails of other animals live on the alimentary juices prepared by the hosts. Since they do not need to see or hear, changed into membranous sacs, they keep adhering to the intestine of that animal in which they live while effortlessly absorbing its nourishment. For these parasites, neither the visible nor the audible world exists. It is enough for them to see and hear those in whose entrails they maintain such worlds.[14]

Knowledge is primarily, therefore, at the service of the instinct of self-preservation, which, more than instinct, is the root force of the human being, human essence itself—since, in accordance with the profound doctrine of Spinoza, the essence of a thing is that effort with which it strives to perpetuate itself in its own being.[15]

And thus it can be said that it is the instinct of self-preservation that creates reality for us and fashions the truth of the sensible world, since it is that instinct which removes us from the unfathomable and unlimited field of the possible and gives what is extant for us.[16] There exists for us all that which, in some way or other, we need to know to be able to exist. In our knowing, objective existence is a dependence on our own personal existence. And no one can deny that there exist aspects of reality unknown to us and even unknowable, because in no way are they necessary for us so to preserve our own existences. What is more, such an unknown and unknowable world should exist.[17]

Yet the human being does not live alone, but forms society, to which he is led by the instinct of self-perpetuation, parent of society. And if there is a reality that is, insofar as known, the work of the instinct of self-preservation, and senses at the service [26] of that instinct, there is another reality, no less real than that one, the work, insofar as known, of the instinct of self-perpetuation and at the service of it.

The instinct of self-preservation, hunger, is the basis of the human individual; the instinct of self-perpetuation, love in its most rudimentary and almost physiological form,[18] is the basis of human society. And just as the human being knows what it is necessary to know for self-preservation, so society, or the human being qua social being, knows what it is necessary to know for individual self-perpetuation in society, so that human society may be preserved.[19]

There is a world, the sensible world, which is the child of hunger, and there is another world, the ideal world, which is the child of love.[20] And just as there are senses at the service of the knowledge of the sensible world, there are senses—today mostly dormant, because the human being is hardly beginning to be socialized[21]—at the service of the knowledge of the ideal world.

And why should we deny reality to the creations of love, of the instinct of self-perpetuation, since we grant it to the creations of hunger, the instinct of individual self-preservation? Why if it is said that these second creations [i.e., of love] are only creations of our fantasy, without objective value, can it not be said that those others [i.e., of hunger] are only creations of our senses? Who tells us that there is not an invisible and intangible world perceived by the inner sense that lives at the service of the instinct of self-perpetuation?[22]

Human society, qua [27] society, has senses that the individual would lack if not for society, the same as this individual, the human being, who is, in turn, a society, has senses that the cells comprising that individual lack.[23] Ear cells, blind in their obscure consciousness, ignore the existence of the visible world, and if spoken to about it, they would consider it the arbitrary creation of the deaf cells of sight. These, in turn, consider the world of sound an illusion that the ear cells create.

I was speaking previously about the parasites which, while living in the entrails of higher animals on the alimentary juices prepared by these hosts, need neither see nor hear, and neither the visible nor the audible world exists for them. And if they could have a certain awareness and could realize that [the animal] at whose expense they live sees and hears, they would judge everything in that world lying beyond their grasp as deviations of the imagination. And thus there are social parasites, as an English writer (Mr. Balfour) perceptively notes,[24] that, while receiving from the society in which they live the motives of their moral behavior, they deny that the belief in God is necessary to ground good behavior, because society gives them already prepared the spiritual juices on which they live. An isolated individual can live a morally good life without believing in God in any way, but the fact is that this individual lives the life of a spiritual parasite; an entire society cannot live such a life.

And I say even more, and it is that if faith in God united to a life of purity and moral elevation is given in a human being, it is not so much that believing in God makes the human good as that being good produces that individual's belief in God. Goodness is the best source of spiritual perspicacity.[25]

And that social sense, child of love, parent of language and of the ideal world born of it, is perhaps nothing else at base than what we call fantasy or imagination. And imagination, the social sense, is the faculty of knowing, which gives us realities. It will be said to me that imagination hammers out capricious images without any basis, but also the senses and the intelligence err, and it cannot be concluded from the errors of imagination that this faculty cannot attain truth, and that there is no truth revealed only to imagination.[26]

And this intimate faculty, imagination, is the social sense, child of love, the one that, at the service of the instinct of self-perpetuation, reveals to us the truth of the existence of God. And God thus turns out to be a social product,[27] the same as the sensible world is an individual product, and not in any other sense.

And to say that God has no existential value outside human society is equivalent to saying that the world we call material does not have it outside our senses. [28] And let it be observed how material things, insofar as known, spring from hunger, and from hunger springs the sensible Universe in which we heap together these material things; and ideal things, insofar as known, spring from love, and from love springs God, in

Whom we heap together these ideal things. For God is the Consciousness of the Universe.[28]

Social consciousness, child of love, of the instinct of self-perpetuation, leads us to socialize everything, to see society in everything, and
finally it shows us how truly all Nature is an infinite Society.

Hundreds of times I have sensed this before thinking it and formulat-
ing it while walking in a wood among the solemn oaks that seemed to see
me and hear me, to introduce themselves to me and to speak to me.[29]

Fantasy, which is the social sense, animates the inanimate and
anthropomorphizes everything, humanizes everything. And the very
labor of the human being is that of super-naturalizing nature, that is, of
divinizing it by humanizing it; making it human, giving it consciousness,
in short. Fantasy humanizes, just as reason mechanizes or materializes.

And just as individual and society are given united and mutually
fertilize one another, with one inseparable from the other without it
being possible to say where one ends and the other begins, with each one
instead being aspects of the same essence,[30] so are given in [29] unity the
spirit, the social element, and matter, the individual element; and in
unity are given, mutually fertilizing one another, the intelligence and
the fantasy, and in unity are given the Universe and God.

And there is a rational faith, a faith in which the imagination fertil-
izes reason and creates its object over the data of the senses; and upon
creating it there is revealed to it what the sensible world bears within
itself, there is revealed to it the truth in God, the truth of God.

The truth is something that is over reason, or under reason, or
within it; the truth is what makes us live, what makes us preserve and
perpetuate ourselves, and what maintains the human being and society.
True water is that liquid which, when drunk, quenches thirst; true nourishment is that which satisfies hunger, no matter what the senses may
tell us.

The senses are at the service of the instinct of self-preservation; and
everything that immediately, ceaselessly, satisfies it through the senses
and causes us to preserve ourselves is a kind of intimate penetration of
reality into us. Is the process of assimilation of nourishment less real
than the process of cognition of nourishing things? No, much more real.
More real and more mine is bread when I make it flesh of my own
instead of when I see it or touch it and say, "This is bread." And as to
this bread thus changed into my flesh and made my own, how can I deny
it the objective reality of when it was outside my body and I saw it with
my eyes and touched it with my hands? For it is the equivalent to denying the [30] objective reality of God, made spirit of society, and of the

whole Universe qua society. God is known only insofar as He is lived, and "Man shall not live by bread alone, but by every word that proceeds from the mouth of God" (*Matthew* 4:4), from the social spirit.

And this lived God—that is to say, God, child of love—is, and by force of love has to be, anthropomorphic, human. Human beings, trivial and external, slaves of reason that externalizes us all, are accustomed to saying that, rather than God having made man in his image and likeness, it is man who in his image and likeness makes God for himself or makes gods for himself. These frivolous people who say so do not notice that if the second alternative is true, it is because the first is no less true.[31]

Yes, each one in the strength of his love imagines for himself God made to measure, and God is as all human beings imagine Him, God is such as results from the fusion of all those human imaginings of Him.[32] And since we cannot arrive at that fusion in which nothing is taken away, but everything, even what seems contradictory, is united to it and completed, God in His perfect truth is unknowable,[33] unimaginable for us. The human being and God make one another mutually.[34]

The Master told us to be perfect as is perfect our Father who is in the heavens (*Matthew* 5:48), and in the order of thinking and feeling, our perfection consists of pressing onward, so that our imagination may arrive at the complete imagination of the humankind of which we form part in God.

There is an idea of God obtained by the maximum of extension and the minimum of comprehension and by removing differences, and this God, the logical God, sinks into nothingness;[35] and there is an image of God, obtained by the maximum of comprehension, and [31] that is the heartfelt God, the living God. And God is God of the living, not of the dead. Let us, therefore, let the dead bury their dead;[36] let logicians and reasoning theologians bury in reason and science their logical God, pure idea without substance; and let us turn our heart and our fantasy to the living God, the heartfelt God, the God of inner revelation, the God that gives life.

This God, the living God, my God, your God, our God, God is in me, is in you, lives in us, and we live, move, and are in Him.[37] And to every one He reveals Himself in accordance with the being of each to whom He may reveal Himself. Your God, poor farmer or innocent child, is much truer than the metaphysical God of the ratiocinators, because God chose what is foolish in the world to shame the wise, and what is weak to shame the strong (1 *Corinthians* 1:27).[38]

Superstition itself is more revealing than theology. The old Father with long beard, Who appears in the clouds while holding the ball of the world in His hand, is more alive than the *Ens realissimum* [the most real Being].[39]

Reason is a corrosive force when, ceasing to act on the form of intuitions—be these of the individual instinct of self-preservation, or of the social instinct of self-perpetuation—it acts on the depths, on the very matter, of those intuitions. Reason orders sensible perceptions that give us the material world, but when its analysis is exercised on the reality of perceptions themselves, it dissolves them for us and it sinks us into a shadowy world of appearances without consistency, because reason, beyond the formal part, is nihilistic and annihilating. And the same fearful function it fulfills when, removing it from its own proper function, we lead it to scrutinize the imaginative intuitions that the spiritual world gives us.[40] For reason annihilates, and imagination integrates, sums up; reason by itself kills, and imagination gives life. Although it is certain [32] that imagination by itself, when giving us limitless life, leads us to be mixed up with everything; and insofar as we are individuals, it kills us also, it kills us through an excess of life. Reason, the head, tells us, "Nothing!"[41] Imagination, the heart, tells us, "Everything!" And between nothing and everything, with the all and the nothingness fusing in us, we live in God, Who is all; and God lives in us, for without Him we are nothing. Reason repeats, "Vanity of vanities, and everything vanity!" and the imagination tells us in opposition to that, "Plenitude of plenitudes, and everything plenitude!" And thus we live the plenitude of vanity, or the vanity of plenitude.[42]

And this vital need to live another world, an illogical, irrational, divine world, arises so deeply from the eternal, innermost recesses of the human being, that all that do not believe in God, or believe they do not believe in Him, believe in any tiny god at all. Or they believe in a little devil or in an omen or in a horseshoe they found by chance while walking on the roads and that they keep on their hearts so that it may bring them good luck and defend them from the same reason of which they imagine they are faithful servants and devotees.

And that is the God of love, and do not ask me, pious reader, how He may be, but consult your heart and let your fantasy picture Him to you far off in the Universe and around you and in you. The one in whom you believe, that one is your God, your God that has lived with you inside you and that was a child when you were a child, and was becoming an adult in the measure that you became an adult, and who dissipates from you when you dissipate, and who is your principle of continuity in your life. That is because He is the principle of your solidarity with yourself, with your successive egos, with your neighbors, with the society on which you live and in which you live, and with the entire Universe, [33] which is, like you, a person.[43]

And if you believe in God, God believes in you, and by believing in you, creates you continually.[44] For you are, at base, the idea that God holds of you, and outside that idea, outside of what you are in society and in nature, in the Universe, you are nothing.

Faith is the substance of things hoped for, that is to say, the depth of hope.[45] If, in fact, faith is the substance of hope, hope is the form of faith, informs it. Faith, before giving us hope, is a formless, vague, chaotic, potential faith, only a possibility of believing in something, a yearning to believe. But one must believe in something. In what does one believe? In what is hoped, in hope. The past is remembered, the present known, and only the future believed. To believe what we did not see is to believe what we shall see. Faith, hence, is faith in hope; we believe what we hope.

In what does love make you believe? In God, on Whom you pin your hope for the future life you await, in which the dream of hope creates you.

Faith is our yearning for heaven, for God, and hope is the yearning for God, for the heaven that comes to meet that faith and raises us up. The human being aspires to God through faith and tells Him, "I believe, give me, Lord, something in which to believe!"[46] And God sends hope in the other life in order to believe in it. Hope is the prize of faith. Only the believer hopes, just as only the hoping individual believes. What do you believe if not what you hope? And what do you hope if not what you believe?

The mystery of love, which is that of pain, has a form, a mysterious form: time. We tie the yesterday to the tomorrow with bonds of anxiety and yearning; and the now, strictly speaking, is nothing more than the effort of the before to become after: the present is nothing but the determination of the past to become future.[47] The now is a point that, hardly pronounced, dissipates; yet nonetheless, in that point is situated all eternity, the substance of time.[48]

All that has been cannot be except such as it was, and all that is cannot be except as it is; the possible stays always relegated to what is to come. And what is to come belongs to the imagination, the freeing power.

[34] Love looks and tends always toward the future, since its work is the work of our self-perpetuation; the characteristic of love is waiting and it only maintains itself on hopes. As soon as love sees its yearning realized, it becomes sad and discovers at that point that its own terminus is not that toward which it was tending, and that God only put that

endpoint there as an enticement to move it toward its work; for its end-point lies beyond, and once again, in pursuit of it, love undertakes its arduous course of deceits and disenchantments through life.[49] And it goes along making memories of its failed hopes. The quarry of our visions of the future lies in the underground of our memory; with remi-niscences, imagination makes us hopes. And at the same time, our hopes, as soon as we touch them, change into memories.[50] Humankind is like a maiden filled with yearnings, hungry for life and thirsting for love. She weaves her days with daydreams and waits, always waits, waits ceaselessly for her eternal lover, who—because he was destined for her since before the before, since long before her furthest memories, since beyond the cradle toward the past—will live with her and for her until after the afterward, until much beyond her final hopes, until beyond the tomb toward the future. And the most charitable desire for this poor girl in love is, as for the maiden who always awaits her lover, that the sweet hopes of the spring of life change for her, in the winter of it, into still happier memories. What essence [35] of peaceable happi-ness, of resignation to destiny, should come in the days of our briefest sun[51] from remembering hopes that were not realized and that, for not having been realized, kept their purity!

Love waits, always waits without ever growing tired of waiting; and love for God, our faith in God, is hope in Him before everything. For God does not die, and whoever hopes in God will live in Him. And our basic hope is the root and trunk of all our hopes, the hope of eternal life.

It was hope that called God Father, and it is hope that keeps giving Him that name pregnant with mystery and consolation. Our fathers gave us life, and give us bread to maintain it; we ask our fathers to pre-serve it for us.

If Christ was the one who with fullest heart and purest mouth called his Father Father and Our Father, if the Christian sentiment rises into the sentiment of the fatherhood of God, it is because, in Christ, the human lineage elevates its hunger for eternity.[52] If Christ did not rise again, we are the most miserable of men, the Apostle taught (1 *Corinthians* 15:19).

God is for the ordinary person, one thinker has said (William James), the Producer of immortality.[53] And thus it is and thus it has to be. The root of our yearnings and the core of our anxieties is the thirst for eter-nity, and the mystery of beyond the grave is the look of the Sphinx.[54] But men of the world who make tolerance an enterprise of their battle-flag, end their tolerance as soon as they hear of the other life.

The *Acts* of the Apostles recounts [36] that wherever Paul went, the zealous Jews were stirred up against him and pursued him. He was stoned in Iconium and Lystra, cities of Lycaonia, despite the wonders he performed in Lycaonia. They flogged him in Philippi of Macedonia, and his brothers pursued him in Thessalonica and Beroea. But he arrived at Athens, the noble city of intellectuals over which the lofty soul of Plato kept watch, and there he debated with Epicureans and Stoics that said of him, "What does this charlatan (σπερμολόγος) mean?" or else, "It seems he is a preacher of new gods!" (*Acts* 17:18). "And taking hold of him they brought him to the Areopagus, saying, 'May we know what this new teaching is which you present? For you bring some strange new things to our ears,[55] and we want to know what that all means'" (17:19–20). The book adds this wonderful characterization of those Athenians of the decadence, of those men with a sweet tooth for curios, since "at that time all the Athenians and their foreign guests concerned themselves with nothing but saying or hearing something new" (verse 21). What a wonderful stroke of the pen that depicts for us what ever happened to those that had learned in the *Odyssey* that the gods plot and achieve the destruction of mortals so that the ones that come after may have something to sing about![56]

Now Paul stands before the refined Athenians, before those learned and tolerant men that admit every doctrine and study every one and neither stone nor flog nor jail anybody for professing this or that. There he stands, where freedom of conscience is respected, and every opinion is heard and listened to. And he raises his voice there, in the midst [37] of the Areopagus, and he speaks to them as befits the learned citizens of Athens, and all, eager for the latest novelty, listen to him. But when he comes to speak to them of the resurrection of the dead, their patience and tolerance is exhausted, and some mock while others tell him, "We will hear you about this some other time!" And a like thing happens to him in Caesarea with the Roman praetor Felix, also a tolerant and learned man, who relieved him of the burden of his prison and wanted to hear him—and in fact did hear him—discuss justice and continence; and when he came to talk about the judgment to come, he told him with dismay, "Go away for now, for I will call you again when it is suitable" (*Acts* 24:22–25).[57] And when Paul was speaking before King Agrippa, and Festus, the governor, heard him talk of the resurrection of the dead, he exclaimed, "Paul, you are mad, your great learning is turning you mad" (*Acts* 26:24).

Whatever may be the truth of Paul's speech in the Areopagus, even if it had never been, the point up to which Attic tolerance extends, and where the patience of the intellectuals ends, is clearly seen in that wonderful story. They all hear us in calm, and sometimes smiling, they encourage you by saying, "It is curious!" or else, "It is ingenious," or "It is suggestive," or "What beauty!" or "That makes me think!" But as soon as you speak to them of resurrection and of life beyond death, their patience runs out and they deprive you of the floor, telling you, "Let it be! We will talk some other day about that!" And about that, my poor Athenians, my intolerant intellectuals, about that I will now speak to you here.

And I will speak to you while exposing myself to your telling me, "You are mad, Miguel, your great learning is turning you mad; it is a delirium of intellectualism that makes you abominate intellectualism."[58] And others will say, "Let us go on our way; now for the present, duty, the work that is presented to us and is at hand; afterwards . . . God only knows." If you feel this way, from this point onward close this book. You continue to read? The fact is you do not feel that way!

I already said, following Spinoza, that each thing strives to persevere in its being,[59] that the effort with which it strives to persevere in it is its own actual essence,[60] and that that effort involves indefinite time,[61] and that [38] the mind, in conclusion, whether in its distinct and clear ideas or in its confused ones, tends to persevere in its being with indefinite duration, and is cognizant of this determination it makes[62] (*Ethics*, part 3, propositions 6–9).

It is impossible for us to conceive ourselves as not existing. There is no effort sufficient for consciousness to take cognizance of absolute unconsciousness, of its own annihilation. Attempt to imagine to yourself in full wakefulness what may be your state of mind in deep sleep; try to fill your consciousness with the representation of non-consciousness, and you will see. It causes anxious vertigo to resolve to understand it. We cannot conceive ourselves as not existing and that is because of the tendency of the consciousness[63] to perpetuate itself, never to end.

The visible Universe, the one that is the child of the instinct of self-preservation, is too tight for me. It is for me like a cage which I find too small, and my soul in its flutterings strikes against its bars; I lack the air to breathe in it. More, more, and yet again more; I want to be myself and, without ceasing to be, want to be everyone else as well: to absorb into myself the totality of visible and invisible things, to stretch into limitless space and to prolong myself into endless time.[64] Unless I were everything forever, it would be as if I were not at all; at least let me be completely myself, though forever and ever. And to be completely myself is to be all the others.

Either all or nothing.[65] And what other meaning can there be in "To be or not to be!" of Shakespeare,[66] the same who caused it to be said of

Martius in his *Coriolanus* (5.4) that he only needed eternity to be god ("He wants nothing of a god but eternity").[67] Eternity! Eternity! This is the yearning; [39] the thirst for eternity is called love among human beings, and the one who loves another in fact wants to eternalize himself in that other. What is not eternal is not real.[68]

This imposing vision of the flow of the waves of life has plucked out cries from the innermost parts of the hearts of poets of all times,[69] from the dream of a shadow of Pindar,[70] to "life is a dream" of Calderón[71] and "We are such stuff . . . As dreams are made on" of Shakespeare.[72] This judgment is even more tragic than the Castilian's, since while Calderón affirms only that our life is a dream rather than we that dream it, the Englishman also makes us over into dreams, dreams that dream.

The vanity of the world and how it slips away and love are the two radical, visceral notes of true poetry. And they are two notes that cannot sound each by itself without the other ringing out too. The sentiment of the vanity of the passing world delivers us to love: the only thing in which what is vain and transitory is conquered, the only thing that fills and eternalizes life. And love, especially when it fights against Destiny, immerses us in the sentiment of the vanity of this world of appearances, and opens to us the glimpse of another world in which, with Destiny conquered, liberty is the law.

Everything slips away! Such is the old refrain of those who have drunk from the fountain of life, mouths to the spigot, of those who have tasted of the fruit of the tree of knowledge of good and evil.[73]

To be, to be forever, to be without terminus; a thirst for being, a thirst to be more! Hunger for God![74] A thirst for eternalizing love! To be forever and to be everything! To be God! "You will be like gods!" *Genesis* (3:5) relates that the serpent said to the first pair of [40] lovers.

"If in this life alone we are to hope in Christ, we are the most pitiful of men," wrote the Apostle (1 *Corinthians* 15:19), and all religion historically gets its start from the cult of the dead (see James, 491, 506, and 507).[75]

Spinoza wrote that the free man thinks of nothing less than of death,[76] but that free man is a dead man, free from the wellspring of life, lacking love, slave to his freedom. That thought, that I have to die and what will there be afterwards?, is the flailing of my consciousness. While contemplating the countryside or while contemplating some eyes from which peers a soul akin to mine, I feel my consciousness swell, I sense the diastolic of my soul and I get saturated with life around me and I believe in my future, but at once the voice of mystery tells me,

"You will cease to be!"; the Angel of Death brushes me with his wing,[77] and the systolic of my soul floods my spiritual innards with the blood of divinity.

Like Pascal, I do not understand those who assure that they do not care a wit about this affair, and that negligence "in an affair in which it is a question of themselves, of their eternity, of their all, irritates me more than it moves me to pity, it astonishes and dismays me"; and the one who feels this way "is for me," as it is for Pascal, whose words are here quoted, "a monster."[78]

A thousand times and in a thousand tones it has been said how it is the cult of dead ancestors that commonly begins primitive religions,[79] and strictly speaking it can be said that what most makes the human being stand out from the other animals [41] is the business of his guarding his dead in some way or other without delivering them carelessly to Mother Earth, who has given birth to everything; the human is an animal serving as a guardian to the dead. And from what does he guard them in this way? From what does the poor human protect them? The poor consciousness flees from its own annihilation, and as soon as an animal spirit, removing itself from its placenta within the world, finds itself face to face with the world—and, as if it differed from it, recognizes itself—it will wish to have a life different from the world's. And thus the earth would run the risk of changing into a vast cemetery before the dead themselves die again.

When not even for the living were anything but huts of earth or cabins of straw made, only to be destroyed by bad weather, tumuli were raised for the dead, and stone was used for tombs before it was for dwelling places. The houses of the dead, rather than those of the living, have conquered the centuries for their strength; not the dwellings of importance, but those of rest and retreat.

This cult, not of death but of immortality, initiates and keeps religions. In the delirium of destruction Robespierre causes the French Convention to affirm the existence of the Supreme Being and the "consoling principle of the immortality of the soul"; the "Incorruptible" became terrified by the idea of having to rot (corromperse) one day.[80]

Sickness? Perhaps—but the one who does not care about sickness is careless about health. Sickness? Perhaps—perhaps it is that, and so is life itself to which it goes prisoner, and the only health death, but that sickness is the wellspring of every powerful action.[81] From the depth of that anxiety, of the abyss of the sentiment [42] of our mortality, one comes out to the light of another heaven, as from the depth of hell Dante came out to see the stars again.[82]

Although at first this meditation of our mortality may cause us anguish, at the end it will be our source of strength.[83] Withdraw into yourself, reader, and imagine yourself slowly coming undone, with the light turning off for you, things falling silent for you and not giving off any sound to you as they surround you in silence, with objects you can grasp melting between your hands, the floor slipping out from under you, memories and ideas departing from you as in a faint, everything dissipating into nothingness, and you dissipating also, without even the awareness of nothingness remaining, like the phantasmagorical handle of a shadow.

I have heard it said of a poor reaper who died in a hospital bed that when the priest went to give him extreme unction, he refused to open his right hand, in which he was grasping some dirty coins, without realizing that once dead that hand would no longer be his, nor would he belong to himself. And thus we close and grasp not our hands, but our hearts, while wishing to grasp the world in them.

A friend once confessed to me that when, in full vigor of physical health, he foresaw that death was near, he only thought about concentrating his life, living it all in the few days he calculated he had left, and imagining he was writing a book about all this.

Should the body die which sustains me and which I call mine to distinguish it from myself, should my consciousness return to the absolute unconsciousness from which it sprung, and [43] should the same happen to the consciousnesses of all my fellow human beings, then our toilsome lineage is nothing more than an ill-starred parade of ghosts that passes from the nothingness to the nothingness, and humanitarianism the most inhumane thing known.

And the remedy is not that of the popular poem that says,

> Each time I pause to think that I
> Will someday surely have to die,
> I stretch my cape out on the ground
> And never tire of sleeping sound.[84]

No! The remedy is to consider it face to face, staring at the staring eyes of the Sphinx,[85] since that is how the curse of its evil eye is undone.

If all of us die altogether, what purpose does everything serve?; What purpose? It is the terrifying "What purpose?" of the Sphinx, it is the "What purpose?" that corrodes the marrow of our souls, it is the parent of anguish, which gives us the love of hope.

There are among the poetic plaints of poor Cowper some lines written under the weight of delirium, and in them, thinking he is the target of divine revenge, he exclaims, "Hell might afford my miseries a shelter."[86]

And here I will confess, as painful as the confession may be, that never in the days of my naïve faith did the descriptions of the tortures of hell make me tremble,[87] and I always felt that the nothingness was much more terrifying than it. The sufferer is alive, and the one who suffers and lives loves and hopes, even though at the gate of the mansion of pain his hell they place the sign, "Abandon ye all hope who enter here."[88] And it is better to live in pain than to be in peace. Suffering, you say? [44] Suffering is not possible without some love,[89] and the lack of love is not suffering, but annihilation.

There is no Christian human being that can believe in an eternity without love, nor is there any hell but the perspective of the nothingness. If we all believed in our sure salvation, in being saved from the nothingness, we would all be better for it.

What is this joy of living of which they now speak to us? The hunger for God, the thirst to survive, will smother forever that poor enjoyment of the life that flees away and does not remain.

It is the unbridled love of life, the love that wants it interminable, that which most impels us toward the yearning for death. "Once I am annihilated, if I must die altogether," we say to ourselves, "the world is all finished for me, all finished, and why will it not get over and done with as soon as possible so that other new consciousnesses come to suffer the grievous deceit of a passing existence made of mere appearances? If the illusory prospect of living forever is undone, living for its own sake does not fill our soul; for what purpose do we live? Death is our only remedy." And thus it is how dirges are sung to interminable repose out of fear of it, and death is called a liberator since we may live in order to set about returning to the nothingness.

The poet of pain, Leopardi, already saw the close kinship between love and death, and how when "there is born deep in the heart an amorous affect, in the breast is felt, languid and produced jointly with it, a desire to die."[90] For the majority of those that put themselves to death, it is love that moves them to strike, it is the supreme yearning for life, for more life, for prolonging [45] and perpetuating life, which leads them to death, once they are persuaded of the emptiness of their yearning.

The head teaches us death, and the heart reveals to us life,[91] although the former may rule the movements of the latter, and the latter, in turn, may refresh the former in blood; science destroys the deceit by showing us the vanity of vanities, but love rebuilds it for us at the same time and gives us the plenitude of plenitudes.[92]

Tragic is the problem, and eternal, and the more we wish to flee it, the more we stumble into it. It was the serene Plato, more than twenty-four centuries ago, who in his dialogue about the immortality of the soul, the *Phaedo*, let slip from his own soul, while he was speaking of the doubtfulness of our daydreams and of the risk that they are without substance, that profound expression, "Beautiful is the risk," καλὸς γὰρ ὁ κίνδυνος,[93]— beautiful is the risk we run that our soul never dies, and this judgment became the germ of the famous argument of Pascal's wager.[94]

With this risk ahead, to prevent our running it, they give me rationales in proof of the absurdity of the belief in the soul's immortality, but these rationales make no impression on me since they are reasons, nothing but reasons, and my heart gathers no sustenance from reasons. I do not want to die; no, I do not want to, nor do I wish to want to; I want to live forever, forever, forever, and to keep myself alive, this poor self that I am to myself, and to feel I am being here and now, and for this reason the problem of the duration of my soul, of my very own, tortures me.

I am the center of my universe, the center of the universe, and in my supreme anguish I exclaim with Michelet, "My self, they are snatching away my self!"[95] To what end does it serve the human being to win [46] the whole world if that individual loses the soul? (*Matthew* 16:26) "Egoism," you say? There is nothing more universal than what is individual, since what becomes of each one becomes of everyone.[96] Every human being is worth more than all humankind;[97] it is not worthwhile for each one to sacrifice to everyone except insofar as this means that everyone sacrifices to each one.

What you call egoism is the principle of psychic gravity, the necessary postulate.[98] "Love thy neighbor as thyself,"[99] it was said to us under the assumption that each one holds some self-love, and it was not said to us, "Love thyself!" Yet we do not know how to love ourselves.

Take away our own persistence and meditate about what they are saying to you. Sacrifice yourself for your children! And you sacrifice yourself for them because they are yours, part and prolongation of yourself, and they, in turn, sacrifice themselves for theirs, and the latter for theirs, and so it will go, without end, a sterile sacrifice from which no one will profit.[100] I came to the world to make myself an "I," to make my ego, and what will become of all of us?

"That art thou!" they tell me with the Upanishads,[101] and I tell them, "Yes, I am that, when that is I, and everything is mine, and mine the totality of things. And I love it as my own, and I love my neighbor because my neighbor lives in me as part of my consciousness, because that person is like me, is mine. God is in the heart of my innermost parts.

Oh, how to lengthen this sweet moment and sleep within it and become eternal within it? Now, here, in the discreet, diffuse light, in this backwater of quiet, where the torment of the heart is placated, and the echoes of the world do not reach me! Insatiable desire is sleeping a dreamless sleep; habit, holy habit, rules in my [47] eternity; there have died with my memories my disappointments and with my hopes my fears.

And they come back and want to deceive us with the deceit of a deceit, and they speak to us about nothing being lost, but everything transforming, mutating, and changing, and that not even the most minute little hunk of matter is annihilated nor does the least stroke of force vanish, and there are those who seek consolation in this. Poor consolation![102] I care neither about my matter nor about my force since they are not mine while I myself am not mine. No, no, it is not to drown in the great All, in infinite and eternal Matter and Force or in God that I yearn; it is not to be possessed by God but to possess Him,[103] to make myself God without ceasing to be myself, the one who is telling you this now. The deceits of monism do not help us; we want mass and not a shadow of immortality.[104]

Materialism? Materialism, you say? Without a doubt, but the fact is that our spirit is also some matter, or else it is nothing.[105] I tremble before the idea of having to be torn away from my flesh; I tremble even more before the idea of having to be torn away from everything sensible and material, from all substance. Yes, this is materialism, and if I latch on to God with all my potencies and senses, it is so that He can carry me in His arms beyond death while looking at my eyes with His sky when my eyes are forever snuffed out. So I am fooling myself? Do not speak to me of deceit, and let me live.

They also call this pride; Leopardi called it "stinking pride,"[106] and they tell us who are we, vile earthworms, to aspire to immortality. [48] For the sake of what? For what purpose? With what right? "For the sake of what?" And for the sake of what do we live? "For what purpose?" And for what purpose are we? "With what right?" And with what right are we? It is as gratuitous to exist as to keep on existing forever. Let us not speak of the sake of anything, nor of a wherefore, nor of a right, for we will lose our reason in a whirlwind of absurdities. I claim no right nor merit at all; it is only a need; I need it to live. "And who are you?" you ask me. And I respond with Obermann, "For the universe nothing, for me everything!"[107] Pride? Pride to want to be immortal? It is a tragic fate, without a doubt, to have to cement the affirmation of immortality on the unsteady and crumbly rock of the yearning for it, but it is vile to condemn the yearning in the belief that it is groundless without giving grounds for holding [immortality] unattainable.

So I am dreaming? Let me dream, if that dream is my life; do not awaken me.[108] I believe in the immortal origin of this yearning for immortality, which is the very substance of my soul. And for what purpose do you wish to be immortal? For what purpose? Frankly, I do not understand the question. It is to inquire into the reason for the reason, the end for the end, the beginning for the beginning.

And the sensible come back at me, those who are not about to let themselves be fooled, and who drum in our ears the whiny old song that it serves no purpose to surrender to madness and to resist in vain, for what cannot be is impossible. The manly course of action, they say, is to resign oneself to luck, and since we are not immortal, let us not wish to be; let us subjugate ourselves to reason, without grieving about what cannot be remedied by darkening and saddening[109] [49] life. That obsession, they add, is a sickness . . . [110]

Sickness, madness, reason . . . the old refrain always heard! Well then, no, I do not submit to reason, and I rebel against it; and I aim to create for myself my God by force of faith and to twist at will the course of the stars, because if we had faith like a grain of mustard seed, we would say to this mountain, "Move on," and it would move, and nothing would be impossible (*Matthew* 17:20).

There you have [Nietzsche,] that thief of energies, as he stupidly called Christ.[111] He wanted to marry nihilism with the struggle for existence, Schopenhauer with Darwin,[112] and he speaks to you of valor. His heart asked of him the eternal all, while his head taught him the nothingness; and desperate and mad, to defend himself, he cursed what he most loved. When he could not be Christ, he blasphemed Christ. Inflated with himself, he wished to be endless, and he dreamed up the eternal return, wretched imitation of immortality;[113] and full of self-pity, he abominated all pity. And you tell me, young people, that that is the philosophy of strong men. No, it is not. My health and my strength impel me to perpetuate myself, and in order to perpetuate myself, to be pious. That is the doctrine of the weak that aspire to become strong, but it does not belong to the already strong, no! Only the weak desire to disappear, yearn for endless rest. In the strong, the yearning for perpetuity surpasses the doubt in achieving it, their surfeit of life spills over into the Great Beyond.

And God gave us a consolation, a supreme consolation, ultimate support of the will, and it is uncertainty, holy uncertainty. [50] Where is there absolute certainty in this business of living? Absolute, complete certainty that death is a complete and definitive and irrevocable annihilation of every personal consciousness, or the complete, absolute certainty that our personal consciousness is prolonged beyond death—both

certainties would make our lives equally impossible.[114] In the most rec-
ondite corner of the spirit, perhaps without the knowledge of the one
avowedly convinced that death is the terminus of individual consciousness, in that hidden place there is still left to that person a shadow, a
vague shadow, a shadow of a shadow of uncertainty. While he tells himself, "Time to move forward and live this passing life, since there is no
other!," the silence of that hidden place answers, "Who knows?" Perhaps the individual thinks he does not hear it, but he does. And also in a
fold of the soul of the believer that keeps more faith in a future life, there
is a muted voice, a voice of uncertainty, that tells him, "Who knows?"
These voices are perhaps like the buzz of a mosquito when the whirlwind roars among the forest trees; we do not take cognizance of that
buzz, and yet, added to the roar of the storm, it reaches our ears. How
could we live without that uncertainty?

I cannot believe those that assure me that never, not even in the
most fleeting wink of an eye, nor even in the hours of greatest inner soli-
tude and tribulation, has there come to the surface of their consciousness that rustle of uncertainty. I do not understand those human beings
who tell me that whatever lies beyond death has never concerned them,
nor that their own annihilation does not unsettle them. It seems to me
that they suffer from spiritual dullness, and I should like to stir up those
poor [51] sleepwalking souls. For myself, I do not wish to make peace
between my heart and my head, between my faith and my reason; I want
them to fight one another and to deny one another reciprocally, since
their combat is my life, and if they take away my life, I am no longer
myself. I cannot believe that reason and the senses are our only means of
communication with eternal reality. I believe that the innermost parts
of the world communicate in an intimate touch with our own innermost parts, and that faith creates its own object.

Intelligence is a fearful power! Intelligence tends toward death, memory toward stability. What is living, which is what is absolutely unstable,
absolutely individual, is unthinkable. Logic aspires to reduce everything
to identities, to genera, to every representation having only one and the
same content in any place or time in which it occurs to us. And this is not
the truth, since there is nothing that is the same in two successive
moments of its being. My idea of God is different every time that I conceive Him. Identity, which is death, is the aspiration of the intellect. The
mind seeks what is dead, since what is living escapes it.[115] It wants to con-
geal the fleeting current into icebergs, it wants to make it fixed. To analyze a body it is necessary to kill it in the mind. Science is no more than a
cemetery of dead ideas. But out of death comes life, like life out of death.

My own thoughts, tumultuous and stirred up in the bosom of my mind, broken away from their root in my heart, set down on this paper and fixed on it in unchangeable forms, are already corpses of thoughts. How, then, will reason open up to the revelation of life?[116] Tragic combat, that of truth with reason! And truth is felt and lived, not understood.

Reality is what is absolutely heterogeneous—there are no two equal leaves of a tree—and knowledge is what is homogeneous. To know is to homogenize, de-individualize. And the arbitrary part is what is truly individual. There are two worlds, that of plurality or outer reality and that of unity or inner reality; a world such as it is for all and a world such as it is for each one. Even for a stone the world is reflected in unity of consciousness. And in God plurality and unity are identified; He is the unity of plurality, the set, and the plurality of unity, richness; His ideas are objects, and objects ideas of His; He thinks by acting and He acts by thinking.[117] When He forgets someone, this one dies; when He remembers that individual, the latter revives.

And logic? Logic was around always, and in the Middle Ages above all, at the service of theology and jurisprudence, both of which began from what had been established by authority. Logic never proposed for itself the problem of knowledge, the examination of metalogical bases. "Western theology," says Stanley, "is essentially logical in its form and is based on the law; the Eastern is rhetorical in form and is based on philosophy. The Latin theologian succeeded the Roman advocate; the Oriental theologian, the Greek sophist."[118]

It is only necessary to read Plato's fearful *Parmenides* to arrive at the tragic conclusion that "the one exists and does not exist, and it and everything else exist and do not exist, appear and do not appear in relation to itself and to others."[119] And I add that all that is real is irrational and all that is rational unreal.[120]

What is rational, in fact, is nothing more than relational; reason is limited to relating irrational elements.[121] Mathematics are the only perfect science insofar as they add, subtract, multiply, and divide numbers, but not real things of substance.[122] Who is capable of extracting the square root of a beech tree or of a village?[123]

And, nonetheless, we need logic, this fearful power, to transmit thoughts and even to think them, because we think with words. To think is to speak to oneself, and speech is social. And just as social, therefore, is thought.[124] But does it not have an individual, irrational, untranslatable content or matter? Is this not its strength?[125]

5   *The Mystery of Mortality*

---

[52] Confronting this fearful mystery of mortality, face to face with the Sphinx,[1] the human being adopts different postures and tries through various means to be consoled about having been born.[2] And it occurs to the individual to take it as a game, and to say with Renan that this universe is a spectacle that God puts on for Himself and that we should serve the intentions of the great Choragus by contributing to make the spectacle as brilliant and varied as possible.[3] And they have made art a religion and a remedy for the metaphysical malady,[4] and they have invented the gibberish of art for art's sake.[5]

And that is not enough for them. Those who may tell you they write, paint, sculpt, or sing for their own recreation, if they give the public what they do, are lying, lying if they sign their writing, painting, statue, or song. They at least want to leave shadows of their spirits.[6] If the *Imitation of Christ* is an anonymous work, it is because its author, seeking the eternity of the soul, did not worry about that eternity of his name.[7] Literary people who may tell you they shun glory lie like rogues.[8]

Of Dante, who wrote those very vigorous thirty-three verses (*Purgatory* 11:85–117) about the emptiness of worldly glory,[9] Boccaccio says that he very much appreciated honors and pomp, perhaps more than was suitable for his distinguished virtue.[10] The most burning desire of his souls in hell was for them to be remembered here on earth and to be spoken about, and this illumines the darkness of his hell.[11] And he himself expounded the concept of monarchy not only for the utility of others but also for the purpose of obtaining the palm of glory (bk. 1, ch. 1).[12] [53] Even of that holy man, the most detached from earthly vanity, poor little Saint Francis of Assisi, *The Three Companions* relate that he said, *Adhuc adorabor per totum mundum,* "You will see how one day I will be adored by the whole world" (2 Celano 1.1).[13] Even of God theologians say that He created the world as a manifestation of His glory. What other need did He have of it?[14]

When doubts invade us and cloud faith in the immortality of the soul, the yearning to perpetuate one's name, to achieve even a shadow of immortality, acquires vigor and painful force.[15] Hence that enormous struggle to distinguish oneself, to survive somehow in others,[16] a struggle a thousand times more fearful than the struggle for life that gives color and tone to our society. Each one wishes self-affirmation, if only in appearance.

Once hunger is satisfied, and it is satisfied quickly, there arises vanity, the need to impose the self and survive in others. Machiavelli's remark that the human being hands over his life before he does his purse[17] can be completed by saying that he hands over his purse out of vanity. He prides himself, for want of anything better, even on his weaknesses and miseries, and is like the child that takes joy in having gotten hurt while strutting around with bandaged finger.[18] And vanity, what is it but a yearning for survival?[19]

What happens to the vain person is the same that happens to the greedy one, who takes the means for the ends and, unmindful of the ends, adheres to the means and persists in them.[20] *Appearing* to be something, which leads to *being* it, ends up by forming our objective.[21] We need for others to think us superior to them in order for us to think [54] ourselves such[22] and to ground our faith in our own persistence, or at least in the continuation of our fame. We are more grateful to the encomiast of the talent with which we defend a cause than to the recognizer of the truth or goodness of that cause. A furious mania for originality blows through the modern world of the spirit; each person embodies it in a different way. "Nobody is more of a brute than I," I once heard a pitiful man say. We prefer to talk nonsense with ingenuity rather than to hit the mark with coarseness.

Writes Rousseau in *Émile,*

> Quand les philosophes seraient en état de découvrir la Vérité, qui d'entre eux prendrait intérêt á elle? Chacun sait bien que son système n'est pas mieux fondé que les autres; mais il le soutient, parce qu'il est à lui. Il n'y en a pas un seul qui, venant à connaître le vrai et le faux, ne préférât le mensonge qu'il a trouvé à la vérité découverte par un autre. Où est le philosophe qui, pour sa gloire, ne tromperait pas volontiers le genre humain? Où est celui qui, dans le secret de son cœur, se propose un

autre objet que de se distinguer? Pourvu qu'il s'élève au-dessus du vul-
gaire, pourvu qu'il efface l'éclat de ses concurrents, que demande-t-il de
plus? L'essentiel est penser autrement que les autres. Chez les croyants
il est athée; chez les athées il serait croyant.

[Were philosophers in a position to disclose the Truth, which of them
would be interested in doing so? Each well knows that his own system
is no better grounded than the others; but he maintains it because it is
his. There is not one of them that, if he came to know what is true and
what is false, would not prefer the lie that he has found to the truth discovered by another. Where is the philosopher that would not willingly
deceive the human race for his own glory? Where is the one that in the
secret of his heart does not propose any other object but that of standing
out? Provided that he rises above the common people, provided that he
outshines his competitors, what more can he ask? Among believers he
is an atheist; among atheists he would be a believer.][23]

Our struggle to the death for the survival of our name goes back to
the past, just as it aspires to win the future. We fight with the dead, who
overshadow all of us, the living. We feel jealous of geniuses who once
lived, and whose names, like milestones of history, leap the ages. The
heaven of fame is not very large,[24] and the more that enter it, the less
famous each becomes. The great names of the past rob from us space in
it. What they may occupy in people's memories will remove it from
those of us who aspire to occupy those memories.[25] And thus we turn
against the greats, and hence the bitterness of the judgments rendered
by those seeking renown in letters about those that already achieved it
and still enjoy it. If literature becomes very rich, the day will arrive for
sifting, and each one will fear being left behind between the meshes of
the sieve. The youth irreverent toward his teachers, during his attack on
them defends himself. The iconoclast or image-breaker is a stylite who
builds himself into an image, an icon.[26] "Every comparison is odious,"
according to quite an appropriate saying, and it is a fact that we want to
be unique. Do not tell [the typical promising young man, whom we shall
call] Fernández, that he is one of the most [55] talented Spanish youths,
since while he feigns gratitude towards you, the praise bothers him; if
you tell him that he is the most talented Spaniard, hurrah!, but even
that is not enough for him; labeling him one of the world eminences
gives him more reason for being grateful, but it only satisfies him that
they tell him he is the first of all nations and all times. The more alone
he is, the closer to immortality he is in appearance—that of the name—
since names mutually diminish one another.[27]

What does that irritation mean when we think that they are robbing
us of a sentence or a thought or an image that we thought was ours,

when they plagiarize us? Robbing us? Is it a fact that it was ours once we gave it to the public? We only want it to be ours, and we live fonder of the false coin that preserves our seal than of the piece of pure gold from which our effigy and legend have been erased. It happens very commonly that when a writer's name ceases to be pronounced, it is when he was most influencing his people, with his spirit spread and infused in the spirits of those who read him, while he was quoted when his utterances and thoughts, clashing with current ideas, needed the guarantee of a name. What was his is now everyone's and he lives in everyone. But in himself he lives sad and faded and believes he is defeated. He no longer hears the applause or the silent heartbeats of those that keep reading him. Ask any sincere artist what he prefers, that his work disappear and his memory survive, or the reverse, and you will see, if he is sincere, what he tells you. When the human being does not work to live and to keep on going, he works to survive. To work for the work [56] itself is play and not work. And play? I will speak of it below.

What a tremendous passion it is that our memory survive over the oblivion of others if it were necessary! From this springs envy, to which, according to the biblical narrative, is owed the crime that opened human history: the murder of Abel by his brother Cain.[28] It was not a struggle for bread, it was a struggle to survive in God, in divine memory. Envy is a thousand times more terrible than hunger, because it is spiritual hunger.[29] Once what we call the problem of living were solved, the earth would change into a hell, because there would arise with even greater strength the struggle for survival.

For an individual's name is sacrificed not life but also happiness. Life, without a doubt: "Let me die, long live my fame!" exclaims Rodrigo Arias in *Las mocedades del Cid* (*The Youthful Deeds of the Cid*) upon falling mortally wounded by Don Diego Ordóñez de Lara.[30] One owes oneself to one's name. "Take heart, Geronimo, for you will be remembered a long time; death is bitter, but fame eternal!" exclaimed Geronimo Oligiati, student of Cola Montano and killer, co-conspirator, along with Lampugnani and Visconti, of Galeazzo Sforza, tyrant of Milan.[31] There are those who yearn even for the gallows to acquire fame, even though infamous.[32]

And what is that but a yearning for immortality, even of a name and a shadow?

There are degrees of this. Those who scorn the applause of the multitudes of today seek to survive in renewed minorities for generations.[33] They wish to prolong themselves in time more than in space. The idols of the multitudes are quickly overturned [57] by the masses themselves, and their statue crumbles at the feet of the pedestal without anyone watching, while those who win the heart of the chosen few will receive fervent veneration for a longer time even in a single chapel, secluded and small, but which will avoid the byways of oblivion.[34] Artists sacrifice the extension of their fame to its duration, yearn rather to last forever in a small corner than to shine a second in the whole universe, would rather be eternal self-conscious atoms than a momentary consciousness of the universe, sacrifice infinity to eternity.[35]

And they come back to vex our ears with that tiresome chorus of pride, stinking pride![36] Is it pride to wish to leave an indelible name behind? Pride? It is like speaking of a thirst for pleasures while interpreting as such the thirst for wealth. No, it is not the yearning to obtain pleasures, but the terror of hell that dragged human beings to the cloister in the Middle Ages; no, it is not pride, it is fear of the nothingness. We tend to be all because we see this as the only remedy to avoid being reduced to nothing. We want to save even the memories of ourselves. How long will they last? At most for the duration of human minds.[37] And what if we saved the memories of ourselves in God?[38]

All this is trivial, as I well know, but from the depth of these trivialities arises new life, and only by drinking up the lees of spiritual pain is it possible to taste honey from the bottom of [58] the cup of life. Anguish leads us to consolation.

That thirst for life everlasting is quenched by many, especially the simple, in the fountain of religious faith, but it is not granted to everyone to drink of it.[39] Further, it poses the risk of each individual making it to measure at will and corroborating its faults with every individual belief instead of correcting them.

And there are those who do not seek to eternalize their names in art, but to taste beauty. Those who do not produce art, if they are not consumers of art, see play in it and do not work, pursuing Beauty, ideal of hope.

In the beautiful the spirit becomes calm and rests,[40] its anguish relieved. The fact is that the beautiful is the revelation of what is eternal,[41] and the beauty of things is nothing but the perpetuation of momentariness.[42]

Just as truth is the ideal of faith, beauty is the ideal of hope.

Nothing is lost, nothing passes away altogether, everything is perpetuated in some way or other; everything after passing through time returns to the eternity from which it arose.[43] The world has temporal roots in eternity and there the yesterday is next to the today and the tomorrow. Scenes pass before us, but the film of the cinematographer of the world stays unified and whole.[44]

Physicists say that not a single atom of matter is lost, nor a sole minuscule blow of force, but they change while persisting.[45] And is a form lost, however fleeting? It is necessary to believe that it is not. In some part it remains filed, reflected, perpetuated, and is a mirror of eternity in which are recapitulated all images [59] that march through time.[46] Every impression that may reach me stays filed in my brain although it may be with such little force that it sinks to the bottom of my subconscious, but from there it animates my life; and if my whole spirit, if the total content of my soul, became conscious, all the fleeting impressions forgotten after hardly being perceived and even those that passed unnoticed would spring up again.[47] I carry within me everything that paraded before me and I perpetuate it with myself and perhaps all of it goes into my roots and all my ancestors live in me completely and will live in my descendents. And all of me, with all this universe of mine, goes into each one of my works, or at least there goes into them the essential part of me, that which makes me be myself, my individual essence.[48]

And this individual essence of each thing, this which causes it to be itself and not something else, what is it if not its beauty? What is the beauty of something if not its eternal base, that which unites its past to its future, that part of it which rests and remains in the innermost depths of eternity?[49] What is my beauty but the formula of my life?

The beautiful is the eternal part of things, their root outside time. And when, conquering time, we die, our beauty will remain. Only the beautiful remains, and everything remains insofar as it is beautiful. And beauty is thus the greatest revelation of the love of God for the human being. God's love gives us the beauty to conquer time and death.

And how is beauty achieved? How does beauty flourish? How is it revealed to us? Through [60] love. Love is the one that reveals to us what is eternal in us and what is eternal in our neighbors; love is the one that takes us with its sweet hand to eternalize our brother in ourselves and to eternalize ourselves in him.[50]

Is it the beautiful, the eternal part of things, that awakens and kindles our love for them; or is it our love of things that reveals the beautiful to us, the eternal part of them? Beauty is a creation of love, the same as the sensible world is a creation of the individual instinct, the instinct of self-preservation,[51] and the supra-sensible world a creation of the social instinct, the instinct of self-perpetuation, and not in any other sense. Beauty, and eternity with it, is a creation of love.

"Our outer man," says the Apostle (2 *Corinthians* 4:16), "goes on wearing away, but the inner man is renewed from day to day." The human being of appearances-that-pass-away wears away and passes away with them; the human being of reality-that-remains, grows. "For this slight momentary affliction is preparing for us an exceedingly high and eternal weight of glory" (verse 17). Our pain gives us anguish, and anguish upon bursting from the fullness of itself gives birth to consolation. "Not by our looking at things that are seen, but things that are not seen; for things that are seen are temporal; but those that are not seen are eternal" (verse 18). Is Beauty seen?[52]

Since love is painful, since love is compassion, it is pity. Beauty arises from compassion, and is nothing but the consolation that compassion seeks. Anguished when we sense that everything is passing, that we are passing, that what is ours is passing, that everything surrounding us is passing, we receive the revelation, offered by anguish itself, of the consolation of what is not passing, of what is eternal, of what is beautiful.

And this beauty thus revealed, this perpetuation of momentariness, is only realized in a practical way, only lives through the action of charity. Hope in action is charity, just as beauty in action is the good. Hope and beauty are something static. As soon as they come out of themselves and spread, hope gives us charity and beauty the good.

[61] The root of charity, which eternalizes all it loves and takes out for us the beauty hidden in it, while giving us the good: the root of charity is love for God,[53] charity towards God, compassion for God. Love, compassion, I said, personalizes everything when it discovers the suffering in everything, and by personalizing everything, it personalizes the Universe itself, which also suffers, and it discloses God to us.[54] For God reveals Himself to us because He suffers and because we suffer; because He suffers He demands our love, and because we suffer He gives us His, and covers our misery with eternal, infinite misery.

This was the scandal of Christianity among Jews and Hellenes,[55] among Pharisees and Stoics. This was the scandal and continues to be so and will be forever. This is the eternal truth before which human beings feel awed. This is, Lord, the revelation of Your heart of hearts, and of the mystery of the world: that You sent Your Son, the Son of Man, to suffer passion and death and to redeem us by suffering. And human beings made him god and discovered through him Your eternal essence, the essence of a God that suffers, that loves, that thirsts for love, for compassion, that is a Person. The one who never knows the Son never knows the Father and the Father only through the Son.[56] The one who does not know the Son of Man that suffers bloody anguishes, rendings of his heart, pain that kills and resurrects, the one who does not know the Son will not know the Father, nor will know of God, of the God that suffers.[57]

[62] What do we have [to do with] that logical and frigid *Ens realissimus* [realest Being], *primum movens* [prime mover], with that impassive entity, and because impassive, no more than a pure idea?[58] How do we want the world to flow and live on an impassive idea? The world itself would be a vain idea, a vain appearance, a shadow of a shadow. But the world suffers and the suffering amounts to feeling the flesh of reality; it is for the spirit to feel itself made of mass and substance, to touch itself, it is immediate reality.[59]

Pain is what is transcendent, pain is the substance of life. And pain is universal and is what unites all us beings; it is divine, universal blood, that circulates through everyone. That which we call will, force, what is it but pain?

And pain has its degrees, in accordance with the degrees of inwardness, from that pain that floats on the sea of appearances to the eternal anguish that goes down to alight on the depths of what is eternal and there arouses consolation,[60] from that pain that causes our bodies to writhe to that anguish that causes us to lie down in the bosom of God and receive there the sprinkling of His divine tears.[61]

Anguish is something deeper and more intimate than pain.[62] One generally feels anguished amidst that which we call happiness and by happiness itself, which produces trembling and refusal to resign oneself.[63] Happy human beings that resign themselves to their apparent bliss (since all bliss is only apparent in the [63] world) may be said to have no substance, or at least have not discovered it in themselves, have not touched it. Such humans are accustomed to being powerless to love and to be loved. At base, they live without pain or glory.

There is no love except in pain (cf. Fray Tomé de Jesús),[64] and in this world we are to choose between love—that is pain—or bliss. And love does not lead to any other bliss that is not that of love itself, which is painful love. From the moment in which love becomes blissful, it is satisfied, it no longer desires, and is no longer love. The satisfied, the blissful do not love; they doze off in customary life, bordering on annihilation.[65] To grow accustomed is to begin to lose one's being.[66] The human being's humanness grows with the capacity for suffering.

When we come to the world it is given to us to choose between love and bliss, and—poor us!—we wish both, the bliss of loving, love in bliss. But Lord, give me love and not bliss, and do not let me doze off into mere custom, for I fear going to sleep altogether, losing consciousness, and not recovering it ever again. May I feel, Lord, may I feel myself in pain.[67]

What is Fate, what is Fatality but the kinship of love and pain, and that fearful mystery that, while love tends toward bliss, as soon as it touches it, it dies off, and with it true bliss dies off? Love and pain engender one another mutually, and love is charity, it is compassion, and love that is not charity and compassion is not such love. Love is resigned despair.

That which mathematicians call a problem of maximums and minimums, that which is called a law of economy, is the formula of all existential movement. In material and social mechanics, in industry and social economy, the whole problem is reduced to achieving the maximum of results with the minimum of effort, the most income with the least costs, the most pleasures with the least pain. And the fearful formula of inner spiritual life is either to achieve the maximum of bliss with the minimum of love, or the maximum of love with the minimum of bliss. Choose. And be sure that as you are approaching the infinite of Love, of infinite love, you will approach the zero of bliss, supreme misery. And when touching this zero, you are beyond your miseries, those that kill.[68]

There is something more anguishing than suffering. [64] That man expected that when he received the dreaded blow, he would suffer so strongly that he would succumb to the suffering, and the blow came to him, and he did not feel the wrenching pain he feared. But later, after recovering consciousness, when he felt insensible, he became seized with dismay, a fearful dismay, of the most dismaying, most painless kind, and he screamed while drowning in anguish: the fact is that he did not exist![69] What would terrify you more: to feel a pain that lacerated your entrails when your breast was pierced with burning iron, or to see that it was pierced in this fashion without your feeling any pain at all? Have you never felt the dismay, the horrible dismay, of feeling without tears and pain? Pain tells us we exist, pain tells us the world in which we live exists, pain tells me that You exist and that You suffer, my God! Pain discloses God to us and causes us to love Him.

To believe in God is to love Him, and to love Him is to feel Him suffering.

He suffers, and since suffering implies limitation, He is certainly limited. He is limited by crude matter in which He lives, by what is unconscious, from which He tries to liberate Himself and liberate us.[70] And we at the same time should try to liberate Him from it.

God suffers, suffers in everyone, and everyone of us suffers in Him. Anguish is nothing but divine suffering, it is to feel that God suffers in me, that I suffer in Him.[71] [65] Universal pain is the anguish of everything to be all without being able to achieve it, the anguish of each one being what it is while being at the same time all that it is not. The base of being is not properly speaking, as Spinoza said,[72] the determination or effort to persist in one's own being, but the effort to become universal and total, to be everything. Every created being tends not to preserve itself within itself, but to perpetuate itself in the others, to invade us, to be all beings while continuing to be itself, to broaden its limits to the infinite but without breaking them. It does not wish to break its walls and leave everything on flat, communal ground, mixing and losing its individuality, but wants to carry its walls to the extremes of Creation and embrace everything within them. I aspire to have the universe be me.

And that vast self within which I wish to insert the Universe, what is it but God? And because I aspire toward Him I love Him; and since I suffer to be Him, He also suffers to be me, to be all and everyone.

A huge current of pain impels some beings toward others and causes them to love and seek and try to complete one another and to be themselves and the others in the case of each of them.[73]

In God everything lives,[74] and in His suffering everything suffers; and when we love God, in Him we love the other creatures, just as when we love the creatures, in them we love God. My soul will not be free, my God, while there is any enslaved creature in this world that You made. You, therefore, Who live in my soul, [66] will be free in it.[75]

And the most immediate element is to feel and love my own misery, to have love of myself.[76] And this compassion, when it lives and overflows, spills over from me to all the others, and from the excess of my own compassion I show pity towards my neighbors.[77] One's own misery is so abundant, that the compassion it arouses quickly brims over, and it reveals universal misery to us.[78]

What is charity if not an excess of compassion, a brimming over of it? What is it if not reflected pain that spills over to pity the ills of others and to exercise charity?[79]

6 *What Is Charity?*

When the fullness of our compassion brings us the awareness of God in us,[1] such a great anguish fills us for the divine misery shed over everything,[2] that we must spill it out in the form of charity. And when we spill it out, we feel relief and the painful sweetness of the good.[3] The contemplator of something beautiful feels the need to make all others participate in it. The impulse to produce is the work of love.[4]

We feel a satisfaction in doing good when we possess the good in excess,[5] when we are bursting with compassion; and we are bursting with it when God fills our souls, and gives us the painful sensation of universal life.[6]

We are not in the world juxtaposed to others, without a common root with them, nor is their lot indifferent to us, but [67] their pain aggrieves us, we feel our community of origin, we feel it even without knowing it.[7] Pain and compassion reveal to us the kinship of all that exists.[8] Francis of Assisi addressed as "Brother Wolf" the poor wolf that feels painful hunger for sheep and perhaps the pain of having to devour them,[9] and that kinship reveals to us the parenthood of God, the fact that God is Father, that is, that God exists.[10] And as a Father, He shelters our common misery.

What is charity, then? It is the impulse to liberate myself and to liberate all my neighbors from pain, to liberate God from it. And how will we liberate ourselves from pain? But previously, let us ask from where the pain comes.

Pain is something purely spiritual and the most immediate revelation of consciousness;[11] the body was given to us only to give occasion for pain to make itself manifest. Whoever has never suffered would have no self-consciousness. The first lament of the human being, at birth, has its cause in the entrance of air into the breast, limiting its owner and seeming to say, "You have to breathe me to live!"[12]

The material or sensible world, the one that the senses create for us, exists only to embody and support the other world, the spiritual or imaginable world,[13] the one that the imagination creates for us. Consciousness tends at every instant to be more consciousness, to engage in consciousness-raising, to have full awareness of its whole self, of all its content. In the depths of our own bodies—in [68] irrational animals, in plants, in rocks, in waters, on the earth, on the sun, in the Universe—there is a spirit that struggles to know itself, to acquire awareness of being, to be itself [*serse*], to be pure spirit;[14] and since it can only achieve this by means of a body, by means of matter, it creates matter, and makes use of it, and is taken and remains a prisoner of it. You can only see your face by means of a mirror, but in order to see yourself you remain a prisoner of the mirror in which you see yourself: and you see yourself just as the mirror deforms you; and if the mirror slips out of your hands and breaks, you no longer see yourself, and if it fogs over, you fog over.[15]

Spirit is limited by the matter in which it has to live and acquire self-awareness, just as thought is limited by the word. Without matter there is no spirit, but matter causes spirit to suffer by limiting it. And pain is the obstacle that matter sets up for spirit, it is the collision with the unconscious.

Pain is the barrier that the unconscious, matter, sets for consciousness, spirit, the limit that the sensible Universe imposes on God;[16] it is the obstacle that consciousness finds when wishing to broaden itself at the cost of the unconscious; it is the resistance that the unconscious sets to consciousness-raising.[17]

Although we believe it by authority, we do not know we have a heart, stomach, or lungs while they do not ache us. It is physical pain that reveals to us the existence of our inner organs.[18] And thus it is with spiritual pain: we do not feel our souls either until they hurt us.[19]

Pain, anguish, is what makes consciousness reflexive, bending back over itself.[20] The individual without anguish knows what he does and what he thinks, but does not know that he is doing it and thinking it. He thinks, but he does not think that he thinks, and his thoughts are as if they were not his. Nor does he belong to himself. Only through anguish does the spirit Unamuno take control of himself.

Pain, which is an undoing, causes us to discover our innermost parts, and in the supreme undoing, that of death, we arrive through pain of annihilation at the eternal interior of our temporal innermost parts, at God, Whom in spiritual anguish we breathe and learn to love.[21]

The origin of evil is that which is called the inertia of matter, and which is sloth in the spirit. And for a good reason it was said that sloth is the mother of all vices.[22]

Consciousness, the yearning for more and more [69] and each time more, the hunger for God,[23] the thirst for the infinite, never is satisfied. Each consciousness wants to be itself and all the others without ceasing to be itself. And matter, the unconscious, tends toward being less, each time less, toward not being anything; it is a thirst for annihilation. Consciousness tends toward the infinite, the unconscious toward zero. Spirit says, "I want to be!" and matter responds to it, "I do not want it!"

And in the order of human life the individual, moved by the mere instinct of self-preservation, creator of the material world, would tend toward destruction, toward the nothingness, were it not for society, which by giving it the instinct of self-perpetuation, creator of the spiritual world, carries it and impels it toward the all, toward immortality. And all that human beings do as mere individuals, vis-à-vis society, for the sake of self-preservation, is bad, and all they do as social entities, for the sake of the society in which they are included, is good because they perpetuate themselves within it.[24] And many that seem to be great egoists and run roughshod over everything to fulfill their works, are merely souls inflamed with charity and overflowing with it, because they submit and subjugate their wretched individual selves to their social selves, which have missions to fulfill in earthly life.[25]

Whoever binds the work of love, of spiritualization, of liberation, to transitory, individual forms, crucifies God in matter. Whoever causes the ideal to serve [70] his or her temporal interests or individual worldly glory perpetrates the same crime. Such a person is a deicide.[26]

The work of charity, of love for God, is that of trying to liberate Him from crude matter, is that of trying to spiritualize and raise the consciousness of everything. This means attempting to make rocks speak, to make everything existing conscious, to resurrect the Word. It is necessary to uncrucify Him, to unnail Him from the Cross, to rescue Him, to dematerialize the world through love.

Do you see this? Do you see this in that Eucharistic symbol? They have captured it in a piece of bread, of material bread, and have done so in order that we may eat it and thereby make it our own, belonging to our body in which the spirit is lodged. May it shake within our heart, and think within our brain, and be consciousness. They have captured it in that bread so that by burying it in our body it may revive in our spirit. Such is the symbol.[27]

I must spiritualize everything. And how will I spiritualize all? By giving to everyone and to all my own spirit, which increases all the more the more I distribute it.

———————

And here you have the supreme precept that rises from love for God and serves as the foundation of all morality: surrender yourself altogether; give over your spirit! This is the sacrifice of life.

Christ gave himself, he surrendered himself completely in a supreme act of generosity, of love.[28]

And the act of surrendering oneself supposes imposing oneself. True morality is, at base, aggressive.

The individual qua individual, the [71] miserable individual that lives imprisoned by the instinct of self-preservation and by the senses, wants nothing but to preserve himself, and is completely obsessed about letting anybody else penetrate into his sphere to disturb him, to interrupt his sloth; and in exchange for this he foregoes penetrating into the spheres of others, interrupting their laziness, disturbing them, taking possession of them. "Do not do unto others what you may not wish for yourself,"[29] it is said, and since he does not want others to insert their spirits into his own, nor to kindle his hunger for God, he does not wish to insert his into those of the others. And he grows smaller and shrivels up and perishes in this spiritual greed.[30]

That is the repulsive morality of anarchistic individualism: everyone out for himself. And since everyone is not himself, he can poorly serve himself.

But as soon as the individual senses himself in society, he feels himself in God, and the instinct of self-perpetuation inflames him with love of God and with charity. He seeks to perpetuate his spirit, that is, to perpetuate the spirit, to unnail God from the Cross, and he only yearns to affix the seal of his spirit on other spirits and to receive their seals on his. He shook off laziness, he shook off spiritual greed.

Sloth, they say, is the mother of all vices, and sloth engenders the two vices that are, in turn, the source of all the others.[31]

Sloth is the weight of matter, inert of itself, within us; and that sloth, while telling us that it tries to [72] preserve us through thrift, in reality tries merely to diminish us, to annihilate us.

The human being has either an excess of spirit or one of matter.[32] And here arises once more the problem of maximums and minimums, of how we shall have the most spirit with the least matter, of how much infinity fits in us so as not to fall into the maximum of matter with the minimum of spirit—the human being has either an excess of spirit or one of matter. When he has too much spirit, he spills it out and sheds it all over, and it increases in company of those of others; when he has too much matter and too little spirit from husbanding it, he lets it get lost, and there happens to him what happened to the individual who received a single talent, and he buried it so as not to lose it, and he later remained without it.[33] For the one who has will be given even more, but the one who has only a little, even this little will be taken away from him.[34]

Be perfect like your heavenly Father,[35] it was said to us. And this terrifying precept, fearful because it is impossible for us to achieve the perfection of the Father, this fearful precept should be the norm of our behavior.[36] And we should aspire to the impossible, and since it is not possible for us to achieve it, we should say to the Father, "I cannot, aid my powerlessness!"[37]

And to be perfect is to be everything, it is to be myself and to be all the others.[38] And I do not find any other road to be all the rest than to give myself to all, and when I am in everything, everything will be in me. [73] Hence invasive morality, which is aggressive, if you will. True charity is invasive. True charity consists of inserting my spirit into the other spirits, of giving them my pain as pabulum and consolation to their pains, of awakening their concerns with my concern, of sharpening their hunger for God with my hunger for Him. Charity is not a dozing off in the inertia of matter, but an arousing of them in the restlessness of the spirit.

And this is generosity, one of the two basic virtues that arise when inertia, sloth, is conquered.

The remedy of pain, which is the clash of consciousness with the unconscious,[39] is not to sink into unconsciousness, but to elevate oneself to consciousness and to suffer more. One must not take opium, but put vinegar and salt in the wound of the soul, for when you go to sleep and do not feel the pain any longer, you cease to be. And one must be.

No, no, do not close your eyes to the anguishing Sphinx,[40] but look at her face to face, and go to her and let her grab you and chew you in her mouth of 100,000 poisonous teeth and swallow you. And you will see what sweetness it is when she has swallowed you, what tasty pain.[41]

The great principle of intimate morality is mutual imposition. Human beings should try to impose themselves on one another, to give their spirits to one another, to leave their seals on each other's souls.[42] And even passively this law is satisfied. Accommodating to the milieu, imitating, putting oneself in another's place—sympathy, in short—besides being a manifestation of the unity of the species, is a way of expanding, of being the others. To be conquered is often to conquer;[43] to take something from another is a way of living in that other.

My glass is small, but I drink from my glass,[44] said an egoistic poet.[45] No, from my glass everyone drinks, I want all to drink [74] from it, I give it to them, and my glass grows in accordance with those that drink from it; and all, when they place their mouth on it, leave in it something of their spirit. And I also drink from the glasses of the others.

The more I belong to others, the more I belong to myself; and the more I am myself, the more I am of the others. From the fullness of myself I spill over onto my brothers and sisters, and on spilling over onto them they enter me.

"Be perfect like your Father" (*Matthew* 5:48), it was said to us, and our Father is perfect because He is Himself and each of His children, who within Him lives, is, and moves.[46] And the end of perfection is that all of us be one thing alone (*John* 17:21), all one body in Christ (*Romans* 12:5), and that finally with all things subjected to the Son, the Son Himself be subjected in turn to the One Who subjected all, so that God may be all in all (*1 Corinthians* 15:27).

The end of charity, the end of love for God, is to cause God to be all in all, and all of us all in God.[47] It is the perfect consciousness-raising of the universe, that is, its socialization, its divinization, that nature be society and society perfect, kinship, family. And then it will be possible to call Him Father openly.

———————

And this society in which we live? This is only society from the outside, in appearance, only an apparent society as well as a mere appearance. The same thing that unites interests within it separates souls. Human beings, the more they associate with one another, the more dissociated they are in spirit. [75] Modern civilization! What a monstrous Greco-Roman idol that awoke in the Renaissance and throttles us![48] Everything is, at base, sensuality; everything is a minute search for passing bliss. Fleeing from pain, we have no love to gain. Thus we flee from love, from the fearful love that causes us to seek not our bliss, but God's.

How much I miss Love, fearful, blind Love, that delivers us to Fatality! It does not speak to us of art, nor of bliss, nor of life, nor does it speak to us of anything but of love. How much better if we could knock down all the proud edifices that human inanity erected, break the marble, burn the fabrics, and spend our lives raising to God a continuous *de profundis* [Out of the depths, as of sorrow]! To change the world into a vast

convent in which souls may burn and be consumed in an infinite yearning for infinity,[49] and while burning and being consumed they would
thus become inflamed and illumined, and the whole earth a conflagration of love: this conflagration would devour our sciences, our arts, our
industries, all our wretched riches.

When it is remarked how apocalyptic and millenary the Gospels
are—all that business of keep watch and pray, as the day is near—we are
told that the Gospels were written under the pressure of the belief in the
nearness of the end of the world.[50] And it was a very just belief, because
the end of the world is very close for each of us, and very near the day of
our death. Let us therefore keep watch and pray and let us spend life in a
continuous yearning.

[76] And for what purpose is that continuous yearning, that sighing,
that praying for mercy if we will thereby gain nothing? Well, precisely
for that reason alone, because we would gain nothing if it is so, and if
something were gained, because we would gain it.[51]

Who say they are happy? No, they are not happy.[52] At most, they
think they are, but the fact is that there is no more fearful unhappiness
than that of the one who thinks he is happy, because his lot is not even
unhappiness, but pure nothingness, unconsciousness.[53] Is the human
being happy in the maternal cloister before being born?[54] For such is the
happiness of those that think they are happy and rest and yearn for nothing. Far better to be a consciousness in pain than an unconsciousness in
repose. An eternal dawn that keeps on growing in clarity without the
sun ever rising; and the clarity grows so great that everything comes to
shine like a sun, and we go on awaiting the sun while [the dawn] surrounds us and inflames us and we live in it.

No, my God, no, not bliss on earth, not that bliss in pursuit of which
our human beings run in anxious haste, no! Illumine them, Lord, so that
they renounce earthly bliss and resign themselves to pain, which is consciousness.[55]

Never has there been so much talk about solidarity, and perhaps
never has there been a vaguer awareness and a more obscure sense of
what solidarity (solidaridad), or better said, welding together (sol-
damiento), is.[56] For there is true welding together in the spiritual union
of a few solitary people that throughout space and time communicate to
one another than in almost all the wretched associations, leagues, and
societies that [77] abound so much today.

This welding together, true solidarity, rises from the excess of individual consciousnesses, which, aching on not knowing inside themselves, spill over onto the outside. The human being truly welded to his

brothers and sisters is the one whose heart bursts out of himself, the one who is seeking to give something of himself, not the one who seeks to receive it. There are no more wretched cooperatives than those for consumption.

And add to all this a raging rudeness that is shown by a poorly veiled hate of ideality—when they veil it at all. This hate, child of the fear bred by powerlessness, characterizes almost all our free-thinking progressives, rationalists, or avant-garde. All religion hurts and vexes them. Incapable of wisdom, they seek refuge under the banner of science, and their ardor increases with their scientific ignorance. Their final prophet has been Nietzsche.[57]

7 *Life in God*

[78] "And that immortality of which you dream and for which you yearn so much, how will it be?" it can be said to me. In other words, how will we live in God? How? Who knows? And this not knowing is our fear and our hope, our consolation and our disconsolateness. Not to know how we shall live in God is not to know what will become of us after death.

Our life in God will be life in truth, in goodness, and in beauty. It will be the life on which God lives, but will we drown in it?[1] Will we maintain the life of God by ceasing to live ourselves the way that those living beings that maintain ours cease to live?[2] Paul says that if one died for all, all are dead, and that Christ died for all so that all who live may no longer live for themselves, but certainly for the one who died and came to life for them (2 *Corinthians* 5:14–15). And do you not recall those Eastern mysteries of Adonis, the god that died to come to life and die again?[3]

How will be our life after death? How will we live in God? By losing our personal consciousness?

We are in the heart of the anguish to assuage, whose pain tends toward all the tedium of the life that passes away.

What will become of this soul of mine? What will become of me?

There are those who do not feel the substantiality of their own spirit, who do not touch it with spiritual touch, who [79] pass like fleeting shadows. I not only know myself, but I feel myself,[4] or to put it better, I am to myself. And vis-à-vis the "vanity of vanities," the hollowness of hollownesses, in which it causes me to burst out with the consideration of what is happening outside me, there escapes from my lips a "plenitude of plenitudes" when I turn to myself and to what is left inside me, and I conquer time.[5] Each memory is a possession of hope, the conquest of a yesterday, a possession for conquering the tomorrow.[6] But my memory does not go beyond my birth, while I then substitute the memory of the society in which I live and it speaks to me of what was before I had being, and thus hope cannot go beyond my death. It then passes into the hope of the society in which my seeds will bear fruits. My spirit, my personal consciousness, began by springing from my unconsciousness, and my spirit will perhaps end by returning to the unconsciousness from which it sprang.

And if it causes me no anguish to think that I was not before I acquired being, why will it cause me anguish to think that I shall not be when I cease to be? Because then I will have no consciousness to feel pain about not existing?

And yet . . .

How will we live in God?

It is a fearful thing, an idea that makes the soul sweat blood, to think about complete annihilation, and it is a fearful thing, too, to think that you will forever be you, you yourself, without being able to cease [80] to be it, condemned to the eternity of yourself.[7] Or will our death be the sowing of a heavenly subject? Will we be caterpillars of heavenly butterflies? Seeds of eternal flowers?

And the butterfly, does it remember when it was a caterpillar?[8] Does the flower remember the seed?

We move in an awesome dilemma. The perspective of our consciousness having to be annihilated one day is a thing that strikes dread in the soul that delves deep into itself;[9] but, on the other hand, the meditation on an eternity of consciousness does not strike less dread in us, because it is so incomprehensible to us, or better said, it is as unimaginable as our annihilation.

Let us try to imagine an individual and personal life everlasting. Within time?[10] This implies change, and change excludes personal eternity.

We can imagine for ourselves an indefinite spiritual growth, a continuing to grow and enrich our consciousnesses, to keep on approaching Universal Consciousness, infinite and eternal, without reaching it ever, the way that several quantities can grow in any progression, some in more and others in less, without reaching the infinite and each one passing through the values through which the other passed.[11] We can imagine for ourselves. . . . But in the possibility of imagination, what is the limit?

And we can also glimpse a state that is neither that of individual personalization, which we enjoy now, nor is it complete [81] impersonalization, that is, annihilation.

And here come to us all those hypocritical doctrines that speak to us of our impersonal persistence, and tell us that nothing gets lost, that the elements comprising me persist,[12] that my ideas remain, as do the effects of my works, etc. But if my individual consciousness, if the consciousness of myself that binds my life in the light of memories disappears, something gets lost.[13]

They tell us that we should renounce personal immortality and even that renouncing it is a religious duty, it is the supreme holocaust to God.[14] And now we are at the heart of this fearful doctrine.

"You keep on growing toward God," it can be said to me.[15] "Well then, imagine that growth takes wing, increases, that you leap the infinite distance that separates you from the Infinite, and that you fuse in God by being absorbed by Him.[16] Would you not accept this lot? For it implies the disappearance of your personality. Would you not accept going on to be absorbed in God? For your being absorbed in Him is equivalent to ceasing to be yourself. You are an instrument in the hands of the Lord, and the Lord proceeds with His work as soon as He dispenses with you."

And to this I say that a religious soul would doubtlessly come to renounce its own personal immortality by placing itself in the hands of its God, but it is by being sure and certain that that God exists in Whose breast it renounces its immortality, and that that God keeps living and fulfilling His work. But do we have this certainty and security?

To cease to be myself in order to go [82] fuse in God, yes, of course; but do I have the certainty that when my consciousness dissolves there remains a Universal Consciousness, a Supreme Person?

This is one of the most dreadful vicious circles. We would renounce our individual immortality if we had the certainty that there exists a universal and eternal Consciousness that gives finality and sense to the Universe and fulfills the work of the spirit, but our belief in that universal and eternal Consciousness, in God, springs from our yearning for immortality.[17] And we are asked to sacrifice for love of God, but what is our guarantee that love is not an empty love, a pure illusion?

Is the universe not something unconscious, pure matter, and consciousness nothing but a passing phenomenon, a lightning flash between two eternities of darkness?

He who sees God dies, the Scriptures say,[18] but we would consider it a good death to die and to die altogether for having seen God, to have our consciousness annihilated at the instant of going to sink into Universal Consciousness, and to be annihilated from the certainty that this Consciousness exists.

We have made God the guarantee of our personality; our personal consciousness asks of us a God. Our egotism is only [83] a reflection of the egotism of the Universe, that wants to be Me;[19] it is the Universe qua conscious, it is the spirit that calls itself "I" within me. When someone strongly believes in God, and asserts it, and because of asserting it suffers until death, it is God Himself Who asserts it in that person; it is Spirit struggling to overcome matter.

The cause of our immortality is reduced, at base and strictly speaking, to the cause of the immortality of the Spirit, that is, of the immortality of God, in other words, of His existence.[20] And the fact that a God may exist means only that there is a Consciousness of the Universe that is individual and personal at the same time, and that joins the greatest personality to the maximum individuality.[21]

For between individuality and personality is a certain inverse proportion, as there is between the extension and the comprehension of an idea. Individuality is for a living being what extension is for a concept: its continent, its form, dividing it from the rest; and personality is for it what comprehension is for a concept: its content, its substance.

A human spirit can separate itself from the rest and strongly acknowledge its individuality by having an extremely poor personality,[22] as there can be a vessel with thick and sturdy walls containing nothing but a homogeneous liquid. There can be, on the contrary, human spirits, as in fact there are, that hardly separate themselves from the rest, that are with them in intimate and frequent communication, giving and taking ideas and thoughts, and filled with spiritual riches, as within a very delicate membrane, through which very active endosmosis and exosmosis is effected, a very rich and very complex protoplasm is enclosed. And experience teaches us that the souls richest in content, the ones bursting with ideas and sentiments, the liveliest ones—that is, those that live in greatest and most active change—are those that separate themselves less from the others. Richness of content rarifies and wears down the density of the continent.

With more abstract, less metaphorical reasons, it could be demonstrated that individuality and personality, understood in this manner, are in inverse proportion to one another.[23]

And God is for us the maximum of personality with the maximum of individuality, the Being richest in content and most closed in continent, because outside Him there is nothing.[24] Pantheism drowns the individuality of God in the plenitude of His personality, and rigid Aristotelian or Islamic monotheism suffocates His personality in His individuality.

The zero is a pure individual without content, and the infinite a pure content, without continent, and the two are two absurdities. And each being is an infinite of zeroes.

The need to save the personality of God is what produced the dogma of the Trinity, the faith in three divine Persons, making God society.[25]

And there will always be someone who says, "And for what purpose will there be an eternal Spirit? For what purpose a Universal Eternal Consciousness? What is the purpose of this purpose?"

And thus is presented to us, in another form, the issue of what is the cause of the cause, the principle of the principle. A first principle needing no prior to be understood is as inconceivable as an ultimate end not serving an end beyond it to justify it. When we enter into the wherefore of the wherefore, we are in such thick, impenetrable darkness as when we enter into the why of the why.[26] And darkness that chills the soul. Let us get out of it.

Let us get out, indeed, but with our souls wounded with despair.

My poor God! How I suffer in You and You suffer in me.[27] You, because we cannot defend each other mutually from death. I would deliver myself completely to You, my God, but is it sure that You exist? Are not You perhaps a mere dream of my anguish, of the anguish of the spirit? If in fact You exist, Universal Consciousness, [84] eternal and infinite Ego, hide me in Your bosom, let me see You face to face, so that I may conquer the certainty that You are, and then let me die from that vision and that certainty so that You may be born from me and may forever be my all.

The Apostle saw this supreme splendid vision when he said that once everything is subjected to the Son, the Son will in turn be subjected to the Father that subjected everything, so that God may be all in all.[28] As soon as the Word, the Idea, changes all into consciousness, and into consciousness everything changes from the grains of sand to the suns and stars, the universal consciousness will enter, with matter conquered, into the supreme Ego. The Apostle had this vision; this vision was the strength of the theology of Origen.[29] This vision is the hidden strong point of religion.[30]

What is religion here on earth but a foreshadowing of that divine life, a sentiment of that dependence on the Spirit which is personal and universal at the same time?[31]

8 *Religion*

[85] The definitions that have been given of religion are as diverse as is, at base, the religious sentiment.[1] And the fact is that in religion more than in any other thing it is sentiment that unites and thought that separates. As soon as human beings try to reduce their religious sentiment to concepts, discords appear.[2]

Nevertheless, it can be said that by religion is understood the relationship of the human soul with a being superior to it,[3] conscious and [willed?],[4] real or fictitious, that is, existing outside us or hammered out by us as a projection of our spirit. Common currency by now is Schleiermacher's notion that religion springs from the sentiment of dependence and from the wish to establish relations with a more perfect being, with a supreme being.[5] Matthew Arnold, for his part, said that religion is ethics accompanied by emotion.[6]

On the other hand, we have the idea that *timor primus fecit deos* (fear first created gods)[7] and the notion of the cult of the dead as origins of religion. And the three concepts can be well harmonized.

The cult of the dead is the primitive form of the spiritual yearning for self-perpetuation, of the need to eternalize our consciousness, the only thing of which we have immediate certainty.[8] At the same time, it is an obscure manifestation of the need, which capacitates the will to live, for giving a spiritual sense to the whole universe by affirming it for the consciousness. The simple human being that instituted the cult of the dead sees everywhere roundabout conscious, animated beings, [86] harmful or beneficial.[9] The basis of fear is insecurity in the face of what is going to come, insecurity based on the ignorance of the law as to why processes of things proceed as they do. And this ignorance of the law, source of insecurity that breeds fear, is the ignorance that causes everything that happens to be attributed to conscious, capricious beings that conceal from us the motives they obey, that is, their law.[10] And that consciousness of the universe, that is not a law imposed on it—strictly speaking, as soon as we know the law it can be said in a certain sense that we give it to the universe[11]—that supreme consciousness established in mystery is the power on which we feel we depend. All this, therefore, the cult of the dead, the dread that creates gods, and the sentiment of dependence, arise from attributing consciousness to the universe, whether as a whole, or whether in its parts, that is, from the need to save consciousness.

This need was reflected in the ancient Greeks and Romans in their cult of heroes, in the making of heroes. The heroes (Amphiaraus, Achilles, Œdipus) did not die but were snatched away to another, underground world, or were assumed—like the Virgin Mary according to Christian legend—and later arose the tendency to convert all into heroes, each family its members, to make them immortal.[12]

And that tendency to assume everything into consciousness, which mixes with the yearning for immortality from which it springs and which it accompanies, is what gave God as Producer of immortality.[13]

Understanding it and feeling it all in the form of consciousness is the basis of the religious spiritual situation. It is completely the contrary of mechanism and even of dynamism; it is a psychism.

The scientific position strives to see it all from without, cosmologically and not anthropomorphically, quantitatively and not qualitatively.[14] Science is eager to reduce everything to weight, number, and measure, to relationships of number and space, to arithmetic and geometry. The ideal of science is to deduce all cognitive foresight from mathematical theorems.[15] The sciences of life, biology, tend to be reduced to chemical sciences, these to physics, and physics in turn to [87] rational mechanics, which in turn is a branch of mathematics.

But they always stumble upon the element called purely material, with the final, irreducible substratum of objective material. Rational mechanics explains the vaguest, most minute movements as you will, but does not explain those ultimate entities, concrete numbers, that which is qualitative. These ultimate irreducible entities—call them atoms, ions, centers of force, etc.—are the material element, and science is purely formal.

And these ultimate entities, conceived and perhaps more precisely than conceived, materially sensed, are in fact conceived and felt anthropomorphically. The human being cannot conceive and sense the universe in any way but humanly, that is, a conscious being cannot conceive the universe except in the form of consciousness.[16]

The religious soul faced by the world feels surrounded by consciousness and sustained by it.[17] Its conception of the universe, derived from its sentiment of it, is not a formal, but a material conception; it is not limited to seeing the relationships of number, position, and measure, among things, but senses our kinship with them.[18] The whole world exists for the purposes and for the sake of consciousness. The human being's religion humanizes the universe, and the lion's, if it had a religion, would "lionize" it.[19]

Science, faithful to its formalism, has combated anthropomorphism, but the latter filters into it everywhere. The teleological conception of law, like everything referring to finality, is a religious conception.[20] With perspicacity it has been said that almost all the attacks addressed against Christianity in the name of science are attacks inspired not by science [88] itself, indifferent of itself to religion, but by a pagan religious sentiment that hides itself under that science. They are attacks by one religion, the pagan, against another religion, the Christian.[21]

Materialist philosophies that claim to be grounded on science are pagan religious conceptions. In them consciousness tries to become matter by diffusing consciousness in subconscious forms.[22]

Such philosophies are today the fruit of a more or less resigned despair, at times of a subconscious despair, but despair in sum. The scientist that denies value to our transcendent hopes by describing them as illusions, in fact despairs at base of not being able to harbor those hopes. That renunciation is a form of spiritual suicide.

Scientific reason, whether it knows it or not, manages to become dehumanized so as to mix with things themselves such as they are outside us. And if they have no knowledge of themselves, if they are not conscious, purely scientific reason will never know them in their essence.[23]

Pure reason seeks truth through science, and that truth does not go beyond being a purely formal equation; faith, for its part, seeks life, that is, consciousness, for religion. There are those who speak of sacrificing life for truth, and others of sacrificing truth for life, and Christ said, "I am the truth and the life."[24]

Science has a divine, religious value when contracted to its proper object, that of giving us knowledge of formal relationships for [89] the practice of our formal or outer life.[25]

And the human being wished to make science religious or rather theological, and hammered out Scholastic philosophy, *ancilla theologiae* (maidservant to theology).[26] He deduced his metaphysics from the concept of an abstract, purely ideal God, in other words, a false one.[27] It was a radically individualistic science at base.[28] And thankfully this individualism was tempered by jurisprudence, which corrected it.[29]

And Scholastic philosophy was not a pure science, it was not a knowing for its own sake and in order to know more, but an applied science, applied to the business of individual salvation. Its hidden ultimate purpose was to convince us of our personal immortality.[30] For its point of departure, whether it knew it or not, it took faith, the *credo ut intelligam* (I believe in order to understand) of Saint Augustine.[31] Science wished to derive itself from religion the way that today religion wishes to derive itself from science.[32] But it was an individual science, although belonging to all individuals. And science, the true science, must be social.[33]

Social science cannot give substantial, personal truths, but formal, collective ones. Only what is formal and collective can be transmitted. There is no science that gives the blind the intuition of color. Science in each era is the adaptation of collective thought, inherited with language, to outer reality, and is a means—nothing more than a means—to act on the world.[34] But it does not give us possession of the world itself, much less possession of ourselves.

Religion must be carefully distinguished from ethics or morality, which, as Socrates saw,[35] is science, the science of doing good works. Political and social needs have caused morals to be placed under the safeguard and shelter of religion, by causing eternal life to depend on our present moral life, on the goodness or wickedness of our moral acts, but this is no more than confusion. Religion is the yearning not to die and is faith in immortality, whatever may be our conviction here on earth.[36] Since it is not suitable for someone else to rob us, nor beat us, nor deceive us, nor enjoy our wives, we have said that punishments await the delinquent in the other life;[37] but strictly speaking, immortality is one thing, and the reward or punishment is another. Immortality is not to be given to us as a reward for our behavior but as the fruit of our faith. To determine our conduct, penal codes exist.[38] Religion cannot depend on morals, although morals may depend on religion.[39]

I conceive another life and I believe in it, or at least I have hope in it, but not under the form of rewards and punishments. If there is another life it is the same for all, and there is no hell.[40] At most those who want to be annihilated are annihilated, and they resign themselves to it; those that violently yearned for immortality are saved, that is, they live always, those that energetically yearned to live, those that could not resign themselves to annihilation.[41] This not resigning oneself is the sign of the predestined, the one that shall not be annihilated. And the one who conforms to it, who willingly agrees to be annihilated without this perspective embittering his life, was born already annihilated. The already immortal feel or await their immortality, even though it may go against all reason.[42] See, therefore, if you find immortality in yourself.[43]

Science—philosophy—poetry—religion.[44]

We can neither feel nor understand religion except in a concrete form, as a religion—for us, Christianity.[45]

9 Christianity

[90] Every cultured European of our days is Christian, willingly or not, knowingly or not. Among us one is born Christian and breathes Christianity,[1] and this applies no less to those who most abominate it. The paganism of those that want to oppose Christ is a paganism that would scandalize a pre-Christian pagan if resurrected and able to see it.[2]

And it is as useful and difficult to wish to define Christianity today as it would be to wish to define modern civilization. Concrete life escapes all definition, which is death.[3] And yet . . .

And yet it is necessary to attempt to characterize Christianity, the religion for us, if we wish to live consciously, to have consciousness of our lives.[4]

In the first place, Christianity arises from the cult of a human being, a concrete human being, whom we have made God, from the cult of the Human—but of the human being that was born, lived, suffered, loved, and died, not of the idea of the human being, like paganism.[5] And its God is unique because the concrete, living human being is also unique for each of us. The concrete, living human being is the one that suffers and dies.[6]

The originality, the deep truth of Christianity, has been to make God a human being, the Human Being, that suffers passion and dies. Such is the madness and the scandal of the Cross (1 *Corinthians* 1:23).

It is God Who becomes human to suffer and to deify in this way, through suffering, the human being.[7] The cult of the idea of the human, of humanity, shuns pain, but the religion of the concrete, living human seeks it.[8] What does not suffer is nothing but idea, form, emptiness. [91] Christianity has made God a human being; it has made of the God that redeems us the same God that created the universe, that lit up Sirius, Aldebaran, the ultimate nebulae.[9] In other words, the universe is a moral creation of the human being, the concrete, living human being, the one that suffers and loves and dies. And is resurrected.

Christianity as a religion, not as a morality—which is something very different—begins to appear in Saint Paul and culminates with Saint Athanasius in the symbol of Nicæa, with the faith in the resurrection of the dead and the life of the age to come.[10] The ethical Jesus, the teacher of morals, the pedagogue,[11] did not need to be god. What is more, it is perhaps better that he was only a human being. For the fact that a human being, a human being like ourselves, had reached that high degree of moral perfection was a guarantee that we other human beings could also reach it.[12] And in this ethical sense Arius was right, and logical Arianism ends up as Unitarianism.[13]

But religion is not morality,[14] and Christianity is not evangelical ethics. It was more a question of the religious Christ than of the historical Jesus.[15] Come what may of our conduct, it was necessary that God, the God Who is both Producer and product of immortality,[16] become a human being, that He suffer, die, and be resurrected as a guarantee of the faith in the resurrection of ourselves the human beings that are born, suffer, and die, as a guarantee of our deification.

God became human to make the human being god.[17] And thus in Nicæa Saint Athanasius won out against Arius, the Christian religion against evangelical ethics (ethics=science), the idiots against the wise men.[18]

[92] In the strict sense, only those deserve the name Christian who believe in Christ's divinity, understood in the broadest and most ancient acceptation, dispensing with theories of Trinitarian consubstantiality.[19] That Christ is God should be understood in the sense in which the Greeks understood the θεὸς [god] applicable to heroes once immortalized. In other words, Christ is personally immortal, the Christ that walked upon the earth keeps living.[20] And in that faith is included everyone from Roman Catholics to Unitarians, and outside it remain those that, while honoring the figure of Christ and perhaps considering the Gospels the purest and most perfect code of morals, nonetheless do not believe in the personal immortality of Christ.[21]

And the one that believes in the personal immortality of Christ, that is, the Christian, believes for that very reason in his personal immortality, the personal immortality of each human being. This is what it means to be Christian, and not simply a Christ-lover:[22] Christianity sprang from faith in the resurrection of Christ, that is, in the immortality of his human soul.

Strictly speaking, Christianity was founded by Saint Paul, who did not know Christ personally and acted out of that absence.[23]

APPENDIX: WHAT IS TRUTH?

The Fourth Gospel tells, in its chapter 18, that when they took Jesus prisoner to the praetorium, Pilate, the intellectual Roman praetor, calling him aside, asked Him if He were king of the Jews; and when Jesus confessed to him that His kingdom was not of this world, and that He had been born to bear witness to the truth, Pilate asked him once more and said, "What is truth?" And without awaiting a response, he went out to tell the Jews that he found no fault in that man.[1]

Already before the birth of Christ, intellectuals that governed or wished to govern peoples would ask, "What is truth?," and without awaiting a response they once more resolved in a lie the affairs that were entrusted to them; and after the death of Christ, as a testimony to truth, the Pilates continue to ask in passing what truth is, and to wash their hands once again in waters devoted to lies. What is truth? I take the treatise of philosophy that I find closest at hand, the one we would carry as a text at the university when I was taking my courses on metaphysics, and it has the inestimable advantage of being a long, wide, and deeply obtuse book, bereft of any originality, an extremely faithful mirror of the abyss of vulgarity, of senility, of stupidity, to which what is called Thomism has sunk among us. It is *Elementary Philosophy Written by the Very Distinguished Don Fray Zeferino González, Bishop of Cordova*—that is what the frontispiece of the second edition says. He is one of the individuals who have written the most stupidities in Spain.[2] I open this detestable book with which they filled my intelligence with cobwebs at the tender age of sixteen, and in the first article of chapter 2 of the second section of his first book, I read that truth is divided into metaphysics, logic, and morals.

Now they are dividing the truth for us, that is, muddying it for us. But let us go on and see what this typical book tells us, written by one of our most representative individuals.

"Metaphysical truth is the objective reality of things insofar as these things, by means of their essence, correspond to the typical idea of those same things, an idea preexisting *ab aeterno* [from eternity] *in the divine understanding.*"[3] Let us leave this mess without setting about to determining whether the things are not already in themselves those typical ideas preexisting in the divine understanding. And let us not set about to ascertain what this business is about things corresponding to their divine idea *by means of their essence,* and what mediation is this matter of the essence, and in what respect the essence is distinguished from the things themselves, for which it serves as a go-between. This intellectual garbage was served to us in our youth.

"*Logical* truth . . . can be defined as follows: *the conformity or equation of the understanding as knowing agent with the thing that is known.*"[4] This is merely a paraphrase in clumsy, awkward language, of Saint Thomas's well-known definition: *adæquatio intellectus et rei* (the correspondence of the intellect and the thing).[5] Let us leave it, therefore; it has been criticized a thousand times. "*Moral* truth is *the conformity or equation of outer language with the inner judgment of the subject.*"[6]

Leaving Fray Zeferino now, let us say that true truth, the root truth, is this second one, the one he calls moral. From it comes the other one, the logical one.

The contrary of logical truth is called error, and the contrary of moral truth is called a lie. And it is clear that one can be veracious, say what one thinks, while in error, and one can say something that is a logical truth while lying.

And now I state that error is born of lying.

More than once before now, I have said a thing that I intend to repeat many times again, and it is that an error in which we believe is worth more than a reality in which we do not believe; for it is not error, but lying, which kills the soul.

The human being lies and learns lying from others. In social intercourse we have learned lying, and since the human being sees everything with human eyes, that human humanizes everything. The human being humanizes nature by attributing to it human qualities and intentions; and since the human says one thing and thinks or feels another, we suppose that nature also usually thinks or feels in one way and manifests itself to us in another; we suppose that nature lies to us. Hence our errors, errors that arise from supposing in nature, in reality, a hidden intention that it is lacking.

What, we wonder, do snow, a lightning bolt, crystallization, parthenogenesis, atavism mean? And they mean nothing more than they say, because nature does not lie.

If we human beings told the truth all the time, if we never lied either by commission or by omission, either by falsification of the truth or by silencing of it, it would never occur to anybody to speak of conformity between outer language and inner judgment, because language and judgment would be one and the same thing. If we did not lie either with words or silences, there would be no distinction made between the form and content of our thought, nor would the word be the vesture of the truth, but the idea itself brought to the outside. Speaking would be nothing more than thinking out loud, thinking for everyone else. And then, transferring this to nature, we would understand and would feel—feeling is something more intimate than understanding—that there is no distinction whatsoever between reality and what appears to us as such, for nature speaks to us while thinking or thinks while speaking to us.

But the fact is that through subtle magic, through mysterious conduct, nature lies to liars.

I am persuaded that if absolute truthfulness took possession of human beings and ruled all their relationships, if lying ceased, errors would disappear and truth would little by little be revealed to us.

The only perfect homage that can be rendered to God is the homage of truth. That kingdom of God, whose advent millions of tongues besmirched with lies pray for daily, is nothing but the kingdom of truth.

Stop trying to reform every vice, every weakness; prostrate yourselves to the lash of pride, wrath, envy, gluttony, lust, greed; but resolve never to lie either by commission or by omission; resolve not only not to tell lies, but also not to silence truths; propose to tell the truth always and in every case, but especially when it most endangers you and when the prudent think it is most inopportune, according to the world; do this, and you will be saved, and all those deadly sins will not succeed in making any impression in your souls. Does pride or envy or lust or greed control you? Well, do not hide it. Do not be a hypocrite, either with the hypocrisy of the one we would call a hypocrite, or with the hypocrisy of cynicism, which wishes to deceive us with the truth, to lie to us by telling what is real. They say that in the confession of sins what is essential to obtain forgiveness for them is contrition, or at least, if this is missing, attrition. No; what is essential is to confess them, to make them public, to tell the truth. The tale in the Gospels does come very clear as to whether the evildoer crucified next to Jesus was contrite when he scolded the other one and confessed his own fault (*Luke* 23:39–41), for which Christ promised him Paradise. He affirmed, it is certain, that he deserved the punishment; but a criminal may affirm the justice of the punishment inflicted on him without feeling repentant for his fault. He spoke to his companion of fear of God, but what is essential is that he confess his sin aloud. He did not lie, either with his words or with his silences.

There are people who are scandalized when spoken to of the kingdom of the absolute truth, of opportune or inopportune truth, and who imagine that it would not then be possible to live in the world. I was speaking of this to a very intelligent lady, and I was telling her that just as paganism culminated in the nakedness of the body, so Christianity should culminate in the nakedness of the soul, and she replied to me, "My God, how horrible! If it were not for clothing, how would the hunchbacked, the crippled, the broken, the oafs, everyone with something to hide, live?"

And I replied to her, "Much better than now, madam! The hunchback is worse off dressed than when naked; clothing only tortures the hump and makes us think it is greater than it really is. So it is that our eyes would grow accustomed to the nude, we would understand physical deformities. I am sure that among savages that go around dressed in nothing but loincloths the hunchbacks go by less noticed than among us."

"The fact is that among them there are hardly any," she answered me.

And I said, "There are not any because they go around naked."

And she said, "Because they are killed shortly after being born with humps." And even if this may be so, it is more worthwhile.

I often hear Shakespeare's expression "Words, words, words" commented upon,[7] and it is said that we need not words, but deeds. And this is what people say who call themselves Christian, and they should have known that according to the Fourth Gospel, in the beginning was the Word, and the Word was toward God, and God was the Word, and all things were made by the Word, and without it nothing was accomplished apart from what indeed was accomplished, and in it, in the Word, was life, and life was the light of men (*John* 1:1–5). And that is what people say who call themselves Christian and that should have known that when Jesus was in the home of Simon the Pharisee he forgave the sinful woman, he performed no *action* whatsoever, either symbolic or non-symbolic; he made no gesture whatsoever with his hand in the air, nor even touched her as he touched the leper when telling him, "I will; be clean" (*Matthew* 8:2–4), but he simply told her, "Your sins are forgiven you; your faith has saved you; go in peace" (*Luke* 7:36–50). He cleansed her of her sin with his word, only with his word. And the Gospels also say that he cast out the demons from the men with the word (*Matthew* 8:16). And it is the word that we need, the one that may cast out the demons.

Jesus did not baptize, nor confirm, nor celebrate Mass, nor perform marriages, nor anoint the dying, but always administered the holy sacrament of the word. And the fact is that the word, when it is the true word, when it is truly the word, and his, Jesus's, was the word of absolute truth, to the point that he was the incarnation of his word; the word, when it is truly the word, is the creative force that raises the human being over inhuman, brute nature. The human is human through the word.

"Down with words; up with facts, facts!" scream the slaves to the lie, without noting that what they call facts are usually nothing but words, and that the word is a more fruitful fact. They call a published law a fact; and what is a published law but a written word?

There is another passage from the Gospels in which the Christian power of the word stands out. And it is that, when Jesus went to cure the centurion's slave, the centurion sent him a message telling him not to trouble himself, since he was not worthy to receive him under the roof of his house, but that He say one word and the slave would heal, because he, the centurion, a man of authority, would say to a soldier, "Come!" and the soldier would come; he would tell him, "Go!" and he would go. When Jesus heard this, he marveled, and turning to those that were following him, he told them, "I tell you that not even in Israel have I found such faith" (*Luke* 7:1–9). And the faith of the centurion, the faith for which he obtained the cure for his slave, was the faith in the word, this faith that is almost quenched in Israel.[8]

Words! Words! Words! And what more would we want than words, if they were words of truth, opportune or inopportune truth? What more would we want than words, if those words were the very thought of the one pronouncing them, whether or not that thought agreed with reality? More than once in the hall of sessions of our Parliament, in that Cathedral of the Lie, this foul-smelling blasphemy has resounded: "That cannot be said here!" or else this other: "That cannot be heard in a mood of calm!" And the only thing that should not be said, neither there nor in any other place, is the lie, and the lie is the only thing that should not be heard in a mood of calm. Everything else must be said there and everywhere, and there and everywhere must be heard in a mood of calm, and when it is an error, a mistake, it must also be answered and rectified in a mood of calm. This very day, December 16, I just read in the summary that a newspaper is carrying of a session of Congress held two days ago that when a republican congressman said that he and his colleagues were not Catholics, murmurs were heard, those stupid inarticulate murmurs that are the way unconscious multitudes express themselves. And most of the murmurers or rumor-mongers were not Catholics either, for the simple reason that most of our congressmen are not, not even the professional Catholics. For these may seem Catholics insofar as they are congressmen, but there is always room for doubt about whether they are insofar as they are human beings. There are many that are not except insofar as they are employees, or journalists, or servants, or children, or husbands, or parents. There is one newspaper that considers itself Catholic when pressed, but has not even one Catholic editor.

Of course, to be precise, in Spain being a Catholic hardly means anything for the vast majority, except simply not being something else. Catholics are those who, having been baptized, do not publicly retract what is supposed to be their creed in accordance with a social fiction. Nor do they think about it either a little or much, either to profess it or to undo it and acquire another or, at least, search for that other.

And in this horrible slough of lying and cowardice there is heard from time to time, "Deeds! Deeds! Deeds! Down with words!" And the supreme deed, the great deed, the fruitful deed, the redeeming deed, would be for each to tell his or her truth. With nothing but this, we would be on the other side of the chasm yawning before our feet.

And there are still wretched individuals who, while not daring to defend lies, stinking lies, try to disguise them as high hopes and speak to us of the power of these and of the relief attained by trying to engage in conscious self-deceit.

No: art is what is furthest from the lie, and the lie is the most deeply anti-aesthetic thing that exists. No: the lie is never consolation, and high hopes that console are not lies.

There is a horrible phrase attributed to Voltaire, and it is that "if God did not exist, it would be necessary to invent Him."[9] That God invented in this fashion to deceive oneself or the people would not be merely a Non-God, but an Anti-God, an absolute devil. That is the only devil that exists, the God invented by those that do not believe in Him in the innermost part of their hearts.

"And what is it to believe in God?" the Pontius Pilates may here ask. And abandoning logical faith, parallel to the so-called logical truth, and adhering to moral faith, which corresponds to moral truth, I will tell them that to believe in God is to want God to exist, to yearn for Him with all our soul. Anyone incapable of conceiving with intelligence the essence of God, while considering the idea of God a mere hypothesis explaining nothing, and deeming the so-called proofs of His existence sophisms, anyone of that sort who harbors a heartfelt wish for God to exist, and adapts to intercourse with Him by giving personality to the Highest Ideal, believes in God much more than that other who is logically convinced that God exists, but either does not take Him into account, or does so only to justify a cult of lying.[10]

One day a zealous Catholic scolded me for what he called my subjectivism, and he told me that I confuse faith with imagination. And he insisted on making me understand—while repeating arguments of the crudest vulgarity, ones that make me sick because I know them from memory—the difference there is between what he called (in a departure from the canons of his school) subjective faith and objective faith.

And I calmly told him, "Do not weary yourself, my friend, by repeating to me all those things: I know very well what you want to tell me. And do not weary yourself by arguing to me with syllogisms and formal rationales. The faith of you people is drowning to death in syllogisms. The cancer of your Church is rationalism, that rationalism against which you never stop railing. You have wanted to make religion a philosophy. Every one of those horrid, arid sermons in which a Jesuit has his say against sect-leaders of modern irreligion, while studding his lecture with "so it is thats" and "therefores" and "it remains clearly demonstrated" and other logical figures of this fashion, each one of those unfortunate sermons is a new blow dealt against true faith. And in them, in those anti-religious lectures, boldfaced lies are customarily told, as the so-called impious are attributed things they never maintained. Or else while speaking of their doctrines, their detractors are aware of not knowing them except through vague references. And this amounts to lying.

"I already know," I went on to tell him, "that at base, even without knowing it, you are a materialist, not because you think that there is nothing but matter, but because you need the material proof of things; you need, like the Jews, signs in order to believe,[11] you need to grab the truth with your two hands, your feet, and your mouth. I already know that you think you are lost if those proofs that your texts carry of God's existence turn out to prove nothing they aim to prove. And yet, my friend, I have not read such proof in the Gospels, nor have I found there any of those Aristotelian "so it is thats" and "therefores." And as soon as one of you finds the Sphinx staring at him and feels the drill of doubt, of holy doubt, mother of true faith, his heart begins to bark at him, he turns his back on the Sphinx, he shakes his doubt away through procedures of spiritual mechanics, says to himself, "Come now, it is better not to think about it!," and surrenders to lies.

"My friend," I went on to say to him, "there are those that consider suicide not so great a crime, but much greater than murder. They think that the killer of oneself is guiltier before God than the killer of one's neighbor. There are those that maintain, and not simply to show ingenuity despite appearances, that in suicide all the aggravating circumstances of murder come together. I do not know, nor does it seem to me possible to know with any certainty; but I do think that lying to oneself is much worse than lying to others. And there are people that live in a perpetual inner lie as they try to silence the truth that springs out of the depths of their hearts.

A poor friend of mine who was going through an intense religious crisis once went to confess, thinking that he would find relief if not a remedy. And he came over to me and told me that the good father confessor had told him, "Do you actually think that those doubts do not occur to others? Dispel them, do not think about them!"

And I said to him, "Welcome them, do not think about anything else!"

And he went on to tell me that the confessor had also told him that he should try to find some distraction, take care of himself, eat well, sleep much, and if those spiritual anxieties oppressed him a great deal, he should come back to that confessor, but also should not forget to consult his doctor. And I told him, "That horrible confessor is nothing but a hardened material-ist!"

My friend took my advice, and today finds more inner peace and consola-tion, and more faith amidst his anguish, restlessness, and uneasiness, than others find in abdicating from truth.

He asked me, "How do I find the truth?"

And I answered him, "By telling it always!"

And he asked me again, "But outer truth, objective truth, logical truth, what is truth?"

And I answered him, "Always and in every case, whether opportune or inopportune, by telling the inner truth, the subjective truth, the moral truth, whatever you believe is true!"

That which we call reality, objective or logical truth, is nothing but the reward given for sincerity, truthfulness. For the one who was absolutely and always truthful and sincere, Nature would hold no secret at all. Blessed are the pure of heart, for they shall see God![12] And pureness of heart is truthful-ness, and the truth is God.

Thousands upon thousands of times it has been said that the majority of arguments are arguments with words, and that, at times, human beings combat for the same cause, given different names by different fighters. And the fact is that rather arguments tend to be arguments using lies, and that human beings combat for these alone. Instead of saying, "I want this, and I want it because I want it without knowing why I want it," or if it is known, truly saying why it is wanted, the individual invents a lie to justify that wish, and fights for the sake of the lie. And in most cases there would be no fight if there were truth.

There are people who say they dispute not for the point of the fight (*hecho*), but for their own right (*derecho*); not for the egg itself, but for their lawful claim to it. If the egg were in fact unencumbered and indisputable, the claim by law would not be needed. If someone tells me, "I am taking this away from you because it belongs to me, in virtue of the fact that you gave it to me or you promised it to me or you took it away from me," I will defend what I think is mine, and I will even come to fight with my adversary by crying, "I did not give it you!" or "I did not promise it to you!" or "I did not take it away from you!"; but if he tells me purely and simply, "I am taking this away from you because I want it for myself and I am stronger than you," I will turn to the others and tell them, "This man is more powerful than I, and because he is, he is taking away from me this thing that is mine," and I will let him take it away from me.

And it accomplishes nothing to say that the man is obscenely selfish and defends what is his fairly or unfairly. No. The sense of justice and truth has deeper roots than that of personal interest and lying. I harbor the faith that all, absolutely all evils we think are the causes of our miseries—selfishness, the will to power, the yearning for glory, scorn for others—everything would disappear if we were truthful. If individuals that seem to scorn their neighbor did not mistrust their scorn and wrap it up and falsify it, all of us, including them, would end up by seeing that such scorn had the opposite meaning, and that when they scorned others they were really scorning themselves. I consider that among those citizens who are most useful to their country and to all their fellow human beings, among the most fertile in spiritual goods, are those called proud, those that do not hide the belief in their own superiority, those heard to complain in some form or other when their countrymen do not show the appreciation they think they deserve. It is one thing for any individual at all to deserve that distinctive appreciation that these subjects to whom I allude think they deserve (if there ever were such superior beings), and it is quite another thing for there to be those who find themselves in that situation of believing themselves superior without hypocritically hiding it. They may be mistaken, but they do not lie.

When at the tender age of fourteen I was a member of the Congregation of Saint Louis Gonzaga, I once heard it read aloud, in the saint's biography, that because he had removed a very little bit of gun powder from his father's soldiers to load up a toy cannon he had, and because he had repeated, without understanding it, a blasphemy he had overheard those same soldiers utter, he thought he was the most sinful of all human beings.[13] This trait, far from edifying me, dis-edified me, I well remember. For since I was unable to believe that there was anybody who for that reason thought he was the greatest sinner, all that seemed to me to be lying to oneself to assume importance as a sinner. Certainly that professional Jesuit saint never succeeded in moving me, even in the days of my most ardent youthful Catholicism. Such as they present him to us—I take pleasure in believing he was probably quite the contrary—he seems like a doll built in accordance with the plans for the perfect model of Jesuit youth, of that Charles Grandison Finney of prudery.[14] And it does not astonish me that as serious a human being, with such a sincere spirit, one as deeply religious as William James, after having dealt with Saint Louis Gonzaga in his book on *The Varieties of Religious Experience*

(1902), adds that when intelligence, as in the case of Louis, is "no larger than a pin's head, and cherishes ideas of God with a corresponding smallness, the result, notwithstanding the heroism put forth, is on the whole repulsive."[15]

And now I seem to be hearing some devotee of the saint: "That cannot be said! That cannot be heard in a mood of calm!" And nonetheless, that, when said, as James says it and as I say it, should be said without a mind to offend anyone, but with a mind to tell the truth. It should be said and heard in a mood of calm by all who love truth, whether they think it exact or not.

It is really revolting to hear what we do so often: someone not wishing to bother or hurt any of his neighbors tranquilly states an opinion disagreeing with the opinion of the listener, who exclaims, "You are hurting my feelings!" On the other hand, it occurs to others, at least to me, that the one who hurts my feelings of love for truth is the one that comes to want to confirm me in what I think without having to think as I do.

There you have a priest of the Church that deems itself the only depository of Christian truth. He does not tolerate certain heretical statements being expressed in his presence. And if it is in public, he exclaims that his religious sentiments are being hurt. And they call this same priest to confess a dying unbeliever, and when he arrives, the unbeliever neither sees nor hears nor understands, or if he sees, hears, and understands, he refuses to make confession; or if he does confess, he states his sins, those he considers as such, and he says nothing about his creed or his faith or affirms that they are neither the creed or the faith of the Church. And the priest, whose religious sentiments feel hurt by serenely telling the truth, absolves him, and afterwards a funeral is held and a burial in sacred ground, and it is said that he died in the bosom of the Church, while it is added, "If those impious ones at the last minute, when they see the evil. . . ." And this horrendous lie of last-minute conversions prospers and spreads like a curse.

"If only the truth were told, it would be impossible to live." Who has said this blasphemy? Who is the coward that maintains and affirms in public that whoever purports to be truthful always will suffer a crash? What is living? What is crashing?

In all orders, death is a lie and truth is life. And if truth leads us to die, it is better to die for truth than to live by lies, to live while dying.

In the innermost order, in the most intimate order, in the religious order, all the misery of this poor Spain, mired down in every kind of lies, the fact is that a lie is perpetuated: the lie that Spain is Catholic. No. Conscious Spain, that of the ruling classes, the Spain of those that think and govern, is not Catholic. Those who, while confessing their Catholicism in public, climb to high positions are not Catholic in the majority of cases. And as long as that lie is not erased, Spain will never end up Christian.

Those disapproving murmurings of rumor-mongering or murmuring congressmen, which burst out when another congressmen or minister simply confesses he does not take communion in the official Church, those murmurings should be kept for occasions when a congressman, a minister, who it is clear to them hardly believes in God or the devil, comes out with a public confession of being a sincere Catholic, something that happens all too often.

Those murmurs should be saved for times when some lying parliamentary hypocrite, when talking against what has been called clericalism, feels the obligation to express reservations; and when so as not to be taken for an anti-Catholic, as he is simply a non-Catholic, he believes he should add that he is a submissive son of the Church.

And in Spain those individuals are not Catholic, not even many of those that think they are and go to Mass every Sunday and holy day, who take communion once a year and eat fish on Lent. For such people turn their backs on the gaze of the Sphinx, and do not wish to think about what they say their creed is.

Being content with so-called implicit faith, while aware it is implicit and different from explicit faith; adhering to the attitude that "I believe what Holy Mother Church believes and teaches"; keeping away from examining what the Church teaches and believes, out of weakness or rather for fear of seeing that there is no such faith, that is the greatest of lies.

"The fact is that we cannot all be theologians," responded to me a friend to whom I said this.

And I replied, "Theologians kill faith." Especially in medicine the science of my physician can heal me, although I may not know the whereabouts of my liver; but in religion, the faith of my confessor cannot save me. In the life of the spirit, only my truth saves me, and my truth is not the truth that I ignore, although this may be the truth of everybody else. As long as I do not know what it means that the Holy Ghost comes from the Father and the Son, not from the Father alone, what difference does it make for the life of the spirit that it may be one thing or another or neither of the two, of what use is it for me to hear them sing at Mass, with the music of Palestrina in Latin, that business of *qui ex Patre et Filioque procedit* (who comes from the Father and the Son)?[16] What hinders harms, and in the soul every herb that yields nothing, every infertile weed, every idea, or rather, every phrase that does not respond to any sentiment at all, every word that evokes no warm, luminous concept constitutes a hindrance.

You that say you are a submissive, faithful son of the Catholic Church and believe everything that it believes and teaches: but what things do you do today that you would not do, or what things that you do not do today would you do, if you believed that the Holy Ghost emerged only out of the Father and not out of the Father and the Son, or if you believed that it emerges out of neither of the two? I tell you here and now, that is not to believe anything.

You speak to me of the Church as a depository of the truths of your faith. The truths that may not be deposited in your soul are not truths of your faith, nor are of any use to you. Your faith is what you believe while fully conscious of it, not what your Church believes. And your Church itself cannot believe anything, because it cannot believe anything as it lacks a personal consciousness. It is a social institution, not a fusion of souls.

———————

Well then, in conclusion, what is truth? Truth is what is believed with all one's heart and all one's soul. And what does it mean to believe something with all one's heart and all one's soul? To act in accordance with it.

To get at the truth, the first thing is to believe in it, in the truth, with all one's heart and all one's soul; and to believe in the truth with all one's heart and all one's soul, that is, what one believes, is true always and in every case, but especially whenever it may seem most inopportune to say it.

And the word is a deed, the most intimate deed, the most creative, the most divine of all deeds. When the word is a word of truth. Blessed be the pure of heart, for they will see God! Tell your truth forever, and God will tell you His. And you will see God and you will die. For the Scriptures also say that whoever sees God dies. And that is the best that can be done in a world of lies: to die from seeing the Truth.

March 1906

Published in *La España Moderna*, 18th. Yr., no. 207
(Madrid: March 1, 1906), 5–20.

NOTES

Translator's Introduction

1. Ortega, the Madrid-born philosopher, journalist, educator, and statesman, studied philology and philosophy in Germany from April through November 1905, from summer 1906 to August 1907, and again in 1911. In Germany, he learned the culture-philosophy of the Marburg neo-Kantians Hermann Cohen and Paul Natorp before developing his own metaphysics of human existence through interaction with E. Husserl's phenomenology in 1913, M. Heidegger's ontology of existence in 1928, and W. Dilthey's philosophy of life in 1929; see my "Ortega y Gasset, José," *Dictionary of the Literature of the Iberian Peninsula,* 1192–99.

2. Unamuno first mentioned the *Tratado* in a May 9, 1905 letter to Jiménez Ilundain; Unamuno says he is writing it "now": Manuel García Blanco, "Introducción" to Miguel de Unamuno, *Obras Completas,* 7:12. Page 34 of the *Tratado* manuscript bears in the right hand margin "27 III 1906," perhaps a date of composition of the text. On December 2, 1906, Unamuno offers to mail the manuscript to Ortega: García Blanco, op. cit., 16. In all likelihood, this is the manuscript I here translate. The antimodernist Papal Encyclical appears in 1907. Unamuno stops writing the *Tratado* and furiously begins reading additional theological texts not present in the *Tratado* but cited in *Del sentimiento.* In a letter of May 14, 1908 to Ortega, Unamuno writes, "He vuelto a mi querido *Tratado del Amor de Dios.* Lo estoy rehaciendo" (I have gone back to my dear *Treatise on Love of God.* I am redoing it). This means that the work, shelved for some time, is undergoing revision into *Del sentimiento trágico.* See my introduction, above, p. xxxi.

3. "Tratado del amor de Dios y no del conocimiento; no de la existencia objetiva de Dios, sino de su existencia subjetiva. Y no guía ni práctica del amor, sino tratado, esto es, disertación del valor subjetivo de Dios. Para amar hay que personalizar." The page, from manuscript series D, has the numbers 1.2/393 in the bottom left hand corner.

4. Saint Augustine (354–430 A.D.), or Augustine of Hippo, a main source of Western Christian thinking, recounted in his *Confessions* (397–400) the process of his conversion to Christianity and the finding of God within: Mark D. Jordan, "Augustine," in *Cambridge Dictionary of Philosophy,* 60. Unamuno also writes of conversion from intellectual atheism to heterodox Christianity, while finding God within.

5. Unamuno helped popularize Kierkegaard in Spain. Søren Kierkegaard (1813–55) was a Danish philosopher, psychologist, theologian, author of fiction,

literary critic, and writer on Christian faith as a way of inward existence: C. Stephan Evans, "Kierkegaard, Søren Aabye," *Cambridge Dictionary of Philosophy*, 468.

6. Athanasius (ca. 297–373), Alexandrian bishop and Church father, in opposing the heresy of Arianism, taught that God the Father and Christ the Son (together with the Holy Ghost) shared the same substance, and that God had taken on human form to make humans divine: Alan E. Lewis, "Athanasius," in *Cambridge Dictionary of Philosophy*, 59.

Origen (185–253), Egyptian-born Christian theologian in the Alexandrian church, acquired fame from his idea of the *apocatastasis*, restoration of all creatures to God, salvation of all, the devil included. Origen viewed hell as a kind of purifying ground or purgatory to ready souls for heaven. Luis P. Pojman, "Origen," in ibid., 636. Unamuno wants to agree with all these notions.

Tertullian (ca. 155—ca. 240), early Church father and Latin theologian, Christianized the Stoic concept of the bodiliness of God and the soul (a doctrine of great interest to Unamuno): Alan E. Lewis, "Tertullian," ibid., 908.

Albrecht Ritschl (1822–1889), Göttingen founder of a theological movement in Germany to liberalize Lutheranism, was one of the thinkers most influential on Unamuno in the *Tratado del amor de Dios* and *Del sentimiento trágico*. Ritschl sought to purify Christian faith by grounding it more on the Gospels and less on dogmas and legal precepts. The Evangelical basis called for the establishment of the Kingdom of God on earth, that is, for a German nation of redeemed believers. Antimaterialistic, antimetaphysical, and antimystical, Ritschl stressed the affirmation of individual personality, capable of mastering the world with faith, or confidence in Providence: Nelson R. Orringer, *Unamuno y los protestantes liberals*, 28–29.

Auguste Sabatier (1839–1901), French Calvinist theologian, displayed a concern for truth, a dualistic, mind/matter worldview, a neo-Kantian epistemology and ethics, and a critical historicism affected by the Ritschlians. In historical, critical, exegetical, and philosophical studies, Sabatier desired a return to the simple doctrine of salvation as he thought Jesus taught it to the multitudes. To Ritschlianism, Sabatier added a tragic point of departure—learned from Blaise Pascal and transmitted to Unamuno—namely, the inner conflict between reason and faith: ibid., 46–47.

Ernest Renan (1823–92), French historian, philologist, and writer whose faith in material sciences and notion of life as a theatrical game for God's amusement do not convince Unamuno: see ch. 5, note 3, below.

7. On Unamuno, see Mary Lee Bretz, "Unamuno, Miguel de," *Dictionary of the Literature of the Iberian Peninsula*, 2:1631; on Ortega, see note 1, above.

8. See note 2, above.

9. Published in Madrid by Renacimiento.

10. See Appendix, note 13, below.

11. See ch. 4, note 87, below.

12. See ch. 4, p. [44].

13. See Antonio Sánchez Barbudo, "El misterio de la personalidad en Unamuno. *Cómo se hace una novela*," in *Estudios sobre Galdós, Unamuno y Machado*, 198, and Pedro Cerezo Galán, *Las máscaras de lo trágico: Filosofía y tragedia en Miguel de Unamuno*, 110n17.

14. Miguel de Unamuno, *Private World: Selections from the* Diario íntimo *and Selected Letters, 1890–1936*, 163–64.

15. See Appendix, note 2, below, on Zeferino González. Jaime Balmes (1810–48) attempted to create a metaphysics that would harmonize Scholastic philosophy with the sciences. He maintained the activism of all psychological phenomena, especially sensations, and affirmed an intellectual intuition superior to the sensible one (Gonzalo Díaz Díaz, "Balmes, Jaime," *Hombres y documentos de la filosofía española*, 1:471). Juan Donoso Cortés (1809–53), essayist, diplomat, and Catholic philosopher, held that Catholicism is a synthesis embracing all. In his main work, *Ensayo sobre el Catolicismo, el Liberalismo y el Socialismo*, 1851 (*Essay on Catholicism, Liberalism, and Socialism*, trans. M. V. Goddard, 1862), he begins with a lyrical vision of God the Principle, descends to the central theme on human existence, and ends by showing the human being elevated to God through Christ: see Gonzalo Díaz Díaz, "Donoso Cortés, Juan," *Hombres y documentos de la filosofía española*, 2:604–5. On Balmes and Donoso Cortés, see Unamuno, *Recuerdos de niñez y de mocedad* (Memories of Childhood and Youth), in *Obras Completas*, 8:144–45.

16. Julián Sanz del Río (1814–69), philosopher and educator, imported the neo-Kantian philosophy of Krausism to Spain. This system, called harmonic rationalism by Sanz, consists of an analytical part and a synthetic part. The first entails an inductive ascent from self-consciousness to God, Primary Infinite Essence; the second, a deductive descent to the plurality of things integrating the cosmos. Krausism, teaching tolerance, opened Spain to multiple systems abroad, and pervaded liberal educational institutions in that country from about 1868 to 1936: Gonzalo Díaz Díaz, "Sanz del Río, Julián," *Hombres y documentos de la filosofía española*, 7:193–94.

17. Eusebio Fernández distinguishes the following five modalities of positivism imported to Spain between 1868 and 1874: the philosophy of Auguste Comte, professed in diluted form by Catalan conservatives; a neo-Kantian positivism centered in Madrid; a naturalistic positivism rooted in the natural sciences; evolutionism taken from Darwin and Spencer; and the Krauso-positivism of Sanz del Río's students, especially Nicolás Salmerón, Francisco Giner de los Ríos, Adolfo Posada, and others: Antonio Jiménez García, "Urbano González Serrano y la fundamentación del krauso-positivismo," 187.

18. Herbert Spencer (1820–1903), British positivist philosopher and social reformer, held that the only trustworthy knowledge is discoverable in the positive sciences. As a consequence, if a positive science can someday give evidence of God, this will be grounds for religious faith (agnosticism). Robert E. Butts, "Spencer, Herbert," *Cambridge Dictionary of Philosophy*, 869–70. Unamuno translated into Spanish portions of Spencer's works *The Principles of Ethics* (1893) and *Essays: Scientific, Political, and Speculative* (1891) for José Lázaro Galdiano of *La España Moderna*, a publishing company and a cultural review that also published *Del sentimiento trágico* between 1911 and 1912: H. Rafael Chabrán, "Young Unamuno: His Intellectual Development in Positivism and Darwinism (1880—1884)," 162–72.

19. Joaquín Costa (1846–1911), jurist, historian, and essayist affiliated with the Spanish Krausists, reflected on the essence of Spain after its disastrous loss in the Spanish-American War of 1898. Costa recommended the Europeanization of Spain, European by essence. He influenced the thinking of the early Unamuno

and of other members of the so-called "Generation of 1898": Gonzalo Díaz Díaz, "Costa, Joaquín," *Hombre y documentos de la filosofía española*, 2:432–34.

20. See note 6, above, on Renan. Also see Unamuno's "Strauss y Renan," in *Obras Completas*, 9:1258–62.

21. Among the post-Hegelians, seeking to develop critical tendencies in Hegel beginning with the historical interpretation of religion, David Friedrich Strauss (1808–74), Max Stirner (1806–56), and Ludwig Feuerbach (1804–72) have occupied Unamuno's attention. Unamuno possessed a French translation of Strauss's *Leben Jesus* (*Life of Jesus*) and criticized it in a 1914 article (see note 20, above); he referred to Stirner's *Der Einzige und sein Eigentum* (The Ego and its Own) in his *Diario íntimo* (in *Obras Completas*, 8:800); and disagreed with Feuerbach's notion that the human being creates God in his own likeness: see ch. 3, note 11, below.

Among major neo-Kantians, the impact of Albrecht Ritschl on Unamuno is inestimable: see note 6, above; Ernst Troeltsch (1865–1923), an independent-minded Ritschlian, appears in *Del sentimiento trágico*, in *Obras Completas*, 7:150, but I have not spotted his presence in the *Tratado*; I have seen a Spanish translation of *Das Heilige* (*The Holy*) by Rudolf Otto (1869–1937) in the Unamuno library.

22. Martin Nozick, *Miguel de Unamuno*, 20, 35. As for Menéndez Pelayo (1856–1912), influential but not mentioned in Nozick's description of the times, this prolific historian, critic, and scholar undertook his research with the breadth learned in the Spanish Renaissance humanist tradition. He polemicized with the Krausists on doctrinal and pedagogical grounds in debates at the Madrid Atheneum probably attended by Unamuno. See Stephen Miller, "Menéndez y Pelayo, Marcelino," *Dictionary of the Literature of the Iberian Peninsula*, 1072–75.

23. On Spencer, see note 18, above. Georg Wilhelm Friedrich Hegel (1770–1831), philosopher and educator from Stuttgart, aspired to devise a system wherein a logic would ground categories of the natural world and categories of practical human activity: Robert B. Pippin, "Hegel, Georg Wilhelm Friedrich," *Cambridge Dictionary of Philosophy*, 365. Perhaps guided by the link between logic and practical (religious) activity, Unamuno felt attracted to Hegel for his own "Filosofía lógica."

24. Miguel de Unamuno, *Recuerdos de niñez y mocedad* (Memories of Childhood and Youth), in *Obras Completas*, 8:144.

25. Enrique Rivera de Ventosa, *Unamuno y Dios*, 91.

26. Martin Nozick, *Miguel de Unamuno*, 21.

27. Georg Wilhelm Friedrich Hegel, *Wissenschaft der Logik*, in *Sämtliche Werke*, 4:87.

28. Ibid., 88.

29. Ibid., 119.

30. Ibid., 118.

31. Ibid., 90.

32. Georg Wilhelm Friedrich Hegel, *Wissenschaft der Logik*, in *Werke*, 3:76.

33. Ibid., 124.

34. For instance, in *First Principles*, Spencer writes, "This conclusion, which brings the results of speculation into harmony with those of common sense, is also the conclusion which reconciles Religion with Science" (p. 99). For Una-

muno in his *Vida de Don Quijote y Sancho* (Life of Our Lord Don Quixote), in *Obras Completas*, 3:108, Don Quixote's servant Sancho Panza often sounds "la voz del sentido común" (the voice of common sense). In philosophy his attitude receives the name of "positivismo" (positivism, coinciding with Spencer's position), or else the names "naturalismo" (naturalism) or "empirismo" (empiricism).

35. Enrique Rivera de Ventosa, *Unamuno y Dios*, 95.

36. "Una desconocida 'Filosofía Lógica' de Unamuno," *Tras las huellas de Unamuno*, 15–32.

37. Herbert Spencer, *First Principles*, 63–64.

38. Ibid.

39. Zubizarreta, "Una desconocida 'Filosofía Lógica' de Unamuno," *Tras las huellas de Unamuno*, 26.

40. This type of allegorizing appears in Unamuno's *Diario íntimo*, in *Obras Completas*, 8:801: "Hay que perderse en esa nada que nos aterra para llegar a la vida eterna y serlo todo. Sólo haciéndonos nada llegaremos a serlo todo; sólo reconociendo la nada de nuestra razón, cobraremos por la fe el todo de la verdad. // En el más vigoroso vuelo de la filosofía humana racionalista, en el idealismo hegeliano, se parte de la fórmula de que el Ser puro se identifica con la Nada pura, es el nihilismo racionalista" (It is necessary to lose oneself in that nothingness that terrifies us in order to arrive at eternal life and be everything. Only by becoming nothing will we come to be everything; only by recognizing the nothingness of our reason, will we acquire through faith the totality of truth. // In the most vigorous flight of rationalistic human philosophy, in Hegelian idealism, the point of departure is the formula that the pure Being identifies with the pure Nothingness; it is rationalistic nihilism).

41. Wolfgang Forster, *Karl Christian Friedrich Krauses frühe Rechtsphilosophie und ihr geistesgeschichtlicher Hintergrund* (Karl Christian Friedrich Krause's Early Philosophy of Law and Its Cultural Historic Background), 1.

42. Stephen Miller, "Krausism," *Dictionary of the Literature of the Iberian Peninsula*, 902.

43. Fernando Martín Buezas, *Teología de Sanz del Río y del krausismo español*, 14.

44. Francisco Giner de los Ríos (1839–1915), Krausist philosopher, essayist, and educator, aspired to restructure education in Spain on all levels in accordance with liberal, Krausist pedagogical principles. He attempted this reform on the university level during the First Republic; and during the Bourbon Revolution—in 1876—Giner, together with other Krausists, founded the Institución Libre de Enseñanza (Free Pedagogical Institute), a center of learning independent of government. Porter Conerly, "Giner de los Ríos, Francisco," *Dictionary of the Literature of the Iberian Peninsula*, 733–35.

45. *El krausismo y la Institución Libre de Enseñanza*, 114.

46. For the titles of the Giner de los Ríos holdings, see Valdés, *Unamuno Source Book*, 98. On Giner, see note 44 above. For the correspondence between Giner and Unamuno, see María Dolores Gómez Molleda, *Unamuno "agitador de espíritus" y Giner de los Ríos*.

47. On the so-called Generation of 1898, see Estelle Irizarry, "Generation of 1898," *Dictionary of the Literature of the Iberian Peninsula*, 707–15.

(1768–1834), one of the most influential theologians of the nineteenth century, his conception of religion as feeling first, belief afterwards, strongly marks the thought of Kierkegaard, Ritschl, Harnack, and, indirectly, Unamuno. Concerning the German philosopher Karl Christian Friedrich Krause (1781–1832), mentioned by Unamuno, he extended Kantianism in a mystical direction with his Pietistic roots. His *panentheism*, discussed above, holds that nature and human consciousness form part of God, Who is not identical to them, but greater than they. The end of history consists for Krause of the apocatastasis, the return of the finite human sphere to infinite being in a universal spiritual order: Jere Paul Surber, "Krause, Karl Christian Friedrich," *Cambridge Dictionary of Philosophy*, 476.

79. On Auguste Sabatier, see note 6, above; his brother Paul (1858–1928), pastor at St. Cierge in the Cevennes, wrote a well-known biography of Saint Francis, *Vie de Saint François d'Assise* (1893), whose 1894 edition shows Unamuno's marginal markings. We demonstrate occasional contributions from this book to the *Tratado*; see ch. 2, note 14; ch. 5, note 13. Alexandre-Rodolphe Vinet (1747–1847), Franco-Swiss Liberal Protestant, had a calling for French literature and morals. His *Études sur Blaise Pascal* (Studies on Blaise Pascal) exercised considerable influence on Unamuno for their stress on veracity in literature and moral life, and on the need for religious doctrine to adapt to the needs of conscience. See my book, *Unamuno y los protestantes liberales*, 42–43. On Paul Stapfer, see my "Introduction," pp. xxii–xxiii, above.

80. Miguel de Unamuno, "Principales influencias extranjeras en mi obra" (1901), in *Obras Completas*, 9:817.

81. Adolf von Harnack, *Dogmengeschichte*, 3:374–75, equates Catholic piety to mysticism insofar as it is not ecclesiastical obedience. Harnack attributes the following values to Catholic mysticism: individualism, intensity of sentiment regardless of content, pantheistic metaphysics, aestheticism, reduction of Christology to the *Ecce Homo*, and inner illumination (ibid., 377). Catholic piety, writes Harnack, on intuiting the responsibility inherent to the individual soul, lacks certainty of salvation and admits only an infinitely gradual approach to God without ever a secure possession (ibid., 375). Apparently, Unamuno finds Harnack describing his own personal piety and may well use this description to model his great devotional poem, *El Cristo de Velázquez* (*The Christ of Velázquez*, 1921): see N. R. Orringer, "Harnack y la fe del pueblo español en *El Cristo de Velázquez*." What the Protestant Harnack sees as limitations of Catholicism, Unamuno tries to turn into its strengths. The Catholic Church's perception of Catholicism does not coincide with Unamuno's and, in 1957, condemned *Del sentimiento trágico* and the book of essays *La agonía del cristianismo* (*Agony of Christianity*, 1925) to the *Index of Forbidden Books:* Martin Nozick, *Miguel de Unamuno*, 18.

82. A main thesis of my 1985 book, *Unamuno y los protestantes liberales*, 229, is that *Del sentimiento trágico* derives a system of doctrines from Ritschl's *Rechtfertigung und Versöhnung*, vol. 3: esteem for individual personality as point of departure; preference of practical over theoretical knowledge; an idea of God as Love, Will, and Personality; linking of God to faith, hope, and love; the idea of sin as finite and not meriting punitive measures; the morality of mastery over the world; and the doctrine of love of enemy. Whereas Ritschl is chiefly concerned with forgiveness of sin, Unamuno substitutes his own obsession with salvation after death.

83. For Adolf von Harnack, Jesus himself regarded adherence to the Gospel possible only with a believing surrender to his person, with every dogmatic utterance being suspect of impiety (*Dogmengeschichte*, 1:69). Life begets life (ibid., 70): "Es handelt sich um ein persönliches Leben, welches Leben um sich erweckt, wie das Feuer einer Fackeln entzündet" (The essence of the matter is a personal life which awakens life around it as the fire of one torch kindles another: Adolf von Harnack, *History of Dogma*, tr. Neil Buchanan, 1:71). Faith propagates faith; dogma creates nothing.

84. "¡Pistis y no gnosis!" in *Obras Completas*, 3:682.

85. This is the thesis of Adolf von Harnack, *Dogmengeschichte*, 1:18: "Das Dogma ist in seiner Conception und in seinen Ausbau ein Werk des griechischen Geistes auf dem Boden des Evangeliums" (Dogma in its conception and in its consolidation is a work of the Greek spirit on the soil of the Gospel).

86. "La fe," in *Obras Completas*, 1:964. The image may come from Phillips Brooks, "The Principle of the Crust," *Mystery of Iniquity and Other Sermons*, 155–57.

87. "¡Pistis y no gnosis!" in *Obras Completas*, 3:683.

88. Ibid., 684–85.

89. Wilhelm Herrmann, *Der Verkehr des Christen mit Gott*, 295.

90. "La fe," in *Obras Completas*, 1:970.

91. "¡Adentro!" in *Obras Completas*, 1:947. On the quotation from Fray Juan de los Ángeles, see the note below, to the epigraphs of this treatise.

92. *Tratado del amor de Dios*, [71].

93. "¡Adentro!," in *Obras Completas*, 1:946.

94. Ibid., 948.

95. On Thoreau, see *Tratado del amor de Dios*, ch. 3, n. 24.

96. "¡Adentro!" in *Obras Completas*, 1:951.

97. Ibid., 950.

98. *Tratado del amor de Dios*, [51]; *Del sentimiento trágico*, in *Obras Completas*, 7:162.

99. "Principales influencias extranjeras en mi obra" (1901), in *Obras Completas*, 9:817.

100. See note 81, above.

101. Ibid.

102. R. S., "Stapfer, Paul," *Grande Encyclopédie*, 30:443.

103. Miguel de Unamuno, *Amor y pedagogía*, in *Obras Completas*, 2:383, according to which Herostratus was the youth who burned down the temple of Diana at Ephesus, merely for fame. Fame takes the place of the immortality of the soul, in which moderns no longer believe: ibid.

104. *De Réputations litteraires*, 197.

105. Ibid., 102.

106. Miguel de Unamuno, "Sobre la lectura e interpretación del 'Quijote,'" *Obras Completas*, 1:1231.

107. Ibid., 1233.

108. Miguel de Unamuno, *Vida de Don Quijote y Sancho*, in *Obras Completas*, 3:232–33.

109. Ibid., 3:228.

110. Ibid., 3:100.

111. Ibid., 3:159.

112. Ibid., 3:187.

113. *Tratado del amor de Dios*, [80].

114. Manuel García Blanco, "Introducción" to Miguel de Unamuno, *Obras Completas*, 1:14–15.

115. Ibid., 19–20.

116. Even in 1921, in *España invertebrada* (Invertebrate Spain), in *Obras Completas*, 3:109, José Ortega y Gasset found Spain comparable to Russia in the numerical disproportion between the intelligentsia and the general populace. On high illiteracy: Gerald Brenan, *Spanish Labyrinth*, 50, 238.

117. Victor Ouimette, *José Ortega y Gasset*, 17–18.

118. Ibid., 37.

119. Ibid., 38.

120. For example, the 1912 article "Los versos de Antonio Machado" (The Verses of Antonio Machado, publicizes the anthology *Campos de Castilla* (*Fields of Castile*) for the poet: José Ortega y Gasset, *Obras Completas*, 1:570–74. Another article, the 1913 "Fiesta de Aranjuez en honor de Azorín" (Festival at Aranjuez in Honor of Azorín), does homage to an exquisite essayist whose books of landscapes will win him prestige in Machado's generation: ibid., 261–63. The examples are legion.

121. Victor Ouimette, *José Ortega y Gasset*, 37.

122. Ibid., 11.

123. In a letter dated December 5, 1906, Unamuno asks Ortega for news about philosophies of religion coming out in Germany. He mentions his acquaintance with those of Otto Pfleiderer and Harald Høffding (both present in the *Tratado*: on Pfleiderer, see ch. 2, note 46, below, and ch. 7, note 3, below; on Høffding, see ch. 7, notes 10 and 11, below). He also alludes to Ludwig Stein (see ch. 4, notes 19, 21, 124, below), in whom he has spotted references to other philosophers of religion. Among them he mentions Paul Natorp, to whom Stein refers in *Die soziale Frage in Licht der Philosophie*, 138, bracketed by Unamuno: "Das hübsche Wort Natorp's: 'Das Individuum ist eine Fiction so gut wie das Atom' mag hier das Richtige getroffen haben" (The fine expression of Natorp, 'The individual is a fiction as well as the atom,' may here have hit the mark): *Epistolario completo Ortega—Unamuno*, Letter 7:53.

124. Victor Ouimette, *José Ortega y Gasset*, 11.

125. "Ahora, además de mi *Tratado del Amor de Dios*, hago versos": *Epistolario completo Ortega—Unamuno*, Letter 3:39.

126. "Si usted quiere le enviaré, certificado, el manuscrito de mi *Tratado del Amor de Dios*, lo lee y me lo vuelve": ibid., Letter 7:50.

127. "Excuso decir que me daría una gran satisfacción enviándome el manuscrito de su «Tratado»": ibid., Letter 8:60.

128. Miguel de Unamuno, *Diario íntimo*, in *Obras Completas*, 8:803.

129. "¿Por qué no se dedica V. más de lleno a Filosofía de la Religión y le hacemos catedrático de nueva creación con máximo de sueldo en Madrid? Creo que le hace falta a V., mi buen Don Miguel, una continencia, una cejuela, un cilicillo; si no nos vamos de cabeza al misticismo energuménico y por ese mero hecho nos colocamos fuera de Europa, flor del Universo": *Epistolario completo Ortega—Unamuno*, Letter 8:60.

130. Ibid., Letter 9:63: "¿Cuándo se convencerá V., mi queridísimo Don Miguel,

que eso que hace V. deben hacerlo los discípulos de V.? ¿Cuándo se convencerá V. de que la misión de V. consiste en hacer lo que no pueden hacer sus discípulos? ¿Y de que sólo haciendo lo que debe puede V. algún día tener discípulos?"

131. "Mi querido Don Miguel: estoy con sed de una carta suya que no me llega y que me traiga la grata convivencia de su alma": ibid., Letter 10:64.

132. "No, tengo más que hacer. He vuelto a mi querido *Tratado del Amor de Dios*. Lo estoy rehaciendo y tengo ya quien me ha prometido traducirlo al italiano que es como aparecerá. El concepto de la inmortalidad es cosa más duradera que cualquier ley contra el terrorismo o a favor de él": ibid., Letter 19:86. According to Laureano Robles, in a letter to Unamuno dated February 2, 1908, Federico Giolli had proposed to publish the *Tratado* (ibid., 18n3). Unamuno never sent the manuscript. In the same Letter 19, Unamuno writes Ortega that someone had told Don Miguel that he was about to offer information about the antiterrorist law, but that Unamuno lacked the remotest idea about such a law: ibid., 85.

133. *Tratado del amor de Dios*, ch. 1, [1].

134. Ibid., ch. 1, notes 9, 11, 12, 13, 14.

135. Ibid., ch. 2, notes 4, 5, 6.

136. Ibid., note 3.

137. Ibid., [10].

138. Ibid., ch. 3, note 17.

139. Ibid., [17].

140. See ch. 3, note 21.

141. See ch. 3, note 22. William James (1842–1910), American pragmatist philosopher and psychologist, believed that human life was constituted by a panorama of personal, religious, and cultural perspectives irreducible to one another: John J. McDermott, "James, William," *Cambridge Dictionary of Philosophy*, 447–48. Unamuno read James some time between 1896 and 1908, finding in him a confirmation of his thesis that the will to believe creates the object of belief. James favors risking belief in immortality despite uncertainty: Martin Nozick, *Miguel de Unamuno*, 45.

142. See ch. 4, notes 7, 8, 13.

143. Ibid., note 23.

144. Ibid., note 27.

145. Ibid., note 32.

146. Ibid., note 53.

147. Ibid., [36–37].

148. *Tratado del amor de Dios*, ch. 5, [52].

149. Ibid., note 23.

150. Ibid., note 25.

151. Ibid., note 49.

152. Ibid., [59].

153. Ibid., ch. 6, note 12.

154. *Tratado del amor de Dios*, ch. 4, note 112.

155. *Tratado del amor de Dios*, ch. 6, note 28.

156. *Tratado del amor de Dios*, ch. 6, note 30.

157. Otto Pfleiderer, *Entstehung des Christentums*, 153.

158. *Tratado del amor de Dios*, [80].

159. Ibid., ch. 7, notes 21, 22.

160. *Tratado del amor de Dios*, [85].

161. Ibid., [88].

162. Ibid., ch. 8, note 38.

163. Ibid., note 41.

164. Ibid., [90].

165. Ibid., [91].

166. Ibid.

167. Ibid., [92].

168. The startling confession in the *Tratado*, [4], "My studies and meditations on philosophy and theology were leading me little by little to the most radical phenomenalism, and with my reason I came to be completely atheistic," never reaches *Del sentimiento trágico*, in *Obras Completas*, 7:209, where subsequent sentences are to be found. Following the passage on Paul before the refined Athenians, Unamuno's self-effacing parody of Acts 26:24, "You are mad, Miguel, your great learning is turning you mad" (*Tratado*, 37), is deleted from *Del sentimiento trágico*. Likewise, Unamuno omits from ibid., 191, the final paragraph on the *Tratado* [9] concerning his personal reaction to the wish to be someone else. From *Del sentimiento trágico*, 7:276, he omits the passages from the final paragraph on the *Tratado*, ch. 6, [75], through the first three lines on ibid. [76]. The prayer on ibid., [76], beginning, "No, my God, no," gets deleted, as do the first two paragraphs on ibid., [77]. From *Del sentimiento trágico*, 7:146, Unamuno eliminates the first paragraph of the *Tratado*, [92]. The list of omissions is not exhaustive.

169. In the *Tratado*, [18], Unamuno writes, "I feel the Universe calling me and guiding me like a person, I hear within its wordless voice"; in *Del sentimiento trágico*, 7:224, appears, "One can feel that the Universe calls him and guides him like one person another, one can hear within its wordless voice." In the *Tratado*, [28], Unamuno writes he has sensed that nature is a society because forest oaks seemed to "see me and hear me, to introduce themselves to me and to speak to me"; in *Del sentimiento trágico*, 198–99, he says that nature is a society because he felt a "sentiment of solidarity with the oaks, which in some obscure way gave one another a sense of my presence."

170. Unamuno was especially sensitive to criticism of this sort from the ferocious literary critic "Clarín" (Leopoldo Alas): cf. Nozick, *Miguel de Unamuno*, 41.

171. Unusually lengthy direct quotations appear in *Del sentimiento trágico*, in *Obras Completas*, vol. 7: James (p. 157), Kierkegaard (p. 174), Robertson (p. 216), Brooks (p. 221), Bonnefon (p. 257). Unamuno may be following the example of William James, *Varieties of Religious Experience*, 102–3, 212–14, 452–53, 464–65, 479–81.

172. Miguel de Unamuno, *Del sentimiento trágico*, in *Obras Completas*, 7:220.

173. Ibid., 122, 131.

174. Ibid., 117.

175. Ibid., 219.

176. Ibid., 210, 216–17.

177. Ibid., 219–20, 223.

178. Ibid., 258–59.

179. Ibid., 272.

180. *Tratado*, ch. 4, [25].

181. Ibid., ch. 8, [89].

182. Ibid., ch. 7, [84].

183. *Del sentimiento trágico,* in *Obras Completas,* 7:268–71.

184. Ibid., 262.

185. For this decree online, see "Church Documents: Lamentabili Sane (1907)," http://www.newadvent.org/docs/df07ls.htm.

186. For the encyclical online, see Pope Pius X, "Encyclical on the Doctrines of the Modernists." http://www.vatican.va/holy_father/pius_x/encyclicals/documents/hf_p-x_enc_19070908_pascendi-dominici-gregis_en.html

187. *Del sentimiento trágico,* in *Obras Completas,* 7:152.

188. Ibid.

189. Pius X, *Pascendi dominici gregis,* in Claudia Carlen, *Papal Encyclicals, 1903–1939,* 73.

190. *Del sentimiento trágico,* in *Obras Completas,* 7:220.

191. Ibid., 147; cf. Pius X, *Pascendi dominici gregis,* in Carlen, *Papal Encyclicals,* 85.

192. See *Tratado del amor de Dios,* ch. 8, [85].

193. A. Vermeersch, "Modernism," *Catholic Encyclopedia,* vol. 10, http://www.newadvent.org/cathen/10415a.htm.

194. *Tratado del amor de Dios,* ch. 8, [89].

195. A. Vermeersh, "Modernism," *Catholic Encyclopedia,* vol. 10.

196. José Ortega y Gasset, *Obras Completas,* 1:128–29.

197. In Spanish, Ortega called Saint John of the Cross "el lindo frailecito de corazón incandescente que urde en su celda encajes de retórica extática": "Unamuno y Europa, fábula," in José Ortega y Gasset, *Obras Completas,* 1:129. On Saint John, see note 52, above. René Descartes (1596–1650) helped revolutionize Western thought by overthrowing Scholastic authority based on Aristotle and substituting reason grounded on geometric logic for master philosophy, physical sciences, psychology, and ethics: John Cottingham, "Descartes, René," *Cambridge Dictionary of Philosophy,* 223–24.

198. Ramón Menéndez Pidal (1869–1968), philologist and literary historian, early distinguished himself for his studies of medieval Spanish epic poetry, especially the *Poema del Cid* (Lay of the Cid) and the legend of the seven princes of Lara. In 1904 he first published his often reedited *Manual de gramática histórica* (Handbook of Historical Grammar), the first systematic exposition of the evolution from Vulgar Latin to Castilian, a Bible for all subsequent philological research in Spanish: Stephen Miller, "Menéndez Pidal, Ramón," *Dictionary of Literature of the Iberian Peninsula,* 1071–72.

199. Américo Castro Quesada (1885–1972), Brazilian-born Hispanist of Spanish parents, studied philosophy and letters in Spain under Ramón Menéndez Pidal (see note 198, above) and Francisco Giner de los Ríos (see note 44, above), and broadened his background in various German universities and at the Sorbonne. During his first period of research, he concerned himself with Castilian as a living language and delved into the honor code in sixteenth- and seventeenth-century literature, as well as into Renaissance and Erasmist themes in Cervantes. In the second phase of his scholarship, initiated around 1936, he explored the impact of Jewish and Arabic culture on Spanish history. See Gonzalo Díaz Díaz, "Castro y Quesada, Américo," *Hombres y documentos de la filosofía española,* 2:271.

200. "Puedo afirmar que en esta ocasión don Miguel de Unamuno, energúmeno español, ha faltado a la verdad. Y no es la primera vez que hemos pensado si el matiz rojo y encendido de las torres salmantinas les vendrá de que las piedras venerables aquellas se ruborizan oyendo lo que Unamuno dice cuando a la tarde pasea entre ellas": José Ortega y Gasset, "Unamuno y Europa, fábula," in *Obras Completas*, 1:132.

201. "El autor de este libro no es un energúmeno, un poseso. Sabe bien á que atenerse. No carece de facultades críticas y es el primero en reconocer la endeblez de sus argumentos desde el punto de vista racional, lógico, científico ú objetivo, pero *quiere* que así sea. Y sobre todo execra á los que se conforman con la razón": on a paper bearing the titles "Amor de Dios" and "*Epílogo*" with the numbers 20. 1.2/392 in the lower left, and gathered in manuscript series D.

202. *Del sentimiento trágico*, in *Obras Completas*, 7:285–86. On Saint Teresa, see note 52, above. The *Critique of Pure Reason*, concerning itself with the cognitive possibility of synthetic a priori knowledge (the principles of Newtonian physics) is probably the greatest work of German philosopher Immanuel Kant (1724–1804). Ortega had studied at Marburg-an-Lahn in the neo-Kantian school of Hermann Cohen (1842–1918). Cohen used Kant as a model for his own critical idealism: see my *Hermann Cohen, 1842–1918*, 18. Unamuno regarded Cohen as a Sadducee, distracting Ortega from concern with the problem of immortality: *Epistolario completo Ortega—Unamuno*, 101–2. Hence, by attacking Kant in *Del sentimiento trágico*, Unamuno attacked both Cohen and Ortega.

203. Ibid., 7:281: "¿Qué significa, por ejemplo, en la historia de la cultura humana, nuestro San Juan de la Cruz, aquel frailecito incandescente, como se le ha llamado culturalmente—y no sé si cultamente—, junto a Descartes?" On Descartes, see note 197, above.

204. Ibid., 7:299.

205. Meister Johannes Eckhart (1260–1328), German theologian, mystic, and preacher, recommended "emptiness" of the soul to birth God. Though posthumously branded a probable heretic, he has affected mystics like Heinrich Suso, reformers like Martin Luther, and modern philosophers like Hegel, Fichte, and Heidegger. Mark D. Jordan, "Eckhart, Johannes," *Cambridge Dictionary of Philosophy*, 252.

On Saint Teresa of Avila, see note 52, above, and Unamuno, *Del sentimiento trágico*, in *Obras Completas*, 7:243; on Saint John of the Cross, note 52, above.

Jakob Boehme (1575–1624), German Protestant mystic, explained his mystic experiences in his writings. He holds that the Godhead, All-powerful Will, resists human comprehension. The world, a creation of God, seeks return to God. Humans undergo self-creation through renewal of faith: John Longeway, "Boehme, Jakob," *Cambridge Dictionary of Philosophy*, 91. In all these positions, Boehme coincides with Unamuno. See *Del sentimiento trágico*, in *Obras Completas*, 7:243.

Emanuel Swedenborg (1688–1772), Swedish visionary, philosopher, and biblical interpreter, became known as the "Spirit Seer," whose speculations in theosophy followed in the tradition of Boehme. Jean-Loup Seban, "Swedenborgianism," *Cambridge Dictionary of Philosophy*, 893. On Swedenborg's angelic vision, see Unamuno, *Del sentimiento trágico*, in *Obras Completas*, 7:200.

206. In *Del sentimiento trágico de la vida*, in *Obras Completas*, 7:178, Unamuno wrote, "Como el pensador no deja, a pesar de todo, de ser hombre, pone la

razón al servicio de la vida" (Since a thinker, despite everything, never ceases to be human, he or she places reason at the service of life). On the same page, he remarked, "No faltará a todo esto quien diga que la vida debe someterse a la razón, a lo que contestaremos que nadie debe lo que no puede, y la vida no puede someterse a la razón" (There will always be someone who may say of all this that life should be submitted to reason, and to that we will answer that no one should do what cannot be done, and life cannot be submitted to reason). Ortega y Gasset will call his thought the philosophy of vital reason. In *El tema de nuestro tiempo* (*The Modern Theme*, 1923), he writes, "La razón, el arte, la ética . . . han de servir la vida" (Reason, art, ethics . . . are to serve life): *Obras Completas*, 3:178. On the same page, remarks Ortega, "El tema de nuestro tiempo consiste en someter la razón a la vitalidad" (The theme of our time consists of submitting reason to vitality).

207. See note 82, above.

Epigraphs

I employ the translation by Harold N. Fowler (215) of this text on the last moments of Socrates, teacher of Athenian philosopher Plato (427–347 B.C.). On Plato's significance in Unamuno, see my article "Unamuno and Plato: A Study of Marginalia and Influence." The same quotation from the *Phaedo* forms the epigraph of *Del sentimiento trágico*, ch. 10, a speculative chapter on "mythology" of the Afterlife: *Obras Completas*, 7:236. If each individual is, for Unamuno, the endeavor to persist in being, then "mythologizing" about this persistence is an affirmation of the individual's being.

Fray Juan de los Ángeles' original text reads, "No seas y podrás más que todo lo que eres" (Cease to be, and you will have more power than everything that you are). Here Fray Juan, Toledan ascetic writer (1548–1609), is glossing *1 Corinthians* 1:25: "For the foolishness of God is wiser than men, and the weakness of God stronger than men." Writes Fray Juan, "That nothingness that you know you are, placed in the hands of God, has more power than all hell taken together" (p. 69). The same quote from Fray Juan, with the same modification made by Unamuno, reappears in *Del sentimiento trágico*, ch. 9 (*Obras Completas*, 7:231). Ceasing to be symbolizes in this work recognizing one's own nothingness, showing compassion for oneself as well as for the universe, and thereby dominating oneself and the universe; that is, being more than what one is.

Chapter 1: Love of God and Knowledge of God

1. This relationship between knowing and loving has classical roots in Xenophon's *Memorabilia* 3.1, where the courtesan Theodote asks the philosopher Socrates (hunter of truths) why he is not at her side like a huntsman's assistant, helping her snare friends and lovers. In Unamuno's 1914 novel *Niebla* (*Mist*), the ironic character Víctor Goti cites from this passage as evidence that philosophy resembles pandering and pandering philosophy: *Obras Completas*, 2:547–48.

2. The aphorism, *Nihil volitum quin praecognitum* (Nothing is wished for

unless previously known), is reversed by Unamuno to read *Nihil cognitum quin praevolitum* (Nothing is known unless previously wished for) in *Del sentimiento trágico* (*Obras completas*, 7:176). The reversal serves different purposes in both works. In the *Treatise on Love of God*, the object of knowledge is God; in *The Tragic Sense of Life*, will and intelligence are said to need one another in an operation of mutual confirmation and negation both in philosophy and in religion. In the latter work (*Obras Completas*, 7:190), Unamuno again quotes the Latin aphorism and his own reversal of it to maintain that nothing can be known well unless loved in the sense of pitied.

3. Unamuno finds these two alternatives in orthodox Catholic sources. Fray Pedro Malón de Chaide, *Tratado de la conversión de la gloriosa Magdalena* (*Treatise on the Conversion of Glorious Mary Magdalen*), 1.284, writes, "Ninguna cosa puede amarse sin que preceda primero el conocella" (no thing can be loved without knowing it coming first); for will, tending toward love, is blind and needs the initial guidance of understanding. This thinking agrees with Saint Augustine, *De trinitate* 10.1, and with Saint Thomas Aquinas, *Summa Theologica*, First Part of the Second Part, Question 3, Article 4, reply to objection 4.

Saint Paul, however, seems to disagree, prioritizing love: "Now I know in part; then [after love comes] I shall understand fully, even as I have been fully understood" (*1 Corinthians* 13:12).

4. Cf. Thomas Carlyle, *Sartor Resartus*, quoted in Unamuno's admired William James, *Will to Believe*, 43–44: "Thus had the Everlasting No pealed authoritatively through all the recesses of my Being, of my Me; and then it was that my whole Me stood up, in native God-created majesty, and recorded its protest.... The Everlasting No had said: 'Behold, thou art fatherless, outcast, and the Universe is mine;' to which my whole Me now made answer: 'I am not thine, but Free, and forever hate thee!'"

5. Unamuno finds himself self-deceived like Job and prays to God for guidance. Cf. Frederick W. Robertson, "The Kingdom of the Truth," in *Sermons Preached at Trinity Chapel*, 1:294–95: "The true man [i.e., Job], wrong, perplexed in verbal error, stood firm: he was true though his sentences were not: turned to the truth as the sunflower to the sun: as the darkened plant imprisoned in the vault turns towards the light, struggling to solve the fearful enigma of his existence." See *Job*, 38–42.

6. In his *Diario íntimo* (*Intimate Journal*), Unamuno wrote, "Con la razón buscaba un Dios racional, que iba desvaneciéndose por ser pura idea, y así paraba en el Dios Nada a que el panteísmo conduce, y en un puro fenomenismo, raíz de todo mi sentimiento de vacío" (With my reason I sought a rational God, Who kept on vanishing because He was a pure idea, and thus He was ending up as the Nothing God to which pantheism leads, and as a kind of pure phenomenism, root of my entire feeling of emptiness): *Obras Completas*, 7:778.

7. In the Greek philosopher Aristotle (384–322 B.C.), the Prime Mover signifies the first cause of change; it is exempt from change by any other agent. See Aristotle, *Metaphysics* 12.7.1072b10. St. Thomas Aquinas Christianized Aristotle's conception of God as Prime Mover, making this notion the first of the five ways to demonstrate His existence: *Summa Theologica*, First Part, Question 2, Article 3.

8. According to Zeferino González, a Scholastic philosopher whose textbook on elementary philosophy confused the young Unamuno, the method for knowing the essence of God is double, a procedure of removing or negation (*via remo-*

tionis) and a procedure using analogy (*via analogiae*). With the existence of God demonstrated and recognized as a First Cause and a Being superior to all things, the researcher removes from Him the imperfections and limits of creatures, while attributing to Him their perfections by analogy. Negation permits Him to be defined, for instance, as increate, infinite, independent, immutable: *Filosofía elemental*, 2nd. ed., "Teodicea," bk. 5, art. 1, 316–17.

9. According to Albrecht Ritschl, the traditional so-called proofs of God's existence do not prove His *objective* existence, but merely his existence in *thought*. The construction of the proofs previously depends on Christian assumptions of God in relation to personal faith: *Rechtfertigung und Versöhnung*, 3:29.185.

10. In manuscript series B, Unamuno has placed a large X over the following paragraph, numbered (1), and made redundant by the passage in his text of series A here footnoted: "Y hay, además, en el fondo de las supuestas pruebas lógicas de la existencia de Dios una extraña pretensión y es la de que tengamos que explicarnos el universo. Reducido á silogismo parece decirse: Es necesario que yo me explique el universo; es así que no me le explico si no admitiendo la existencia de un Dios, luego es necesario admitirla. Y aquí digo que niego lo mayor, y que puedo quedarme sin explicación alguna del universo. El negador de Dios á quien se le arguya: pues, entonces, [¿] cómo se explica usted el universo? puede contestar: de ninguna manera: no me le explico, y vivo" (And there is, furthermore, at the base of the supposed logical proofs of God's existence a strange aspiration, and it is that we have to explain the universe to ourselves. Reduced to a syllogism, it seems to say: it is necessary that I explain the universe to myself; it is thus that I do not explain it to myself unless admitting the existence of a God; therefore it is necessary to admit it. And here I say that I deny the greater part, and that I can remain without any explanation of the universe. The denier of God to whom is argued, "Well, then, how do you explain the universe?" can answer, "In no way; I do not explain it to myself, and yet I live").

The idea of God conceived as a hypothesis may stem from William James, *Varieties of Religious Experience*, 517–18: "A good hypothesis in science must have other properties than those of the phenomenon it is immediately invoked to explain. . . . God, meaning only what enters into the religious man's experience of union, falls short of being a hypothesis of this more useful order. He needs to enter into wider cosmic relations in order to justify the subject's absolute confidence and peace."

11. Likewise, Albrecht Ritschl finds it an error to adduce the creation of nature as proof of God's existence. Such an argument simply gives a different twist to the old cosmological argument, which is that, given the series of causes and effects, the first cause must be its own cause, *causa sui*, hence, God; but Ritschl questions whether this cause, immanent in nature, is really God, a goal-setting intelligence: *Rechtfertigung und Versöhnung*, 3.29.186.

12. According to Albrecht Ritschl, ibid., 3.29.185, the cosmological and teleological proofs of God's existence ought to demonstrate the coherence of the natural world necessarily and legitimately through God. The cosmological proof denotes the chain of natural causes culminating in God as the cause of everything else and of Himself; the teleological proof designates the purposes of all beings serving the divine world-plan. However, in both proofs, the conception of God is attained because the religious notion of the cosmic totality cooperates as the secret motif.

13. In the *Critique of Judgment*, remarks Ritschl (ibid., 29.187), Immanuel Kant insists that the necessity ("Notwendigkeit") of the notion of God is adequately demonstrated only for the practical use of our reason.

14. According to Ritschl (ibid. 32.212), "Diese beiden Formeln, dass etwas gut sei, weil Gott es will, und dass Gott etwas wolle, weil es gut ist, sind beide gleich ungenügend" (Both of these positions, that a thing is good because God wills it, and that He wills a thing because it is good, are equally unsatisfactory": *Justification and Reconciliation*, tr. Mackintosh and Macaulay, 248). As Ritschl here explains, Socinian heretics objected that divine justice, imposing on God's will the necessity for punishment, makes natural necessity a power higher than God. On the other hand, Ritschl finds it equally unjustified to suppose that God's will is unprincipled, capable of acting in either of two contrary ways and thereby casting aside any fixed plan in favor of capricious equity.

The whole preceding paragraph in the text comes from manuscript series B, where Unamuno indicates it with number (6), and so I have inserted it in my translation of manuscript series A where Unamuno has written number (6).

15. According to William James, *Varieties of Religious Experience*, 438n1, "order and disorder, as we recognize them, are purely human inventions." The reason is that "any state of things whatever that can be named is logically susceptible of theological interpretation. The ruins of the earthquake at Lisbon, for example: the whole of past history had to be planned exactly as it was to bring about in the fullness of time just that particular arrangement."

16. Cf. ibid., 31–32: "Modern transcendental idealism, Emersonianism, for instance, also seems to let God evaporate into abstract Ideality. Not a deity *in concreto*, not a superhuman person, but the immanent divinity in things, the essentially spiritual structure of the universe, is the object of the transcendentalist cult."

17. The same Latin quote from John Scotus Erigena (810?–877?), Irish-born Scholastic philosopher, appears in ibid., 417n2. For James, Scotus Erigena illustrates the mystic tendency to journey to the positive truth of divinity through absolute negativity. The comparison of the Aristotelian God to cannon holes, extending to the end of the paragraph, stems from manuscript series B, Unamuno's number (4). I have inserted this comparison precisely where Unamuno has written number (4) in manuscript series A.

18. Nineteenth-century physics, affected by analogies between light-waves and sound-waves (or other mechanical disturbances), rejected the notion of a wave without a medium. Hence physicists then hypothesized that an ether existed, filling all space and acting as a medium for light-waves. But in 1905, shortly before Unamuno began writing his treatise, Einstein postulated that the speed of light, c, in free space has the same value in all inertial frames of reference and all directions. With all reference frames yielding the same value, and none special, the postulate that an ether exists to propagate light became unnecessary: Halliday and Resnick, *Fundamentals of Physics*, 857.

19. See note 6, above.

20. Pindar's *Pythian Ode* 8.5.95 holds that the human being is a dream of a shadow (σκιᾶς ὄναρ). Pindar (518–438 B.C.), a lyric poet from Boeotia, wrote *Epinician Odes* to celebrate the victors in the Olympian, Nemean, Isthmian, and Pythian Games. See James H. Mantinband, "Pindar," *Dictionary of Greek Literature*, 321.

21. Cf. Heinrich Suso (Seuse), *Schriften*, 137: "Gott ist eine überwesentliche Ursache" (God is a super-essential Cause), a passage indicated by Unamuno in his personal edition.

Chapter 2: What Is Love?

1. To the love-god Cupid, German philosopher Arthur Schopenhauer, once translated by Unamuno, attributes a deadly dart, blindness, and wings (signifying fickleness). Fickleness comes with disillusionment following on the heels of dissatisfaction. For passion rested on the delusion that the loved had value for the individual, when it merely had value for the improvement of the species. Hence, once the species attains its end, the deception vanishes: *Welt als Wille und Vorstellung*, 2:639 (*World as Will and Idea*, tr. E. F. J. Payne, 2:556–57).

2. "Do amor . . . terreno, não há quem não experimente com quanta fúria corre ao que ama. . . . E sem mais razão que a afeição, por tudo passa, por tudo rompe, tudo comete e só sente não alcançar o que deseja" (Of earthly . . . love, there is no one who does not experience with how much fury he runs to the one he loves. . . . And with no motive but captivation, he passes through everything, breaks through everything, undertakes everything, and only laments that he does not achieve what he desires): Fray Thomé de Jesus, *Trabalhos de Jesus*, 1:104.

3. "Denn alle Verliebtheit, wie ätherisch sie sich auch geberden mag, wurzelt allein im Geschlechtstriebe, ja, ist durchaus nur ein näher bestimmter, specialisirter, wohl gar im strengsten Sinn individualisirter Geschlechtstrieb": Schopenhauer, *Welt als Wille und Vorstellung*, 2:610. ("For all amorousness [no matter how ethereally it may behave], is rooted in the sexual impulse alone, is in fact absolutely only a more closely determined, specialized, and indeed, in the strictest sense, individualized sexual impulse": tr. E. F. J. Payne, 2:533.)

4. According to Pedro Malón de Chaide, *Conversión de la Magdalena* (*Conversion of Mary Magdalen*), 58.307, Plato finds love bitter since "muere el que ama" (the one that loves dies): love implies forgetting of self and living within the beloved. Plato's *Symposium* 207c12–d3 holds that in love the mortal nature seeks immortality through generation, leaving another new creature (νέον) in place of the old (παλαιοῦ).

5. Plato's *Symposium* 191d5–7 compares each lover to half a broken die (keepsake of friendship) and to a flatfish sliced in two.

6. Perhaps with the help of the Anglican preacher Frederick W. Robertson, Unamuno Christianizes Jean-Marie Guyau, *Esquisse d'une morale sans sanction ni obligation* (Sketch of a Morality without Sanction or Obligation), 177, suggesting that extremes of pain and pleasure seemingly fuse: "Les spasmes de l'agonie et ceux de l'amour ne sont pas sans quelque analogie. . . . Les souffrances fécondes sont accompagnées d'une jouissance ineffable" (The spasms of agony and those of love are not without some analogy to one another. . . . Fruitful sufferings are accompanied by an ineffable enjoyment). For Robertson, "God's Revelation of Heaven," in *Sermons Preached at Trinity Chapel*, 1:10: "Call it friendship, love, what you will, that mystic blending of two souls in one, when self is lost and found again in the being of another."

7. Remarks Schopenhauer, *Welt als Wille und Vorstellung*, 2:44.637: "Endlich verträgt sich die Geschlechtsliebe sogar mit dem äussersten Hass gegen ihren

Gegenstand; daher schon Platon sie der Liebe der Wölfe zu den Schaafen ver-
glichen hat" (Finally, sexual love is compatible even with the most extreme
hatred towards its object; hence Plato has compared it to the love of the wolf for
the sheep: *World as Will and Idea*, tr. E. F. J. Payne, 2:555–56).

8. For Schopenhauer, *ibid.*, 640, even marriages for love serve the species, not
individuals. The true aim of spouses, unknown to them, is to bring forth an individual possible only through them. Unamuno plays with this notion in his 1902
novel *Amor y pedagogía* (Love and Pedagogy), in *Obras Completas*, 2:317–410.

9. For Søren Kierkegaard, *Entweller/Oder*, 4, certain insects die upon fertil-
ization; in all joy, the most brilliant instant of enjoyment brings death.

10. For Plato, *Phaedrus* 234e4–8, the lover ruled by desire lives enslaved
(δουλεύοντι) to pleasure. He takes pleasure in anything not antithetical to him,
anything better than or equal to him. Hence, he strives to weaken or abase any
lover superior or equal to himself.

11. Schopenhauer, *Welt als Wille und Vorstellung*, 1:60.387–88.

12. In "Amore e morte" (Love and Death), *Canti* 27, Giacomo Leopardi writes,
"Fratelli, a un tempo stesso Amore e Morte / Ingenerò la sorte": *Canti* 27:264
(Twinborn are Love and Death: on one same date / were they conceived by Fate:
Leopardi, *Poems*, tr. Geoffrey L. Bickersteth, 293); see Unamuno, *Del sen-
timiento trágico de la vida*, in *Obras Completas*, 7:187, and Kerrigan and Noz-
ick, in Unamuno, *Tragic Sense of Life*, 427n146.

13. On despair in love: see note 2, above; through prayer, writes Auguste
Sabatier, *Esquisse d'une philosophie de la religion*, 23, "le sentiment écrasant de
ma défaite devient le sentiment joyeux et triumphant de ma victoire. Chacun de
ces états se change en son contraire" (the crushing feeling of my defeat becomes
the joyful, triumphant feeling of my victory. Each of those states changes into its
opposite). Unamuno resorted to prayer at the moment of maximum spiritual
prostration: *Diario íntimo*, in *Obras Completas*, 1:781.

14. Marked in Unamuno's edition of Paul Sabatier, *Vie de S. François d'Assise*,
26, is the following passage: "La douleur est le ciment de l'amour. Pour s'aimer
vraiment il faut avoir mêlé ses larmes" (Pain is the cement of love. To love one
another truly it is necessary to have mixed the tears of one another together).

15. When only a few months old, Unamuno's third child Raimundo Jenaro, in
fall 1896, contracted meningitis, which led to hydrocephalia. Unamuno saw this
mishap as divine punishment directed against himself for his own loss of faith
and excessive reliance on intelligence: *Diario íntimo* in *Obras completas*, 1:775.
In March 1897, he awoke one night anguished by dreams of falling into the nothingness, experienced tachycardia, and discovered a mother in his consoling wife
Concha, who embraced him and called her his son. References to the well-
known "crisis of 1897" recur in the *Diario íntimo*, personal correspondence,
novels, and plays. See Kerrigan and Nozick, "Notes" to Unamuno, *Tragic Sense
of Life*, 428n149. For Schopenhauer, *Welt als Wille und Vorstellung*, 1:67.444,
pure love (*die reine Liebe*) is by nature fellow-feeling, called by the ancients
ἀγάπη or *caritas*.

16. This entire paragraph stems from manuscript series B, Unamuno's number
(7). I have inserted my translation of paragraph (7) precisely where Unamuno has
written (7) in manuscript series A.

17. Unamuno's description of self-pity followed by fellow-feeling may show
the impact of Schopenhauer, Sénancour, and Guyau. For Schopenhauer, *Welt als*

Wille und Vorstellung, 1:64.144, fellow-feeling arises either when we imagine ourselves vividly in the sufferer's place, or else see in his destiny the lot of all humanity in its finiteness and, as a consequence, our own destiny. In Unamuno, self-pity precedes fellow-feeling, as in J. M. Guyau, *La Morale anglaise contemporaine,* 20: "L'amour de soi, après s'être fait sympathique, se fait philanthropique" (Self-love, after having become sympathetic, becomes philanthropic). Unamuno's expression of self-pity suggests his self-identification with Sénancour's hero Obermann in the homonymous novel (p. 86, passage marked by Unamuno): "Accident éphémère et inutile, je n'existais pas, je n'existerai pas: je trouve . . . ma idée plus vaste que mon être; et si je considère que ma vie est ridicule à mes propres yeux, je me perd dans des ténèbres impénétrables" (Ephemeral, useless accident, I did not exist, I shall not exist: I find . . . my idea [of myself] vaster than my being; and if I consider that my life is ridiculous in my own eyes, I get lost in impenetrable darkness). Cf. *Diario íntimo,* in *Obras Completas,* 8:778.

18. Cf. Frederick W. Robertson, "The Sympathy of Christ," in *Sermons Preached at Trinity Chapel,* 1:111: "The rich man who goes to his poor brother's cottage, and . . . enters into his circumstances, inquiring about his distresses, and hears his homely tale, has done more to establish an interchange of kindly feeling, than he could have secured by the costliest present by itself."

19. Besides universalizing his own wife's motherly compassion towards him (see note 15 above), Unamuno may have read in Schopenhauer, *Parerga und Paralipomena,* 2:379, 652, that woman's fellow-feeling and human love are superior to man's, and in Kierkegaard, *Stadier paa Livets Vei* (*Stages on Life's Way*), in *Samlede Vaerker,* 6:146, that a woman acquires maturity, completion—even reality—with motherhood.

20. Lizabetta (Isabella) and Lorenzo, the unfortunate lovers in a tale by Giovanni Boccaccio, were the victims of Lizabetta's brothers, who murdered Lorenzo. Lizabetta dug up the body and retained the head as a keepsake in a pot where she grew basil. The English poet John Keats (1795–1821), in his poem *Isabella* or *The Pot of Basil,* retold the story. Unamuno owned a two-volume 1928 Italian edition of Boccaccio's *Decameron* (Valdés, 32) and an 1899 edition of Keats's poetry (Valdés, 130).

Romeo and Juliet, belonging to feuding families, are the star-crossed lovers of Shakespeare's tragedy taking their names for its title, with Romeo and Juliet each committing suicide out of grief for the death of the other.

In Shakespeare's tragedy *Othello, the Moor of Venice,* Othello's wife Desdemona, before dying victim to her husband's murderous jealousy, falsely claims instead, in order to exonerate him, that she has committed suicide. Unamuno possessed an 1864 four-volume edition of Shakespeare's works (Valdés, 227).

Finally, Paolo and Francesca were adulterous lovers, wafted around hell forever in a wind, and portrayed in the *Inferno* 5.73–142 by Florentine poet Dante Allighieri (1265–1321). There Francesca's shade expresses her love for Paolo, which survives his death.

This entire paragraph on woman's love stems from manuscript series B, Unamuno's number (13). I have inserted it into my translation of manuscript series A precisely where Unamuno has written (13) there.

21. See note 2, above.

22. A clear echo of Sénancour, cited above in note 17.

23. Unamuno refers to what Paul Stapfer, in his "Confession d'un égoïste," calls "l'espèce d'égoïsme qui est commun aux hommes et aux bêtes" (the type of egoism that is common to humans and beasts): *De Réputations littéraires*, 87. The "flesh of your soul," however, reflects Unamuno's fascination with the Church Father Tertullian's doctrine that everything real is bodily, including God and the soul (marked by Unamuno in Ueberweg, *Die patristische und scholastische Philosophie*, 9.51). Self-love is perfectly compatible with spiritual love, however, as Unamuno has read in his admired Fray Juan de los Ángeles, "Triunfos del amor de Dios," in *Obras místicas*, 17: "Ama á Dios y ámate á ti, y ama los dones de Dios por Dios. Ámale a Él para gozarle, y ámate á ti para que seas amado de Él" (Love God and love yourself and love the gifts of God for God's sake. Love Him in order to enjoy Him, and love yourself in order to be loved by Him).

24. Schopenhauer, *Die Welt als Wille und Vorstellung*, 2:567, writes the following: "Das Ende der Person ist eben so real, wie es ihr Anfang war, und in eben dem Sinne, wie wir vor der Geburt nicht waren, werden wir nach dem Tode nicht mehr sehn" (The end of the person is just as real as was its beginning, and in just that sense in which we did not exist before birth, shall we no longer exist after death: tr. E. F. J. Payne, 2:495).

25. This sense of human nothingness returns to Sénancour; see note 17, above.

26. Prof. Thomas Franz here discerns the influence of the Spanish Romantic poet José de Espronceda (1808–42), whose poem "A una estrella" (To a Star), is addressed to a star that has lost its light (as the lyric subject has lost his beloved) and which receives the lyrical subject's compassion ("y un vago padecer mi pecho siente": and a vague suffering my breast feels: *Poesías líricas*, 253). Franz also proposes an allusion by Unamuno to "Al sol. Himno" (To the Sun. Hymn), wherein Espronceda's lyrical voice advises the sun to enjoy its youth before the universe explodes and the solar light dies (ibid., 182). Such compassion has inspired one of Unamuno's own moving poems, "Aldebarán," addressed to a star: *Obras Completas*, 6:545–48.

27. Here is the basic premise of Unamuno's *Tratado:* every being is an effort to be itself and, at the same time, to be everything else. All creatures imitate God in His progress toward the apocatastasis, the final self-affirming ingathering or restitution of all creatures to God.

28. In his moral treatise *Virtud militante contra las cuatro pestes del mundo* (Militant Virtue against the Four Plagues of the World, 1651), the Spanish neo-Stoic moralist, philosopher, and poet Francisco de Quevedo writes (p.1229) that envy "no quiere ser lo que es, y quiere que los otros sean lo que no son" (does not want to be what it is, and wants others to be what they are not). Unamuno quotes from this work by Quevedo in his own essay, "Comentarios quevedianos" (Commentaries on Quevedo), *Obras Completas*, 3:1062–63.

29. *Ecclesiastes* 1:2–3: "Vanity of vanities, says the Preacher, vanity of vanities! All is vanity. / What does man gain by all the toil at which he toils under the sun?"

30. "Erstens sind die Objecte der Liebe nothwendig dem liebenden Subjecte gleichartig, nämlich geistige Personen. Spricht man von Liebe zu Sachen oder zu Thieren, so wird der Begriff unter seine eigentliche Geltung degradirt": Albrecht Ritschl, *Rechtfertigung und Versöhnung*, 3:34.238 (First, it is necessary that the objects which are loved should be of like nature to the subject which loves, namely, persons. When we speak of love for things or animals, the conception is

degraded beneath its proper meaning: *Justification and Reconciliation*, tr. Mackintosh and Macaulay, 277).

31. This powerful statement simply means that everything endowed with consciousness wishes to overshoot its spatiotemporal limit but vaguely or clearly understands that it cannot.

32. "Nur in Einer oder in vielen geistigen Personen können wir das Object vorstellen, welches seinem Wesen als Lieben correlat ist": Albrecht Ritschl, *Rechtfertigung und Versöhnung*, 3:239 (Only in one or many spiritual persons can we represent the object which is correlate to [God's] essence as love). Ritschl adds that if God's reason for being is to create many spirits, perfect them, and reveal Himself as Love to them, Nature is conceivable as a means to that end (ibid., 240).

33. Unamuno may have recalled reading in the Portuguese poet Antero de Quental's double sonnet "Redempção" (Redemption) that spirit is tormented by its inability to escape matter: "Vozes do mar, das árvores, do vento! / Quando às vezes, num sonho doloroso, / Me embala o vosso canto poderoso, / Eu julgo igual ao meu vosso tormento . . ." (Voices of wind, of branches, and of foam! / At times, when in a painful slumber deep, / The power of your singing rocks my sleep, / I judge your torment equal to my own). Unamuno translated the double sonnet into Spanish as "Redención," in *Obras Completas*, 6:926–27. The texts in the original Portuguese appear in his essay, "¡Plenitud de plenitudes y todo plenitud!" in *Obras Completas*, 1:1181. See Antero de Quental, *Sonetos completos*, 111–12.

34. This thinking may be inspired by the first tercet of Antero de Quental's first of the two sonnets comprising "Redempção" (ibid.): "Um espírito habita a imensidade: / Uma ânsia cruel de liberdade / Agita e abala as formas fugitivas" (A spirit lives within the immensity: / A cruel yearning simply to be free / Shakes up and moves about the fleeting forms).

35. "Ce choc perpétuel, cette lutte du moi et du monde, c'est la cause première et l'origine de toute douleur. Ainsi refoulée sur elle-même, l'activité du moi se replie au centre que s'échauffe comme l'essieu d'une roue en mouvement. Bientôt l'étincelle brille et la vie intérieure du moi s'éclaire. C'est la *conscience*" (That perpetual clash, that struggle of the ego and the world, is the first cause and origin of all pain. Thus driven back over itself, the activity of the ego coils up to its center that heats up like the axle of a moving wheel. Rather the spark shines and the inner life of the ego comes aglow. It is *consciousness*): Auguste Sabatier, *Esquisse d'une philosophie de la religion*, 15.

36. "L'homme ne se peut connaître, sans se connaître limité" (The human being cannot know himself without knowing that he is limited): ibid., 16.

37. See ch. 6, note 3, below, on charity as an overflow of painful sweetness.

38. Unamuno puns on the word *consentir*, to consent, from *con-*, with, and *sentir*, to feel, which suggests sym-pathy or com-passion. Cf. Jean-Marie Guyau, *La Morale anglaise contemporaine*, 386: "Sympathiser, c'est-à-dire, suivant l'étymologie même du mot, pâtir ensemble, souffrir ensemble" (To sympathize, that is, following the very etymology of the word, to drudge together, to suffer together).

39. Cf. *Del sentimiento trágico de la vida*, *Obras Completas*, 7:196–97, criticizing with Schopenhauer Darwin's superficiality in his book, *The Origin of Species*. On March 1, 1860, Schopenhauer wrote the following to Adam Ludwig

von Doss: "Aus Darwin's Buch habe einen ausführlichen Auszug in den *Times* gelesen: darnach ist es keinwegs meiner Theorie verwandt, sondern platter Empirismus, der in diese Sache nicht ausreicht" (Of Darwin's book [I] read a detailed abstract in the [London] *Times:* according to that, it is in no way related to my theory, but vulgar empiricism, which in this matter is inadequate): Eduard Grisebach, *Schopenhauer's Briefe*, 382–83. The British naturalist Charles Darwin (1809–82) held that changes in all species come about through chance variation and natural selection. In the struggle for existence, some individuals, better adapted to their environment, proliferate more than individuals less well adapted: David Leech Anderson, "Darwinism," 204. In a letter of March 1, 1859, written to Johann August Becker, Schopenhauer enclosed a copy of his work "Über den Willen in der Natur" (On Will in Nature) to clarify his own, deeper metaphysical doctrine of will: "In dieser kleinen Schrift ist der eigentliche Kern meiner Metaphysik deutlicher, als irgendwo, dargelegt, und sie ist besonders geeignet, die so nöthige Ueberzeugung hervorzubringen, dass das innere Wesen aller Dinge, mithin das allein Reale in der Welt, . . . eben jenes uns so Vertraute und doch so Geheimnissvolle ist, was wir in unserm Selbstbewusstseyn als den Willen finden und welches vom Intellekt gänzlich verschieden ist" (In this brief writing the real core of my metaphysics is set down more clearly than elsewhere, and it is especially appropriate for eliciting the necessary conviction that the inner essence of all things, hence, the only reality in the world, . . . is precisely that which is so familiar to us and yet so secretive, that which we find in our self-consciousness as will and which is entirely different from intellect): Eduard Grisebach, op. cit., 91. On the manuscript copy of *Tratado del amor de Dios*, numbered page 12 by Unamuno, he has written vertically up the right hand margin in large letters "Berkeley Schopenhauer." The final version of this page 12 will evidently evolve into *Del sentimiento trágico de la vida*, in *Obras Completas*, 7:196. Here Unamuno mentions Schopenhauer's "On Will in Nature" and connects it to the British idealist George Berkeley's assertion that not matter, but only mind exists (analogous to Schopenhauer's ubiquitous Will).

40. Here Unamuno equates Schopenhauerian will to his own doctrine of being as the effort of every entity to persevere in being and, at the same time, to be everything else. Certainly Schopenhauer holds, as does Unamuno, that in every individual the will-to-live exhibits itself both as an impulse to self-preservation and as an impulse for self-perpetuation throughout all time: *Welt als Wille und Vorstellung*, 2:4.45.651. But in Schopenhauer's metaphysics the *universal* will is the only reality (see note 39 above); in Unamuno, reality is the *individual* desire to persist and to extend itself throughout all time.

41. For Jean-Marie Guyau, *Esquisse d'une morale sans obligation ni sanction*, 101, the cells of the human brain and the heart aspire to live and develop with a thrust of moral life.

42. Cf. Blaise Pascal's essay on the cognitive incapacity of the human being, despairing in the face of the two infinities, the immense one above him, the miniscule beneath him. If he removes his vision from his surroundings and raises them to lofty heights of nature, he can imagine the earth as a point in comparison with the revolution of the sun; this vast revolution as a point from the perspective of the distant stars; the whole visible world as but an imperceptible trace in the bosom of nature. We can produce only atoms at a cost of reality, an infinite sphere with a center everywhere and a circumference nowhere. The

greatest sensible characteristic of God's omnipotence, nature loses our imagination in thought: quoted in Alexandre-Rodolphe Vinet, *Études sur Blaise Pascal*, 143, annotated by Unamuno.

43. In a tentative scheme to a chapter of the *Tratado*, Unamuno writes, "Cuerpo de Dios. v. Tennemann VII 171" (MS. hand-numbered page 11), referring to Wilhelm Gottlieb Tennemann (1761–1819), German historian of philosophy of the Kantian school, and author of the eleven-volume *Geschichte der Philosophie* (*History of Philosophy*). In Tennemann, op. cit., we learn that most Church Fathers at first depicted God as being associated with space and time like a bodily being, although this vision underwent subsequent corrections. Tennemann cites Tertullian, *Adversus Praxean* (*Treatise against Praxeas*), ch. 7, and Arnobius, *Adversus Gentes* (*Against the Heathens*), 1.17. Tertullian, op. cit., ch. 7–9, holds that Christ has the form of God, and that God is body (*deum corpus est*), even though spirit. For spirit is body of its own kind, in its own image (*spiritus enim corpus sui generis in sua effigie*). Arnobius, op. cit., bk. 1, maintains that God is the space (spatium) in which the bases of all things rest, though He is illimitable, unconfined as to place, and displaying no bodily shape. Unamuno could well have combined the two visions to imagine the universe as the body of God, a metaphor he apparently takes literally.

44. "Le moi . . . est pour la psychologie contemporaine une illusion, . . . il n'y a pas de personnalité séparée, . . . nous sommes composés d'une infinité d'êtres et de petites consciences ou états de conscience" (The self . . . is for contemporary psychology an illusion, . . . there is no separate personality, . . . we are composed of an infinity of beings and tiny consciousnesses or states of consciousness): Jean Marie Guyau, *Esquisse d'une morale sans obligation ni sanction*, 115. Hence neither my pleasure nor my pains are absolutely mine: ibid.

45. This fleshly conception of God harks back to the early Church Fathers. See note 43 above.

46. Otto Pfleiderer, *Religionsphilosophie auf geschichtlicher Grundlage* (Philosophy of Religion on Historical Bases), 464–65, holds that scientifically compelled, "exact" proofs of God's existence lie beyond the scope of religion and philosophy (despite claims of individual Scholastic philosophers). On the other hand, he deems it a useless if pious frivolity to discredit demonstration of rational grounding of faith in God in the whole world order, so as to resort to positive authorities. On a tentative scheme of ideas for this chapter (though labeled III), Unamuno has jotted down, "Pretendidas pruebas Pfleiderer 464" (so-called proofs Pfleiderer 464): manuscript series D.

Chapter 3. What Is Faith?

1. This question and answer stem from the Catechism of Father Gaspar Astete (1537–1601), learned by Unamuno in elementary school. Cf. *Hebrews* 11:1, defining faith as "the conviction of things not seen." Unamuno's essay "La fe" (1900) begins with the same question and answer: *Obras Completas*, 1:962.

2. For Phillips Brooks, *Mystery of Iniquity and Other Sermons*, 95 (emphatically marked by Unamuno), "in its fullest exercise faith is personal. We speak indeed of faith in principles . . . ; but the fullest trust comes with the perception of a trustworthy character, and the entire reliance of one nature on another."

3. "Our reason is quite satisfied . . . if it can find a few arguments that will do to recite in case our credulity is criticized by someone else. Our faith is faith in someone else's faith." William James, *The Will to Believe*, 19.

4. James, ibid. 17, contrasts mere belief by volition with "submission to the icy laws" of outer scientific fact.

5. For Richard Hooker, *Of the Laws of Ecclesiastical Polity*, 2 (marked by Unamuno), "faith is more certain than any science. That which we know either by sense, or by infallible demonstration, is not as certain as the principles, articles, and conclusion of Christian faith."

6. An extension of *Mark* 2:27: "The Sabbath has been made for man, not man for the Sabbath."

7. For Albrecht Ritschl, *Rechtfertigung und Versöhnung*, 3:19.86–87, faith is not the recognition of the accuracy of an inherited fact, not the recognition of a theoretical truth, as this limits the role of will. Rather, faith is "eine Willesbewegung direkter Art, weil dessen Object der Werth einer praktischen Wahrheit hat, welche auch als Inhalt einer anerkannten Ueberlieferung, oder in der Form einer allgemeinen Wahrheit darauf bezogen ist, den Willen direkt entweder anzuziehen oder abzustossen" (a movement of the will of a direct kind, because its object has the value of a practical truth, related to it as the content of a recognized tradition, or in the form of a universal truth, either to attract the will directly or to repel it); ibid., 87.

8. For Saint Thomas Aquinas, *Summa Theologica*, Second Part of Second Part, Question 4, Article 2, "The assent of faith to believe anything proceeds from the will obeying God. Therefore it seems that faith owes all its praise to obedience. But obedience is in the will. Therefore faith is in the will, not in the intellect." This passage appears quoted in Latin in A. Ritschl, *Rechtfertigung und Versöhnung*, 3:19.87n, cited by Unamuno.

9. I use "psychic" to translate Unamuno's adjective *anímica*. Phillips Brooks, *Mystery of Iniquity and Other Sermons*, 95, speaks of fiducia or confidence and trust as a "faculty" within faith, as the "power" of admiration for someone greater. It is a "life-giving faculty" obliging "all other faculties" to perform optimal work: ibid., 96. For Frederick W. Robertson, "Third Advent Lecture—The Barbarian," *Sermons Preached at Trinity Chapel*, 239, faith is a "power in the soul, quite separate from intellect."

10. The following notion appears in Georg Simmel, *Einleitung in die Moralwissenschaft*, 1:404–45: "Das Objekt, von dem irgend ein Glaube gilt, steht uns doch nicht immer als äussere, von uns unabhängige Realität rein beobachtbar gegenüber; sondern auf praktischen, psychologischen, sozialen Gebieten machen wir erst das Objekt, über das wir reflektieren, es entsteht und besteht in Wechselwirkung mit der Vorstellung von ihm, die allmählich auf die Umgestaltung der Wirklichkeit in ihren Sinne wirkt" (The object to which a faith applies does not stand over and against us as a purely observable outer reality independent of us, but in practical, psychological, social spheres we initially *make* the object of our reflection, it originates and persists in reciprocal action with its image, which gradually has an influence on the transformation of the meaning of the reality).

11. Ludwig Feuerbach corrected *Genesis* 1:26 by affirming that God did not create man in His own image, but man the gods in his: Ludwig Stein, *Die soziale Frage in Licht der Philosophie*, 157 (marked by Unamuno). Yet August Sabatier,

Esquisse d'une philosophie de la religion, 34, repeats with Pascal that piety is "Dieu sensible au cœur" (God perceptible to the heart). Hence religious revelation is "la création, l'épuration et la clarté progressive de la conscience de Dieu dans l'homme individual et dans l'humanité" (the creation, purification, and progressive clarity of the consciousness of God in the individual human and in humankind).

12. "Al fine de le sue parole il ladro / le mani alzo con amendue le fiche, / gridando: Togli, Dio, ch'a te le squadro!" (At the end of his remarks the thief / raised both hands, making the [obscene] sign of the fig, / and shouting, "Take that, God, for at Thee I aim them"): See Dante Alighieri, *Divine Comedy*, tr. H. R. Huse, 118. Vanni Fucci, one of Dante's political enemies in life, in Dante's hell suffers horrible punishments for having robbed in 1293 the Church of San Zeno (Pistoia). No wonder he obscenely blasphemes against God.

13. *James* 2:19.

14. For Auguste Sabatier, *Esquisse d'une philosophie de la religion*, 28, the self-proclaimed atheist is so only from the standpoint of others' God. He denies his priest's God but keeps his own, hidden in his soul and worshipped under a private name. Sabatier, with Pascal, has an inner struggle between faith, which yea-says salvation, and reason, which nay-says it: ibid., 4.

15. Cf. Unamuno's 1917 novel, *Abel Sánchez*, whose protagonist, Joaquín Monegro, calls a devout housemaid a hypocrite and dismisses her out of envy of her simple piety: *Obras Completas*, 2:724.

16. In *Einleitung in die Moralwissenschaft*, 1:404–5, the Berlin Neo-Kantian culture-philosopher Georg Simmel (1858–1918) writes that faith sets the dividing line between objectively recognized anthropomorphisms and no longer admissible ones. Faith wishes (German *will*) to set that limit on bases no longer relevant to knowledge. The virtuously pious, convinced about going to heaven, already feel happy on earth. Often, our originally false images so reform reality that they one day come true.

17. "Seek and ye shall find": *Matthew* 7:7, *Luke* 11:9. "For those that seek will find [Him] and finding Him will praise Him. May I seek You, Lord, invoking You, and may I invoke You believing in You": Saint Augustine, *Confessions*, bk. 1, prayer 1:3. In *De trinitate* 15.51, Saint Augustine prays, "Give strength to seek, You Who made me find You, and gave [me] hope of finding You more and more." As to the wicked unresponsive to God's wisdom, "They will seek Me diligently but will not find Me": *Proverbs* 1:28.

18. In a tentative outline of the present chapter, Unamuno writes, "A Dios no se llega por la cabeza Robertson II 109" (God cannot be reached with the head Robertson II, 109). The reference is to *Sermons Preached in Trinity Chapel*, 2:109, by Frederick W. Robsertson, intellectually independent of dogma and affirming the individual as such, personal immortality, and the superior veracity of feeling over intelligence.

19. *Matthew* 5:8.

20. Unamuno holds that to believe is to create. He puns on the double meaning in Spanish of the verb *creo* (meaning, "I believe," when interpreted as the first person present of the verb *creer*, to believe, but signifying, "I create," when seen as the first person present of the verb *crear*, to create).

21. Cf. A. Ritschl, *Rechtfertigung und Versöhnung*, 3:63.545, for whom faith in divine providence gives religious dominion over the world. By this view, a

supramundane God loves us as a Father and thereby fills us with self-esteem, making us confident that all worldly events serve our good because we are objects of God's special care. Ritschl adds that faith in divine providence asserts God's goodness as each individual's own conviction based on experience, not on a scientific law: ibid., 3:63.536.

22. Cf. very similar words of a twenty-seven-year-old believer quoted by William James, *Varieties of Religious Experience*, 71: "Something over a year ago I was . . . in the direst perplexity. . . . before long . . . I could hear distinctly a passage of Scripture: 'My grace is sufficient for thee.' . . . God has frequently stepped into my affairs very perceptibly, and I free that he directs many little details all the time."

23. "Go therefore and make disciples of all nations": *Matthew* 28:19. Cf. William James, *Varieties of Religious Experience*, 318, quoting R. Philip's 1842 biography of George Whitfield. In 1898 Unamuno wrote to his friend Pedro Jiménez Ilundain that when most devout, at age fifteen or sixteen, he once opened the Gospel at random with the resolution to follow the instruction at hand. He came to touch *Matthew* 28:19, which he interpreted as a command to be a priest: Kerrigan and Nozick, in Unamuno, *The Tragic Sense of Life*, 440n213. Perhaps out of a secret desire to become the Spanish Luther and one day reform Spanish Catholicism, Unamuno mathematically calculated Luther's age at many stages of life, as if to compare his own progress in M. Lenz's 1897 biography, *Martin Luther*, 38, 44, 45, 47, 50, 142, 162, 168, 175, 176, 221, 222.

24. Henry David Thoreau in *Walden* (cited in William James, *Varieties of Religious Experience*, 275) describes a like experience. A gentle rain made him suddenly sensitive to a "sweet and beneficent society in Nature." Thoreau found that "every little pine-needle expanded . . . with sympathy and befriended me. I was so distinctly aware of the presence of something kindred to me, that I thought no place could ever be strange to me again."

25. Here Unamuno paraphrases Plato, *Symposium* 211 c 1–d 1, describing induction from particulars to universals—for instance, from beautiful bodies to the essence of beauty itself.

26. William James, *Varieties of Religious Experience*, 57, quotes the passage from Plato paraphrased by Unamuno (see note 25, above) to the effect that abstractions like Beauty polarize and magnetize us, attract and repel us, are sought, held, hated, and blessed by us as any concrete beings are. Unamuno differs from James in envisioning the ascent from the particular to the universal as ending in the love of Love (=God). In notes to his manuscripts, Unamuno attributes the idea to Alonso Rodríguez. In *Ejercicio de perfección y virtudes cristianas*, pt. 1, treatise 3, 7:169–70, Rodríguez finds suspect any love based on hope of receiving some benefit from the beloved: pure love expects nothing in return because no interest moves it. It derives its content from itself and is its own reward. "And the cause to love God is to be loving Him; and the fruits of loving Him is to be loving Him; and the end of loving Him is to be loving Him: . . . I love in order to love": ibid., p.170.

27. The anonymous *Theologia Deutsch* or *Germanica*, published by Luther in 1516, recommends annihilation of self-will and absorption of the soul in God. Ch. 32 says that where the One (God) lays hold of a creature to perceive what is His own, that creature no longer says it loves itself, but belongs to Him insofar as it is needed for Him to be a Person.

Heinrich Suso or Seuse (1295–1366), German mystic of the Dominican Order, stresses self-detachment. See *Deutsche Schriften*, 354, note 2, translating *Büchlein der Wahrheit*, ch. 6: "Every person is one with Being, and if one observes only Being as such, no difference is seen in God. This [difference] enters, though, as soon as individual persons are observed, who differ by means of their relationships among themselves."

28. *1 John* 4:8; *1 John* 4:16.

29. See ch. 2, note 35, above.

30. George Berkeley, *A Treatise concerning the Principles of Human Knowledge*, 413.

31. Cf. Thomas Aquinas, *On Being and Essence*, ch. 4, 7–8:57, holding that all creatures are composites of essence and being, two terms related to each other as potency is to act. Creatural being means actualization of potential. Being also means existing. Hence to exist is to act, to act is to exist, as Unamuno expresses the idea.

32. According to ibid., ch. 4, 6:55–56, God is incomposite, comprised of pure being. His essence is His existence. He is pure act. Scholars debate whether this reasoning, derived from an early work of Aquinas, constitutes a "sixth proof" of God's existence, different from the other five of his mature work, the *Summa Theologica*. See A. Maurer, "Translator's Introduction," ibid., 25–26.

33. *1 Corinthians* 1:22.

34. *John* 18:38.

Chapter 4: What Is Truth?

1. *John* 18:38.

2. *Matthew* 27:24.

3. In Unamuno's text, between parentheses, appears a remark that I have omitted: "(See my essay "What Is Truth" from *La España Moderna* and let it be moved here)." The essay appears translated by me in the Appendix, below. Unamuno there attributes the distinction between logical and moral truth to Zeferino González. See Unamuno's *Obras Completas*, 3:855.

4. "Un vrai savant peut être sincèrement modeste, et il est même difficile de concevoir une grande science réelle qui ni soit pas alliée à beaucoup de modestie, je dirai plus d'humilité" (A true sage may be sincerely modest, and it is even difficult to conceive a great science of reality unallied to a great deal of modesty, or better still, humility): Paul Stapfer, *Des Réputations littéraires*, 22.

5. Arthur Schopenhauer, *Ueber den Willen in der Natur* (*On Will in Nature*), 96–97, attributes will to objects of science, cites many examples of language usages pointing to will in animals and abstract principles, and mentions French and German chemists who do the same with regard to chemical substances.

6. The physical sciences demand "submission to the icy laws of outer fact." William James, *Will to Believe*, 17.

7. In *Ueber den Willen in der Natur*, 69, Arthur Schopenhauer reminds that in animals cognitive capacity, like every organ, has arisen only for their preservation (*Erhaltung*). This capacity varies by stages with the need of each species. A plant, with many fewer needs than animals, requires no further knowledge. To the same effect, see Arthur James Balfour, *Foundations of Belief*, 74.

8. In *Ueber den Willen in der Natur*, 51, Schopenhauer holds that human needs greatly surpass those of animals and multiply to the infinite. They include lack of natural arms and natural shelter, together with weak muscular power. Consequently, human understanding far outstrips that of other species and is supplemented by abstract reason.

9. *Genesis* 3:5–7. Cf. Arthur Schopenhauer, *Welt als Wille und Vorstellung*, 2:60.388, using the narrative of Original Sin to confirm his own doctrine that sexuality serves the species, not the individual. By identifying each individual with Adam, falling through sexual passion into sin, suffering, and death, the Bible equates the individual with the Savior, representing the denial of the will to live, inviting participation in his self-sacrifice, and causing the individual to be redeemed (*gerettet*) from sin and death: *Romans* 5:12–21.

10. Aristotle, *Metaphysics* 1.1.980a22.

11. Alexandre-Rodolphe Vinet, *Études sur Blaise Pascal*, 28.

12. Arthur Hugh Clough, quoted by William James in *Will to Believe*, 17, as a fanatical believer in science, acquires life from truth, however bitter: "It fortifies my soul to know / That, though I perish, Truth is so."

13. Arthur James Balfour, *Foundations of Belief*, 73, writes: "With the great mass of natural fact we are probably brought into no sensible relation at all. I am not referring here merely to the limitations imposed upon such senses as we possess, but to the total absence of an indefinite number of senses which conceivably we might possess, but do not. There are sounds which the ear cannot hear, there are sights which the eyes cannot see." Unamuno quotes from this work in *Del sentimiento trágico*, in *Obras Completas*, 7:125n1.

14. Arthur James Balfour, *Foundations of Belief*, 87–88. This whole paragraph comes from manuscript series B and is numbered (2) by Unamuno. I have placed it in the text of manuscript series A after Unamuno's number (2).

15. Baruch (Benedict) Spinoza (1632–77), Dutch philosopher of Judeo-Portuguese origin, wrote in his *Ethics*, part 3, proposition 6, "Unaquaeque res, quatenus in se est, in suo esse perseverare conatur: *Ethica*, 175 (Every thing, in so far as it is in itself, endeavors to persevere in its being: *Ethics*, tr. W. H. White, 398). Various authors affecting Unamuno quote this conception of being: Jean-Marie Guyau, *Esquisse de la morale sans obligation ni sanction*, 88, 92; Auguste Sabatier, *Esquisse d'une philosophie de la religion*, 10 (applied to the religious sentiment of the human being).

16. See note 13, above.

17. Arthur James Balfour, *Foundations of Belief*, 73, speculates that "there must be countless aspects of external Nature of which we have no knowledge; of which, owing to the absence of appropriate organs, we can form no conception; which imagination cannot picture nor language express."

18. Recall that for Unamuno all love is rooted in sexual impulse striving for self-perpetuation. See ch. 2, note 3, above.

19. Ludwig Stein, *Die soziale Frage in Licht der Philosophie*, 50 (marked by Unamuno), finds a teleology immanent in society as there is in nature. A regulative principle governs voluntary acts of sociable individuals. Hence Unamuno applies the teleological principle of self-preservation to the natural human being and the teleological principle of self-perpetuation to the human being qua social.

20. Auguste Sabatier, *Esquisse d'une philosophie de la religion*, 14, distinguishes between two worlds, the animal and the moral. In developing self-

consciousness, the human being forms two essences: an empirical ego and a moral or ideal ego (*moi ideal*). The struggle between them generates pain needed for human progress. Otherwise spiritual life could not be born out of physical life. "Tous les enfantements sont douloureux" (All childbirths are painful): ibid., 15–16. Perhaps the association of sexual love with childbirth may have inspired Unamuno to trace the birth of the ideal, spiritual world to love. All love for him seeks immortality.

21. Progress from unconscious to conscious formation of society is hardly a century old, writes Ludwig Stein in 1897: *Die soziale Frage in Licht der Philosophie*, 33 (passage indicated by Unamuno).

22. Against scoffers, Auguste Sabatier, *Esquisse d'une philosophie de la religion*, 36, also defends the rights of the faculty of imagination (*l'imagination*): "Le mythe n'est mensonger qu'en apparence. Quand le cœur a été pur et sincere, les voiles de la fable laisent toujours transparaître le visage de la vérité" (Myth is only deceitful in appearance. When the heart has been pure and sincere, the veils of fable let the face of truth show through).

23. Georg Simmel, *Einleitung in die Moralwissenschaft*, 1:446, holds that the social totality transmits to us "die Ausbildung der Organe, mit denen wir die verschiedenen und oft schwer zu vereinigenden Seiten der Welt auffassen" (the formation of organs with which we comprehend the different sides of the world, often to be integrated with difficulty). Paul Stapfer, *Des Réputations littéraires*, 70, writes that, according to sociologically oriented philosophy, societies are complex organisms with their own life, while "les individus, à leur tour, sont eux-même des sociétés" (individuals, in turn, are themselves societies). The ego consists of a multiplicity of states of consciousness.

24. Arthur James Balfour, *Foundations of Belief*, 87–88. Balfour (1848–1930) was a philosopher, statesman, and one-time prime minister of Great Britain (1902–5).

25. The last two paragraphs of text stem from manuscript series B, where Unamuno includes them under his number (3). Accordingly, I have intercalated them into my translation of manuscript series A precisely at the point there indicated (3) by Unamuno.

26. See note 22, above.

27. According to Georg Simmel, *Einleitung in die Moralwissenschaft*, 1:445, we depend for our religion on society extended in space and time. Our bonding to something more universal and lofty from which and into which we flow, to which we surrender ourselves, from which we expect elevation and redemption, from which we differ yet to which we are identical—all this converges on God as on an imaginary focal point (*focus imaginarius*), yet is reducible to our individual relationships with past generations and with our contemporaries.

28. See ch. 3, note 21.

29. Cf. ch. 3, note 24, above.

30. Georg Simmel, *Einleitung in die Moralwissenschaft*, 1:445.

31. See ch. 3, note 11, above.

32. Given a prayer service attended by worshippers of varied educational backgrounds, "pour tous, . . . Dieu subsiste, et c'est parce que Dieu est présent et vivant chez tous, que le mot se prête à tant d'acceptations différentes; mais ce mot n'est vivant . . . que parce qu'il sert d'expression à une piété ressentie et commune" (For everyone . . . God exists, and it is because God is present and liv-

ing in everyone that the word lends itself to so many different acceptances; but that word is living . . . only because it serves as an expression of a felt, common piety): Auguste Sabatier, *Esquisse d'une philosophie de la religion*, 304.

33. A student of Kant attending the prayer service imagined by Auguste Sabatier (see note 32, above) knows that "toute idée positive de Dieu est contradictoire, et . . . se réfugie, par échapper à la contradiction, dans celle de l'Inconnaissable" (every positive idea of God is contradictory, and . . . he takes refuge, to escape the contradiction, in the idea of the Unknowable): ibid.

34. Here Unamuno is once again saying that to believe (*creer*) is to create (*crear*), and if I create God within myself, God re-creates me from within, making me a new man. See ch. 3, note 11, above.

35. This is the intellectualistic God mentioned in ch. 1, note 8.

36. *Matthew 8:22.*

37. *Acts 17:28.*

38. This biblical quote stems from manuscript series B, bears Unamuno's number (5), and accordingly I insert it into my translation of manuscript series A, precisely where Unamuno has indicated number (5).

39. The *ens realissimus* (most real substance) forms part of the fourth argument of God's existence in Saint Thomas Aquinas's *Summa Theologica*, First Part, Question 2, Article 3: in any genus the maximum member is the cause of the whole genus (fire, maximum heat, causes all hot things). It follows that there is a cause of all being, and this uttermost Being we call God. But see ch. 1, note 11, above, for Ritschl's refutation of the cosmological argument. With irony, Unamuno denies reality to the *ens realissimum*. As to the widespread, innocent concept of God as the white-bearded father-figure, in Auguste Sabatier's imagined prayer service, a poor old woman still recalls the colored illustrations of her great Bible showing the "Père eternal avec une grande barbe blanche" (eternal Father with a great white beard): *Esquisse d'une philosophie de la religion*, 303. Sabatier considers this conception of God as valid as any. See note 32, above.

40. Unamuno follows Alexandre-Rodolphe Vinet, *Études sur Blaise Pascal*, 309, who explains that discursive (abstract) reason, when used for skepticism, behaves as a "destructeur sans pitié, corrosive éprouvé dont l'action ne laisse après soi qu'un vide parfait" (pitiless destroyer, demonstrated corrosive whose action leaves only a perfect void behind). Pascal writes that clashing the principles of reason together would make religion absurd and ridiculous. Those lacking religion by sentiment cannot obtain it through reasoning, unless this is accompanied by divine grace: ibid., 314.

41. See ch. 3, note 14, above. Unamuno adopts the language of Pascal, *Pensées*, sec. 2, 72, 350, asking what the human being is in nature, and responding "un néant à l'égard de l'infini, un tout à l'égard du néant, un milieu entre rien et tout" (a nothingness with respect to the infinite, an all with respect to the nothingness, a midpoint between nothing and all). Infinitely removed from understanding the extremes, he finds the end and beginning of things hidden. Equally veiled to him are the nothingness from which he is drawn and the infinite into which he is absorbed.

42. See ch. 7, note 5, below.

43. Unamuno harks back to Auguste Sabatier's conception of progressive personal and universal revelation of God in human beings and humankind; see ch. 3, note 11, above.

44. Unamuno returns to the idea that believing (*creer*) is creating (*crear*). See note 34 above.

45. *Hebrews* 11:1. Unamuno has written (12) here, which in manuscript series B corresponds to (12), followed by the remainder of the paragraph on faith, together with the succeeding two paragraphs that end with the two questions linking believing with hoping.

46. Here Unamuno paraphrases one of his favorite biblical passages, for him equating faith with uncertainty. In *Mark* 9:24, the father of the possessed boy cries out to Jesus, "I believe; help my unbelief!" Unamuno glosses this passage in *Del sentimiento trágico* (*Obras Completas*, 7:180). Even Adolf von Harnack, *Dogmengeschichte*, 1:83n1, invoking this prayer, confesses the impiety of acting as if faith in life eternal and in Christ were easy.

47. This conception of time seems to combine Albrecht Ritschl's with Benjamin Paul Blood's. Ritschl, *Rechtfertigung und Versöhnung*, 3:37.261, suggests that our knowing and planning overcome temporal succession, but our whole individual self-consciousness (*das gesammte Selbst-Bewusstsein*) stays fettered (*gefesselt*) to the form of time. We respect self and surrounding objects as *real* only in the present, while seeing as *unreal* what was and what is not yet. To say this with greater immediacy, Unamuno uses Blood's mystical experience of the multiple forms of the other (=creatures) being absorbed into the One (=God) over the course of time. Blood calls such an experience the "anæsthetic revelation" of how, with the observer forgetting and forgotten, "the present is pushed on by the past, and sucked forward by the vacuity of the future." This passage, handwritten in English, appears in series D, Unamuno's notes to the *Tratado*, also mentioning Blood, together with William James, and the page number from James's *Variety of Religious Experience*, 389n2.

48. Cf. James, *Varieties of Religious Experience*, 389n2: "The real secret would be the formula by which the 'now' keeps exfoliating out of itself, yet never escapes." Ritschl, *Rechtfertigung und Versöhnung*, 3:37.261, writes that when reviewing the past or glimpsing the future, we temporally suspend awareness of time passing. Hence, much of what was but no longer is in the same form, still persists as a cause in recognizable effects; and, to a lesser extent, things of the present seem to survive as causes despite changes in present form. Henri-Frédéric Amiel, *Journal intime*, 303, holds that eternal life is not future life, but life in God. Any being apperceiving itself under the category of time, can become aware of the "substance de cet temps, laquelle est l'éternité" (substance of that time, which is eternity).

49. An echo of the first paragraph of ch. 2, above.

50. One of Unamuno's deepest poems expresses this notion. I copy and translate the first ten lines of this untitled ballad: "Con recuerdos de esperanzas / y esperanzas de recuerdos / vamos matando la vida / y dando vida al eterno / descuido que del cuidado / del morir nos olvidemos . . . / Fue ya otra vez el futuro, / será el pasado de nuevo, / mañana y ayer mejidos / en el hoy se quedan muertos" (With memories of hopes / and hopes of memories / we keep on killing life / and giving life to these / eternally neglected / —forgotten?—cares of dying . . . / The future fled again, / The past will come back flying, / tomorrow and yesterday / mix now and pass away"): Miguel de Unamuno, *Antología poética*, 96.

51. In the original manuscript, page 35, Unamuno has crossed out the adjective "poniente" (=setting) after the noun "sol" (=sun).

52. "En lui c'est l'homme qui appelle Dieu père! et c'est à l'homme que Dieu répond: mon fils" (In him [Jesus] is the human being that calls God, 'Father!' and it is to the human being that God responds, 'My son'): Auguste Sabatier, *Esquisse d'une philosophie de la religion*, 192. All who call God their Father, according to Sabatier, ibid., 185, have elevated their inner life to hope in eternal life and are the true posterity of Christ throughout history.

53. *Varieties of Religious Experience*, 524: "Religion, in fact, for the great majority of our own [human] race *means* immortality, and nothing else. God is the producer of immortality; and whoever has doubts of immortality is written down as an atheist without farther trial."

54. The Sphinx is a mythological creature with head and breasts of a woman, torso of a lion with eagle's wings, and a serpent's tail. She terrorized ancient Thebes by posing great riddles and by devouring those who guessed wrong (Bell, 402–3). Unamuno makes the Sphinx a metaphor for the anguish caused by posing to oneself the riddle of the Afterlife and by arriving at no solution.

55. On manuscript page [36], this passage reads, "porque traes á nuestros oídos cosas peregrinas," which I have translated, "because you bring strange new things to our ears." However, "traes á" replaces "pones en" (you place in), and "cosas peregrinas" replaces "unas nuevas cosas; queremos" (some new things; we want).

56. In the *Odyssey* 8.577–580, Penelope's suitor Alkinoös asks the nostalgic Ulysses, disguised, "Tell us also why you are made unhappy / on hearing about the return of the Argive Danaans from Troy. / The gods arranged all this, and sent misfortunes to humans / in order that future generations might have something to sing about" (εἰπὲ δ᾽ ὅ τι κλαίεις καὶ ὀδύρεαι ἔνδοθι θυμῷ/Ἀργείων Δαναῶν ἠδ᾽ Ἰλίου οἶτον ἀκούων./τὸν δὲ θεοὶ μὲν τεῦξαν, ἐπεκλώσαντο δ᾽ ὄλεθρον/ἀνθρώποις, ἵνα ᾖσι καὶ ἐσσομένοισιν ἀοιδή.).

With irony, Unamuno criticizes the aestheticism, the attitude of living life for the sake of outward beauty, visible in the Greek spirit; cf. *Obras Completas*, 8:779, 818. Like criticism appears in Frederick W. Robertson, "First Advent Lecture—The Grecian," in *Sermons Preached in Trinity Chapel*, 1:173–75.

57. Here Unamuno writes (14), a number which in manuscript series B is followed by the remainder of the paragraph on Paul with King Agrippa and Festus.

58. Unamuno parodies *Acts* 26:24. This entire paragraph containing the parody stems from manuscript series B, Unamuno's number (15). I have inserted my translation of this paragraph in my English version of manuscript series A, precisely where Unamuno has written (15).

59. See note 15, above.

60. This statement equating effort to essence comes from Spinoza, *Ethics*, part 3, proposition 7: *Ethics*, tr. W. H. White, 399.

61. The statement on indefinite time comes from ibid., proposition 8.

62. This statement on perseverance of the mind comes from ibid., proposition 9.

63. On manuscript page 38 "conciencia" (consciousness) has been substituted for "mente" (mind).

64. "L'épanouissement libre du moi, ses velléites de s'étendre et de s'agrandir sont comprimés par le poids de l'universe qui, de toutes parts, retombe sur lui" (The free flowering of the ego, its whims to extend and expand, are compressed by the weight of the universe which, from everywhere, falls back over it): Auguste Sabatier, *Esquisse d'une philosophie de la religion*, 15.

65. See note 39 above.

66. See the famous soliloquy in *Hamlet*, act 3, scene 1, lines 56–61, in which the Danish prince debates with himself whether or not to avenge his father's murder. Vengeful action is here equivalent to being, and inaction to nonbeing.

67. The full quotation concerning Martius is, "He wants nothing of a god but eternity and a heaven to throne in" (act 5, scene 4, lines 25–28).

68. From the artistic viewpoint, according to Paul Stapfer, *Des Réputations littéraires*, 70, immortality assumes two forms: the real (*réelle*), when the work survives and continues to be admired, and the nominal, when all that remains is the author's name and the titles of his works. From the Christian point of view, fame or survival in the memory of others is an imaginary life, while real life (*vie réelle*) belongs to that of the soul freed from matter and returned to God: ibid., 99. In both cases, real = immortal.

69. In series C of the manuscripts, labeled, "Mi confesión" (My Confession), with Unamuno's page number 2, there is a primitive version of this sentence that coincides with the final, printed version in *Del sentimiento trágico*, in *Obras Completas*, 7:132: "Gritos de las entrañas del alma ha arrancado a los poetas de los tiempos todos esta tremenda vision del fluir de las olas de la vida" (This imposing vision of the flow of the waves of life has plucked out cries from the innermost parts of the hearts of poets of all times: my translation). Between the lines, atop the words "de los tiempos todos esta tremenda," appear Unamuno's words, identifying the poetry he has in mind: "The Task. I. 284 sigs. Wordsworth. Ode, pág. 313." "The Task" is the poem with that title by William Cowper, in *Poetical Works*. In the part of this long poem with the title, "The Winter Walk at Noon," lines 995–1000 on pp. 284–85 may have affected Unamuno: "So life glides smoothly and by stealth away, / More golden than that age of fabled gold, / Renowned in ancient song; not vexed with care / Or stained with guilt, beneficent, approved / Of God and man, and peaceful in its end. / So glide my life away! And so at last, / My share of duties decently fulfilled, / May some disease, not tardy to perform / Its destined office, yet with gentle stroke / Dismiss me weary to a safe retreat, / Beneath the turf that I have often trod."

Unamuno has placed a mark comprised of four vertical parallel lines crossed by a single horizontal line next to the title of Wordsworth's famous ode "Intimations of Immortality from Recollections of Early Childhood," from *Poetical Works*, 313. This poem begins with the lines, "There was a time when meadow, grove, and stream, / The earth, and every common sight / To me did seem / Apparelled in celestial light, / The glory and the freshness of a dream. / It is not now as it hath been of yore— / Turn wheresoe'er I may, / By night or day, / The things which I have seen I now can see no more." There appears a mark composed of a large Greek letter Π with three feet next to the lines, "Full soon thy soul shall have her earthly freight / And custom lie upon thee with a weight, / Heavy as frost and deep almost as life!": p. 316. Finally, on the same page, Unamuno places a mark resembling a right angle next to the lines, "Upon us, cherish, and have power to make / Our noisy years seem moments in the being / Of the eternal silence; truths that wake."

70. See ch. 1, note 20, above.

71. The play *La vida es sueño* (*Life Is a Dream*, 1636) by Spanish Golden Age playwright Pedro Calderón de la Barca (1600–1681), is based on a Baroque philosophy of human life as disenchantment with worldly pursuits (metaphorically

called dreams). The protagonist Segismundo's famous soliloquy at the end of act 2 makes it clear that "toda la vida es sueño, / y los sueños sueños son" (all life is a dream, / and dreams are also dreams).

72. The quotation comes from Shakespeare's fantasy play (1610?), *The Tempest* 4.1.156–57.

73. A reference to the fall of Adam and Eve, *Genesis* 3:6: they ate of the forbidden tree of knowledge of good and evil, and in punishment were condemned to death: ibid., 3:19.

74. Unamuno attributes to the Jesuit Fr. Alonso Rodríguez an "appetite for divinity" ("La locura del doctor Montarco," in *Obras Completas*, 1:1131), and he may be referring to Rodríguez's statement "que tenemos un apetito de divinidad y una locura y frenesí de querer ser más de lo que somos" (that we have an appetite for divinity and a madness and frenzy for wanting to be more than we are): *Ejercicio de perfección y virtudes cristianas*, treatise 8, ch. 15, quoted in *Vida de Don Quijote y Sancho*, in *Obras Completas*, 3:244.

75. The page references are to *Varieties of Religious Experience* by William James. The pages enumerated do not prove that religion originates in the cult of the dead, but that it stems from concern for personal destiny: 491, 506, 507n1. On Erwin Rohde, from whom Unamuno surely found information on worship of the dead, see note 79, below.

76. Baruch Spinoza held, "A free man thinks of nothing less than of death; and his wisdom is not a meditation upon death but upon life" (*Ethics*, part 4, proposition 67, p. 444).

77. A striking image drawn from Frederick W. Robertson, "Jacob's Wrestling," in *Sermons Preached at Trinity Chapel*, 1:47, describing God as a Being which at times "sweeps through the soul . . . as a desolation, like a blast from the wings of the Angel of Death."

78. Unamuno quotes from French philosopher, mathematician, and scientist Blaise Pascal (1623–62), *Pensées* (*Thoughts*), section 3, 194 (417): "Cette négligence en une affaire où il s'agit d'eux-mêmes, de leur éternité, de leur tout, m'irrite plus qu'elle ne m'attendrit; elle m'étonne et m'épouvante, c'est un monstre pour moi" (That negligence in an affair in which it is a question of themselves, of their eternity, of their all, irritates me more than it moves me; it astonishes and appalls me, it is a monster for me). Note that the monster here in this particular context is for Pascal the negligent attitude, not as for Unamuno the negligent person.

79. Erwin Rohde, *Psyche: The Cult of Souls and Belief in Immortality among the Ancient Greeks*, 4. Here anthropologists are said to view worship of bodiless souls as one of the most primitive (if not the original) form of reverence rendered to invisible powers.

80. Irish-born French lawyer and revolutionary who rose to dictator in the French Revolution, Maximilien Robespierre (1758–94), overly self-righteous, became the butt of ridicule in Thomas Carlyle's *French Revolution: A History* (1851), which Anthony Kerrigan and Martin Nozick identify as Unamuno's source in *Tragic Sense of Life*, 387–88n47. Carlyle describes him as "an incorruptible Robespierre, most consistent, incorruptible of thin acrid men": Vol. II, Book 2.III, ch. 2.3.III. As President of the National Convention and opponent of the extreme Left, "he . . . made the Convention decree . . . the 'Existence of the Supreme Being,' and likewise 'ce principe consolateur (that consoling principle) of the Immortality of the Soul.'"Vol. III, Bk. 3. VI., ch. 3.6.IV.

81. Of "liberal" preachers, concerned with "healthy-mindedness" as opposed to the "morbidness" of traditional theology, William James writes, "They look at the continual preoccupation of the old-fashioned Christian with the salvation of his soul as something sickly and reprehensible rather than admirable; and a sanguine and 'muscular' attitude, which to our forefathers would have seemed purely heathen, has become in their eyes an ideal element of Christian character": *Varieties of Religious Experience*, 91.

82. Unamuno translates the final line of Dante's *Inferno*, the famed canto 34, line 139, describing Dante's emergence from the darkness of hell to Purgatory outside with the stars once more in view: "E quindi uscimmo a riveder le stelle" (And out we came to see the stars anew): A. Kerrigan and M. Nozick, in Unamuno, *Tragic Sense of Life*, 388n47.

83. Frederick W. Robertson, "Realizing the Second Advent," *Sermons Preached at Trinity Chapel*, 1:163, praises the "power of meditation . . . to bring danger in its reality before the imagination." He writes, "It is good for a man to get alone, and then in silence think upon his own death, and feel how time is hurrying him along" (ibid., 164).

84. "Cada vez que considero / que me tengo que morir, / tiendo mi capa al suelo / Y no me harto de dormir." Unamuno remarks of these verses, "Hay un cantar andaluz hermosísimo, que revela el último fondo del beduinismo indolente y fatalista que aquí ha dominado": "Examen de conciencia," in *Obras Completas*, 7:418 (There is a very beautiful Andalusian folksong that reveals the ultimate depth of indolent, fatalistic Bedouinism that has dominated here [in Spain]).

85. On the Sphinx, see note 54, above. Cf. Frederick W. Robertson, "The Israelite's Grave," *Sermons Preached at Trinity Chapel*, 1:317: "Let us look the truth in the face, You cannot hide it from yourself. 'Man is born to sorrow as the sparks fly upward.'"

86. The verse quoted comes from the poem "Lines Written During a Moment of Insanity," in *Poetical Works*, 23. Cowper (1731–1800) was an English poet and satirist, subject to bouts of depression and mania.

87. On a handwritten page of notes numbered 1.2/392, included in manuscript series D, and headed "Amor de Dios" with a subtitle "Pecado" [Sin], Unamuno confesses, "Salí del catolicismo por lo de la eternidad de las penas del infierno; eso se me resistía" (I left Catholicism for that business of the eternity of the punishments of hell; that [notion] resisted me).

88. Unamuno here translates Dante's *Inferno* 3.9: "Lasciati ogne speranza, voi ch'intrate," the last line of the inscription above the gate to hell.

89. On sorrow born of love, see Oscar Wilde, *De profundis*, mentioned by Unamuno on a sheet of paper (from manuscript series D) with a tentative outline of his *Treatise* and with Roman numerals II, III, IV, V, with one numeral in every quadrant of the page, as if to indicate planned chapter numbers. Here is the probable text from Wilde, op. cit., 59–60: "Now it seems to me that love of some kind is the only possible explanation of the extraordinary amount of suffering that there is in the world. I cannot conceive of any other explanation. I am convinced that there is no other, and that if the world has indeed, as I have said, been built of sorrow, it has been built by the hands of love, because in no other way could the soul of man, for whom the world was made, reach the full stature of its perfection. Pleasure for the beautiful body, but pain for the beautiful soul."

90. Unamuno is directly translating lines 27–31 of the poem "Amore e morte" by Count Giacomo Leopardi: "Quando novellamente / Nasce nel cor profondo / Un amoroso affetto, / Languido e stanco insiem con esso in petto / Un disiderio di morir si sente": *Canti* 27, 266 (When newly self-confessed / Deep in the lover's heart / The flame of love is burning, / Instantly doth a weary, languid yearning / For death spring up beside it in his breast: Leopardi, *Poems*, tr. Geoffrey Bickersteth, 295).

91. In other words, reason leads us to fear of the nothingness, while faith takes us to hope in salvation.

92. See ch. 7, note 5, below.

93. *Phaedo* 114 d 69.

94. Cf. William James, *Will to Believe*, 16, on Pascal's wager: "He tries to force us into Christianity by reasoning as if our concern with truth resembled our concern with the stakes in a game of chance. Translated freely his words are these: You must either believe or not believe that God is—which will you do? Your human reason cannot say. A game is going on between you and the nature of things which at the Day of Judgment will bring out either heads or tails. Weigh what your gains and your losses would be if you should stake all you have on heads, or God's existence: if you win in such case, you gain eternal beatitude; if you lose, you lose nothing at all. If there were an infinity of chances, and only one for God in this wager, still you ought to stake your all on God; for though you surely risk a finite loss by this procedure, any finite loss is reasonable, even a certain one is reasonable, if there is but the possibility of infinite gain. Go, then, and take holy water, and have masses said; belief will come and stupefy your scruples,—*Cela vous fera croire et vous abetira*. Why should you not? At bottom, what have you to lose?" See Blaise Pascal, *Pensées*, 233, 437–41.

95. Unamuno remakes the remark of French historian Jules Michelet (1848–1915), "Je me perdis de vue, je m'absentai de moi" (I lost sight of myself, I spirited myself away from myself) when he tried to change himself into a contemporary of the historical figures he studied. See J. de Crozals, "Jules Michelet: l'homme et l'œuvre," *L'Encyclopédie de L'Agora*, http://agora.qc.ca/reftext.nsf/ Documents/.

96. "Der Egoist, auf das immanente Verhältniss seiner Willensakte unter einander angesehen, ist eine sittliche Gemeinschaft im Kleinen, die sittliche Gemeinschaft ein Egoist im Grossen" (With a view toward the immanent interrelationship of his voluntary acts, the egoist is a moral community in miniature, the moral community an egoist writ large). The urge to form psychic contents into norms, the sacrifice, the counterstriving, all this reflects in the individual the reference of his totality to the community, viewed as normative for his moral conduct. Georg Simmel, *Einleitung in die Moralwissenschaften*, 1:180.

97. Albrecht Ritschl (*Die christliche Lehre von der Rechtfertigung und der Versöhnung*, 27.184) defines as the basic principle of Christian self-evaluation the following notion: "Dass der einzelne Mensch mehr werth ist als die ganze Welt, und dass er dieses in dem Glauben an Gott als seinen Vater und in dem Dienst an dem Reiche Gottes erprobt" (That the individual is worth more than the whole world, and that each soul can test and prove this truth through faith in God as his Father, and by service to Him in His kingdom: tr. Macintosh and Macaulay, 27.211).

98. For Paul Stapfer, *Des Réputations littéraires*, 10, "L'amour-propre est si

peu le principe du mal moral, qu'on a pu donner de la vertu cette définition pure-
ment égoïste: La vertu est le sacrifice d'un intérêt immédiat et passager à l'intérêt supérieur et durable de l'être moral qui est en nous" (Self-love is so far from
being the principle of moral evil that virtue has been capable of being given this
purely egoistic definition: "Virtue is the sacrifice of an immediate, passing interest to the higher, durable interest of the moral being which is within us").

99. *Leviticus* 19:18.

100. Cf. Arthur Schopenhauer, *Welt als Wille und Vorstellung*, 2:652: "Eben
darauf, dass der Erzeuger im Erzeugten sich selbst wiedererkennt, beruht die
Vaterliebe, vermöge welcher der Vater bereit ist, für sein Kind mehr zu thun, zu
leiden und zu wagen, als für sich selbst, und zugleich dies als seine Schuldigkeit
erkennt" (Paternal love, by virtue of which the father is ready to do, to suffer, and
to take a risk more for his child than for himself, and at the same time recognizes
this as his obligation, is due to the very fact that the begetter recognizes himself
once more in the begotten): tr. E. F. J. Payne, 2:569.

101. In Hinduism, *Upanishads*, or "mystic teachings," expound main Vedic
doctrines like self-realization, yoga and meditation, karma and reincarnation.
Schopenhauer explains that "Tatoumes," or more correctly, "tat twam asi,"
meaning, "This thou art," refers to a principle of eternal justice, promising expi-
ation in a following life for sufferings inflicted in this one (for example, animal-
eaters now become those animals eaten later), or else the reward of rebirth in
nobler forms. According to the Vedic myth, all beings, living or dead, are brought
before the student's gaze while over each is pronounced that same three-word
formula: *Welt als Wille und Vorstellung*, 1:420. William James interprets the formula otherwise, as an expression of the integration of the individual into the
cosmos, the unity of man and God: *Varieties of Religious Experience*, 419. Unamuno synthesizes both meanings for his aspiration to be himself while being
everything else forever.

102. See ch. 5, note 45, below, on the Principle of Law of Conservation of
Energy.

103. With Albrecht Ritschl, Unamuno conceives God as personal, with individuality and personality like himself. That conception is distinguishable from
limitless being taken as cosmic substance or from an impersonal First Cause
clear only to a mechanistic worldview. The idea of God is for Ritschl not to be
distorted into pantheism or deism: *Rechtfertigung und Versöhnung*, 2:30.194.

104. Monism refers to fusion into a supposed single substance of the universe.
This would reduce the individual to a mere shadow, lacking mass or a kind of
bodily substance in the Afterlife, as taught by the Church Father Tertullian. See
ch. 2, note 23, above.

105. Frederick W. Robertson, "The Israelite's Grave," *Sermons Preached at
Trinity Chapel*, 1:327, writes that Christianity "grants all that the materialist
and all that the spiritualist have a right to ask. It grants to the materialist, by the
doctrine of the resurrection of the body, that future life shall be associated with a
material form. . . . It simply pronounces that the spirit shall have a body."

106. "Stinking pride" ("hediondo orgullo," although Unamuno has crossed out
"fétido orgullo") translates Leopardi's phrase "fétido orgoglio" from his 1836
poem "La Ginestra o il fiore del deserto" (The Broom or the Desert Flower). Unamuno made a Spanish translation, "La Retama, de Jacopo Leopardi," in *Obras
Completas*, 6:322–29. Lines 98–104 read in the original: "Magnanimo animale /

Non credo io già, ma stolto, / Quel che nato a perir, nutrito in pene, / Dice, a goder son fatto, / E di fetido orgoglio / Empie le carte, eccelsi fati e nove / Felicità, quali il ciel tutto ignora": Canti 34.338 (Great-souled I do not rate / That creature, but a fool, / Who, born to perish, suckled on sorrow, cries: / I am made for happiness; / And, swollen with rank pride, / Fills pages promising unheard-of bliss": Leopardi, *Poems*, tr. Geoffrey L. Bickersteth, 345). Prof. Thomas Franz of Ohio University, in his close reading of the manuscript of the present translation, points out to me that the apology of arrogance supposed in the quest for immortality has previously appeared in *Vida de Don Quijote y Sancho*, 1st pt., ch. 5. See Unamuno, *Obras Completas*, 3:82.

107. In the 1804 autobiographical, epistolary novel *Obermann*, by Étienne Pivert de Sénancour (1770–1846), the protagonist confesses (p. 194): "Mais tout mon être, c'est trop: ce n'est rien dans la nature, c'est tout pour moi" (But all my being is too much: it is nothing in nature, it is everything for me!).

108. Unamuno is role-playing as Segismundo, protagonist of Calderón de la Barca's play *Life Is a Dream* (see note 71, above). In act 3, scene 4, lines 231–35, Segismundo, finding himself called to rule over Poland, says to himself, "I'm off to start my reign, Oh Fortune; / do not rouse me if I sleep, / and if this is true, don't let me slumber." If worldly fortune is a dream, Segismundo does not wish to awaken just yet, but if he must rule, he hopes to stay alert.

109. Up the right hand margin of the manuscript page 48, perpendicularly to the final two paragraphs, Unamuno scrawls, "no querer hablar de ello, de mal gusto, fol 36–37" (not wanting to talk about it, in poor taste, folios 36–37). His manuscript folios 36–37 refer to Saint Paul in the Areopagus.

110. See note 81, above.

111. In his 1895 polemical work *Der Antichrist* (The Anti-Christ, 7), German vitalist philosopher Friedrich Nietzsche (1844–1900) holds that in the Christian religion suffering becomes contagious through compassion, often causing a loss of vital energies disproportionate to the cause (Christ's death).

112. Unamuno equates nihilism with Schopenhauer's thought and the struggle for existence with Darwin's. German philosopher Arthur Schopenhauer (1788–1860) regarded all being as ruled by a will to live, engendering suffering, which, as Buddhism holds, can be eliminated forever by ending desire: Kathleen Marie Higgins, "Schopenhauer," 820. Unamuno equated this goal to nothingness. British naturalist Charles Darwin (1809–1882) held that changes in all species come about through chance variation and natural selection. In the struggle for existence, some individuals, better adapted to their environment, proliferate more than individuals less well adapted: David L. Hull, "Darwinism," 204. To Nietzsche's philosophy Schopenhauer contributed the notion of will as moving force of human life vis-à-vis the tyranny of reason. An optimist, not a pessimist like Schopenhauer, Nietzsche applies Darwinism to human "evolution": he looks forward to the development of the "superman," overcoming obstacles and surviving as the fittest of the human species. The "superman" produces the "death of God" as a superfluous Super-being. Therein lies Nietzsche's nihilism for Unamuno.

113. The eternal return (*die ewige Wiederkunft*) springs out of Nietzsche's concern for passing time. Ancient Greek philosophers like Anaximander, Empedocles, and others may have accepted the concept, denoting indefinite repetition of events in the same way. Nietzsche has perceived the eternal return as the

main conception of his work *Thus Spoke Zarathustra* (*Also sprach Zarathustra*, 1883), though the notion dawned on him in August 1881. The work cited, pt. 3, states that all things repeat eternally and we along with them, and we have existed infinite times and with us all things. Zarathustra affirms that, for want of any other spouse, he chooses eternity as the woman he loves. See Luis Jiménez Moreno, *Nietzsche*, 48–49. On a handwritten sheet of notes titled "Erostrato" and "Lucifer," Unamuno has written, "El pobre Nietzsche. El ansia de eternidad" (Poor Nietzsche. The yearning for eternity). Herostratus was the youth so obsessed with achieving the eternity of his name, that he burned down the temple of Diana at Ephesus for that purpose (Paul Stapfer, *De Réputations littéraires*, 12). The implication is that Nietzsche lives so obsessed with immortality, he will destroy anything sacred.

114. For Søren Kierkegaard, *Afsluttende uvidenskabelig efterskrift*, in *Samlede Vaerker*, 7:445 (*Concluding Unscientific Postscript*, tr. Hong and Hong, 1:455), uncertainty (*Uvisheden*) is the sign to the existing person of a relationship to God, whereas certainty signals the absence of such a relationship. Certainty of salvation is life in the inauthentic, aesthetic mode. Certainty of annihilation is a break with the God-relationship.

115. "Vouloir tout réduire à l'unité, c'est faire du règne de la vie le domaine immobile de la mort. Depuis longtemps j'ai renoncé, pour ma part, à ce que l'on a appelé justement la philosophie de l'identité, à cette dialectique abstraite qui, ramenant toutes choses à leur point de départ logique, rend parfaitement incompréhensible et superflu le développement éphémère qu'elles ont dans notre conscience et dans l'histoire" (To want to reduce everything to unity is to make the kingdom of life the immobile realm of death. For a long time I have renounced, for my part, what has justly been called "the philosophy of identity," that abstract dialectic which, by leading all things back to their logical point of departure, makes perfectly incomprehensible and superfluous the ephemeral development that they have in our consciousness and in history): Auguste Sabatier, *Esquisse d'une philosophie de la religion*, ix.

116. This beautifully formulated question condenses Auguste Sabatier's doctrine of religious revelation as an ongoing process defying discursive reason: "La création de Dieu n'est point achevée. . . . Mais le peu que j'aperçois de l'œuvre divine me démontre qu'elle est progressive, qu'elle élève et enrichit la vie à chaque degré, et que ce progrès tient précisément aux antinomies essentielles où ma raison se perd et où mon cœur adore" (God's creation is not at all finished. . . . But the little that I apperceive of the divine work demonstrates to me that it is progressive, and that it elevates and enriches life at every step, and that that progress tends precisely toward essential antinomies wherein my reason gets lost and where my heart worships). *Esquisse d'une philosophie de la religion*, viii–ix.

117. For Unamuno, God is both plural and one, both the Trinity and One God. He consists of Personality (implying richness) and Individuality (implying singularity). Albrecht Ritschl, *Rechtfertigung und Versöhnung*, 3:34.236, points out that individuality (*Besonderheit*) is a pervasive trait of the religious representation of God, historically undeniable. If He were not an Individual, He would be indistinguishable from the world. Human personality, on the other hand, embraces within itself every possible psychic content: ibid., 30.198. God's personality must contain the highest possible receptivity to universal relationships

of things and to the common interests of human beings, and the highest possible active efficacy upon them in all directions: ibid., 198–99. Hence for Unamuno, His words are acts, creations. Kierkegaard writes as follows (*Afluttende uvidenskabelig Efterskrift*, in *Samlede Vaerker*, 7:321): "Gud tœnker ikke, han staber; Gud existerer ikke, han er evig" (God does not think, he creates; God does not exist [existere], he is eternal]: *Concluding Unscientific Postscript*, tr. Hong and Hong, 1:332. See Unamuno, 7:200.

118. Arthur Penrhyn Stanley (1815–81), English clergyman and author, is cited by name, together with the pertinent work, *Lectures on the History of the Eastern Church*, in *Del sentimiento trágico*, in *Obras Completas*, 7:163n1. See Stanley, op. cit., 71–72. This entire paragraph and the preceding one on manuscript page 51 stem from manuscript series B, Unamuno's number (21), a number repeated on manuscript page 51.

119. *Parmenides* 166c3–7. Whether or not Plato is practicing sophistry here, this is the ending of his dialogue, displaying problems in the Eleatic doctrine of being (that things cannot have both being and non-being), placing these problems on the lips of Parmenides, founder of the Eleatic School, and exhibiting to Unamuno the limitations of mere ideas.

120. Unamuno parodies the German philosopher Hegel (1770–1831) in the preface to his *Philosophie des Rechts* (*Philosophy of Right*, xviii): "Was vernunftig ist wirklich, und was wirklich ist vernunftig." This is variously translated as "what is reasonable is actual, and what is actual is reasonable," or "what is real is rational, and what is rational is real," a statement positing the identity of reality (=Absolute Mind) and the process of reasoning. If for Unamuno reality means the desire to persevere in being, such perseverance has little rational about it in the case of the human being, whom reason deems perishable.

121. We find the following opinion in Arthur Schopenhauer, *Welt als Wille und Vorstellung*, 2:22.323: "Ein solches, anschliesslich zu praktischen Zwecken vorhandenes Erkenntnissvermögen wird, seiner Natur nach, stets nur die Relationen der Dingen zu einander auffassen, nicht aber das eigene Wesen derselben, wie es an sich selbst ist" (Such a faculty of knowledge, existing exclusively for practical ends, will by its nature always comprehend only the relations of things to one another, not their inner nature as it is in itself): *World as Will and Representation*, tr. E. F. J. Payne, 2:285.

122. Arthur Schopenhauer, *Welt als Wille und Vorstellung*, 1:12.64 (*World as Will and Representation*, tr. E. F. J. Payne, 1:54).

123. Cf. Immanuel Kant, *Kritik der Urteilskraft*, B338, holding it impossible to cognize organized essence in accordance with mechanical causation; hence, it is nonsensical to hope that one day a Newton may arise who can make conceivable the production of a blade of grass with natural laws.

124. According to Ludwig Stein, *Die soziale Frage in Licht der Philosophie*, 124, the historian, philosopher, and writer Johann Gottfried von Herder (1744–1803) had already recognized that reason is conditioned by speech and speech by reason. But Stein quotes his contemporary Lazarus Geiger on the subject: "Der Sprache is überall primär; der Begriff entsteht durch das Wort. . . . [d]ie Sprache hat die Vernunft erschaffen; vor der Sprache war der Mensch vernunftlos" (Speech is everywhere primary; the concept arises through the word. . . . Speech created reason; before speech the human being was irrational). Moreover,

Stein holds that speech arises instinctively among social groups (ibid., 54n). Unamuno marks both passages in Stein's book with small brackets.

125. The final three paragraphs of this chapter stem from manuscript series B, Unamuno's number (19). Next to this number (19) he writes, "a la pag. 51" (to page 51). Accordingly, I have translated to English the three paragraphs and inserted them on page 51 of my English version of manuscript series A, precisely where Unamuno has written (19).

Chapter 5: The Mystery of Mortality

1. See ch. 4, note 54, above.

2. Paul Stapfer, *Des Réputations littéraires*, 3, speaks of several different ways or means to aspire to everlasting life.

3. Ernest Renan (1823–92), French philosopher, historian, and writer, is quoted by William James, *Will to Believe*, 170n1: "Cet univers est un spectacle que Dieu se donne à lui-même. Servons les intentions du grand chorège en contribuant à render le spectacle aussi brillant, aussi varié que possible" (The universe is a spectacle that God puts on for Himself. Let us serve the intentions of the great Choregus by contributing to make the spectacle as brilliant, as varied, as possible). Unamuno has marked this passage in his personal copy of James's book.

4. On the *mal du siècle*, an inner wasting affecting cultivated minds, a war of the human self against itself, with clarity of thought in inverse proportion to the energy of the will, see August Sabatier, *Esquisse d'une philosophie de la religion*, 18.

5. The *modernista* movement in vogue in Hispanic literature when Unamuno wrote made a healing religion of art for its own sake. We find this cult in the Colombian *modernista* poet José Asunción Silva. In his prologue to a 1908 edition of poetry, Unamuno praises Silva's subtlety but criticizes the cold, empty musicality of pseudo-*modernistas*, Silva's bad imitators (*Americanidad*, 124).

6. Cf. Blaise Pascal, quoted in Paul Stapfer, *Des Réputations littéraires*, 98: "Ceux qui écrivent contre la gloire veulent avoir la gloire d'avoir bien écrit" (Those that write against glory want to have the glory of having written well).

7. "*L'Imitation de Jésus-Christ*, si elle était ornée du nom de son auteur, serait une choquant contradiction, moins celle de l'humilité chrétienne avec la vanité littéraire, que celle de la réalité d'un bien infini avec l'ombre chimérique d'un bien d'imagination" (The Imitation of Christ, if it were adorned with the name of its author, would be a blatant contradiction, less that of Christian humility with respect to literary vanity than that of the reality of an infinite good with respect to the whimsical shadow of a product of fantasy): Paul Stapfer, *Des Réputations littéraires*, 99. The *Imitation of Christ*, first published anonymously in 1418, has in the twentieth century been attributed to Thomas à Kempis (1379/80?–1471). This devotional work aims to teach the soul Christian perfection with Christ as model.

8. See note 6, above.

9. Dante Alighieri (1265–1321), greatest Italian poet, wrote the epic poem *The Divine Comedy* (1310–14) about the quest of a Christian soul for salvation. The poem has a threefold division, *Inferno, Purgatory*, and *Paradise*.

10. Around 1364, Dante's first biographer, Italian novelist Giovanni Boccaccio (1313–75) wrote his *Life of Dante*, containing his critique of Dante's hunger for fame. This appears in ch. 4, deploring that Dante, learned in philosophy and aware of the ruin of powerful kingdoms in history, nonetheless lacked the knowledge or power to resist the desire for worldly splendor and entered Florentine politics (*Tratadello in laude di Dante*, in *Opere minori in volgare*, 332–33): "Fermossi adunque Dante a volere seguire gli onori caduci e la vana pompa de' publici ofici" (So Dante decided to pursue the fleeting honors and vain pomp of public office): tr. J. G. Nichols, 24.

11. Jakob Burkhardt, *Die Kultur der Renaissance in Italien* (Vienna), 82, writes that Dante's Divine Comedy retains the intuition of the nothingness of fame while betraying in a certain sense the fact that his heart is not fully free of the yearning for it. The pitiful souls in Hell often ask him to renew and increase their fame on earth. Burkhardt (337n285) offers the examples of the *Inferno* 6.89, 13.53, 16.85, and 31.127.

12. *De Monarchia*, 1.1: "Cumque, inter alias veritates occultas et utiles, temporalis Monarchiae notitia utilissima sit et maxime latens et, propter non se habere immediate ad lucrum, ab omnibus intemptata, in proposito est hanc de suis enucleare latibulis, tum ut utiliter mundo pervigilem, tum etiam ut palmam tanti bravii primus in meam gloriam adipiscar" (However knowledge of temporal monarchy may be most useful, especially hidden among other concealed and useful truths, and tried by all as it is of no immediate profit, I propose to extract the nub of this from its hiding-places, both so that I may keep ever vigilant in a way useful to the world, and also so that I may obtain the palm of my glory, the first of so many rewards).

13. Unamuno read in Paul Sabatier, *Vie de saint François*, 15, that at age twenty, Francis imagined life the way troubadours depicted it, dreamed of great adventures, and always would say, "Vous verrez qu'un jour je serai adoré par le monde entire" (You will see that one day I will be adored by the whole world). The *Three Companions* or the *Legenda de S. Francisci Assisiensis quae dicitur Legenda trium sociorum* contained a biography of Saint Francis by his companions, Brother Angelus, Leo, and Rufinus. Unamuno here cites from Thomas of Celano's 1247 life of the saint: Kerrigan and Nozick, *The Tragic Sense of Life*, 393n58. Sabatier (15n1) refers to the young Francis's quotes as found in both sources. Unamuno mentions Sabatier's book in *Obras Completas*, 1:851.

14. Cf. *Psalm* 19:2–3: "The heavens are telling the glory of God / and the firmament proclaims his handiwork." Unamuno echoes this psalm in *Obras Completas*, 8:778. His notes to the *Treatise on Love of God* reveal that the "theologian" he has in mind is the Jesuit playwright Calderón de la Barca. On a manuscript page of series C, numbered 28, Unamuno has written, "Contra Calderón." In *The Great World Theater*, Calderón's best appreciated auto sacramental, or brief allegorical drama in honor of Corpus Christi, the protagonist God is about to create the world the way an author would set a scene to acquire glory (lines 39–42): "Una fiesta hacer quiero / a mi mismo poder si considero / que sólo a ostentación de mi grandeza / fiestas hará la gran Naturaleza" (A feast I want to celebrate / To my might when I meditate / that only to display my own magnificence / Nature will stage feasts of great significance).

15. "Voilà donc, à défaut de l'immortalité substantielle, une manière d'échapper au néant qui ne le cède à aucune autre: vivre dans la mémoire reconnaissante

du monde" (Here we have, then, for want of a substantive immortality, a way to escape the nothingness without equal to any other: to live in the grateful memory of the world): Paul Stapfer, *Des Réputations littéraires*, 10.

16. "L'espérance d'une immortalité littéraire peut être regardée depuis la Renaissance, pour emprunter un terme au vocabulaire de la chimie, comme un succédané de la croyance éteinte ou expirante à l'immortalité personnelle des âmes" (The hope for literary immortality can be seen since the Renaissance as a succedaneum, to borrow a term from the vocabulary of chemistry, for the dead or dying belief in the personal immortality of souls): ibid., 99.

17. However, Unamuno has written in the margin of his manuscript, "There is no such remark" (*No hay tal dicho*). Niccolò Machiavelli (1469–1528), Florentine diplomat, civil servant, political observer, and thinker, in his famed political writing *Il Principe* (*The Prince*, 1513), examines in chapter 16 the desirability of lavishness in a prince to gain supporters. He holds that anyone wishing to maintain a reputation for being generous must avoid no attribute of magnificence, so that a prince thus inclined will consume in such acts all his property.

18. Schopenhauer, *Die Welt als Wille und Vorstellung*, 1:67.446, remarks that children that feel pain usually cry when they are pitied because of the representation of pain, not the pain itself. Unamuno maintains that they cry to attract attention. Schopenhauer was a bachelor; Unamuno, the father of a large family. He is more convincing than the German philosopher.

19. Paul Stapfer, *Des Réputations littéraires*, 10, quotes Lucien Anatol Prévost-Paradol to the effect that self-love leads to seeking one's advantage in this world and one's salvation in the next. The general order of nature has made self-love, understood as the need to be and to last, the very principle of self-preservation of the universe.

20. For Albrecht Ritschl, *Rechtfertigung und Versöhnung*, 3:41.306, sin is no end in itself (*Zweck an sich*), no good (*Gut*), being the opposite of the universal good. Accordingly, Unamuno jots down on a handwritten page of notes numbered 1.2/72 and headed "Eróstrato" the notation, "Avaricia. V. su definición en la *Summa* de St. Tomás. Tomar el medio por fin. Su relación con la soberbia" (Greed. See its definition in the *Summa Theologica* of Saint Thomas. To take the means for the end. Its relationship with pride). For Saint Thomas Aquinas, the human being's universal goal is heavenly bliss, fruition of God: see ch. 8, note 29, below. Therefore, every other human purpose is a mere means. In the *Summa Theologica*, First Part of Second Part, Question 84, Article 1, reply to objection 2, Saint Thomas interprets 1 *Timothy* 6:10, calling money the root of all sin. He writes that human beings seek riches for a *temporal* end (goods purchased), not for a universal good. By implication, covetousness mistakes means for an end in itself. As to the relationship between greed and pride, this is covered in ibid., Article 2, reply to the objection 1: pride consists of a desire to excel. Human acquisition of temporal goods fulfills a desire for excellence. Hence, pride is the "beginning" of every sin. However, covetousness is the "root" of every sin in offering opportunity from the outset for sinning. (Consequently pride prolongs the error of taking the means for the end.)

21. "Nous voulons vivre dans l'idée des autres d'une vie imaginaire, et nous nous efforçons pour cela de paraître" (We wish to live in others' idea of an imaginary life, and we strive for the matter of appearances): Blaise Pascal, cited in Alexandre-Rodolphe Vinet, *Études sur Blaise Pascal*, 12.

22. Blaise Pascal finds vanity so anchored in the human heart, that even a camp-follower, a scullion, and a porter boast to acquire admirers: ibid., 13. On page 53 of manuscript series A, Unamuno originally wrote, "Necesitamos creernos superiores á los demás" (We need to think we are superior to others), then scratched out the last five words and substituted, "que los demás nos crean superiores" (for others to think us superior), closer to Pascal's text.

23. Jean-Jacques Rousseau (1712–78), Geneva-born French philosopher, essayist, and novelist, has achieved renown for his ideas on social freedom and social rights, religion, and pedagogy. In *Émile or Education* he outlines in lavish detail a theory for educating the natural gifts of his pupil, uncorrupted by bourgeois society (represented in the quote by the philosopher) which hinders individual development. See Joseph Bien, "Rousseau, Jean-Jacques," *Cambridge Encyclopedia of Philosophy*, 800–801. The long quotation in French comes from manuscript series B, Unamuno's number (25). I have inserted it into my translation of manuscript series A, precisely where Unamuno has written (25).

24. Paul Stapfer, *Des Réputations littéraires*, 2, 102, 145.

25. On a sheet of notes numbered 28, Unamuno has written, "Celos de Shakespeare; quita sitio en la gloria cuantos más á menos toca. Si se enriquece la lit. universal habrá más que no lleguen á tener tiempo de leerme" (Jealousy of Shakespeare; he takes space away in glory[;] the more there are [in glory], the fewer can have their turn. If universal lit[erature] gets enriched, there will be more that will not come to have time to read me).

26. Stylites, or Christian ascetics living atop narrow pillars for long intervals, followed the example of the first of their number, Saint Simeon (born in 389 A.D.), who, starting in 423 A.D., resided thirty-seven years on a column about seventy-eight feet high at its maximum height. He kept heightening the pillar to escape the crowds gathering around the base, but the throngs increased in number (Kerrigan and Nozick, in Unamuno, *Tragic Sense of Life*, 393–94). Abbots in Antioch and monks in Egypt criticized him for his ostentatious display of piety. Perhaps for this reason, Unamuno compares an iconoclast to a stylite. An iconoclast, equivalent in Greek to an idol-breaker, gets more puffed up with himself, rises higher, the more idols he breaks. A breaker of idols, he ironically makes a new idol out of himself.

27. Originally Unamuno had written, "los nombres se matan los unos á los otros" (names kill one another), then substituted "se menguan los unos á los otros" (diminish one another).

28. *Genesis* 4:8. See the classical study on the theme, Carlos Clavería, "Sobre el tema de Caín en la obra de Unamuno," *Temas de Unamuno*, 97–129. The notion of Cain as father of human history may stem from German historian of law Rudolph von Jhering and from Albrecht Ritschl. Claverías, op. cit., 100, notes that Unamuno alludes in an essay ("Ciudad y campo," in *Obras Completas*, 1:1037) to Jhering's opinion that civilization began in cities, and hence the Bible too harshly condemns Cain for his evil, as he built the first city (Enoch). In *Rechtfertigung und Versöhnung*, 3:269, Ritschl, opposing Augustinian pacifism, points out that coercion joins people to the general human experience, endows them with culture, and teaches them love of enemy. This notion appears in *Del sentimiento trágico* (in *Obras Completas*, 7:273), but not in the *Tratado*, with its apocalyptic overtones. The Cain-Abel theme forms the basis of one of Unamuno's finest novels, *Abel Sánchez: Historia de una pasión* (Abel Sánchez: His-

tory of a Passion, 1917). This work has generated excellent criticism. See, for instance, Thomas Franz, "Nietzsche and the Theme of Self-Surpassing in *Abel Sánchez," Perspectivas de la novela*, 59–81; by the same author, *Parallel but Unequal: The Contemporizing of "Paradise Lost" in Unamuno's "Abel Sánchez,"* and "The Painting of the Banquet Scene in Abel Sánchez." An extremely provocative interpretation appears in Gayana Jurkevich, *Elusive Self*, 106–133.

29. According to *Virtud militante contra las cuatro pestes del mundo: invidia, ingratitud, soberbia, avaricia*, 1228 (Militant virtue against the four world plagues: envy, ingratitude, pride, greed), a moral treatise by Francisco Quevedo examined by Unamuno in "Comentarios quevedianos" (Quevedan Commentaries), in *Obras Completas*, 3:1062–64: "La invidia está flaca porque muerde y no come. Sucédela lo que al perro que rabia. No hay cosa buena en que no hinque sus dientes, y ninguna cosa buena le entra de los dientes adentro" (Envy is thin because she bites and does not eat. The same happens to her as to the rabid dog. There is nothing good into which she does not sink her teeth, and nothing good comes into her from inside her set of choppers).

30. In the original Spanish, "Muera yo, viva mi fama." The quotation comes from part 2, act 3, line 2537, 271. After besting Don Diego Ordóñez de Lara in singular combat, because Ordóñez's horse steps out of bounds, the speaker, Rodrigo Arias, falls to the sword of his adversary. The judges declare the dying Rodrigo victorious, but the city of Zamora for which Ordóñez has fought Rodrigo goes free. *Las mocedades del Cid*, a three-act play in two parts, was written by Valencian playwright Guillén de Castro y Bellvis (1569–1631). Unamuno quoted the same line in his 1895 series of essays, *En torno al casticismo* (*On Authentic Tradition*, in *Obras Completas*, 1:832), to show the extremes to which Castilian individualism goes, sacrificing life for the barbarous law of the honor code.

31. The historical background of Oligiati's statement appears in Jakob Burckhardt's *Die Kultur der Renaissance in Italien (The Civilization of the Renaissance in Italy)* read by Unamuno (Valdés, 38): Kerrigan and Nozick, *The Tragic Sense of Life*, 394–95n62. Burckhardt (1:61–62) argues that Oligiati, in conspiring to rid Milan of its tyrant in 1476, followed ancient classical models of tyrannicides, as suggested by Oligiati's humanist teacher Cola de' Montani. Accordingly, Oligiati pronounced the valiant words (quoted by Unamuno) while the executioner was breaking his ribs.

32. According to Paul Stapfer, *Des Réputations littéraires*, 12n1, "Rien, dit Voltaire, n'est aussi désagréable que d'être pendu obscurément. La brillante publicité donnée aujourd'hui aux crimes les plus vulgaires rend ce «désagrément» moins commun" ("Nothing," says Voltaire, "is as unpleasant as being hung in obscurity." The brilliant publicity given today to the most vulgar crimes makes that "unpleasantness" less common).

33. Ibid., 51.

34. The cult of literary fashion, according to Paul Stapfer (ibid., 29–30), resembles no other because of the identity between the worshippers and their idol, the multitude. The great ball they stage quickly gets swallowed in oblivion, while only a few distinguished individuals survive.

35. Of the true writer, Paul Stapfer remarks that to master space like a live wire is for him less desirable than to take possession of time. Had he to choose

between an immediate, universal conquest without future and one coming due to him at a slow, obscure, silent but durable pace, he would take the distant promise of glory that he would never live to see: ibid., 91.

36. An expression of Leopardi. See ch. 4, note 106, above.

37. Paul Stapfer, *Des Réputations littéraires*, 10, reminds that although living in the memory and recognition of the world is a way to escape the nothingness, "la mémoire et la reconnaissance de l'humanité sont courtes" (the memory and recognition of humankind are brief).

38. Cf. Paul Stapfer, ibid., 60, praising Blaise Pascal for subordinating artistic considerations in his anonymous *Lettres provinciales* (1656–57), a critique of Jesuit casuistry and anti-Jansenist persecution, to his religious and moral purposes: "certainment il anéantissait sa propre gloire dans la gloire du Dieu qu'il amait" (certainly he annihilated his own glory in the glory of the God he loved).

39. "Ceux à qui Dieu a donné la religion par sentiment de cœur sont bienheureux et bien persuadés. Mais pour ceux qui ne l'ont pas, nous ne pouvons la leur procurer que par raisonnement, en attendant que Dieu la leur imprime luimême dans le cœur; sans quoi la foi est inutile pour le salut" (Those to whom God has given religion through a heartfelt sentiment are blessed and well persuaded. But for those that do not have it, we can obtain it for them only through reasoning while waiting for God to impress it Himself in their hearts. Without that, faith is useless for salvation). Blaise Pascal, cited in Alexandre Rodolphe Vinet, *Études sur Blaise Pascal*, 51.

40. The anguished Frederick W. Robertson nevertheless appreciated the spirituality of sensual beauty: "He whose eye is so refined by discipline that he can repose with pleasure upon the serene outline of beautiful form, has reached the purest of the sensational raptures": "God's Revelation of Heaven," in *Sermons Preached at Trinity Chapel*, 1:3. Also, Cervantes, in justifying his exemplary novels as a pastime healthful for the soul, writes, "Horas hay de recreación, donde el afligido espíritu descanse" (Times there are for recreation, when the afflicted spirit may rest): "Prólogo al lector" (Prologue to the Reader), *Novelas ejemplares*, in Miguel de Cervantes, *Obras Completas*, 770, quoted in Miguel de Unamuno, "Prólogo" to *Tres novelas ejemplares y un prólogo* (Three Exemplary Novels and a Prologue), in *Obras Completas*, 2:971.

41. Explaining *1 Corinthians* 2:9–10 ("Eye hath not seen, nor ear heard, neither have entered into the heart of man, the things which God hath prepared for them that love him. But God have revealed them unto us by his Spirit"), Frederick W. Robertson distinguishes between the "perishable beauty" attainable by the eye and the "Eternal Loveliness" for which the human spirit yearns: *Sermons Preached at Trinity Chapel*, 1:4.

42. An allusion to *2 Corinthians* 4:17, as translated by Unamuno, who writes in *Del sentimiento trágico de la vida* (*Obras Completas*, 7:229) that the human being who lives by passing appearances wears out and passes away along with them, but that the human being concerned with reality remains and grows: "Porque lo que al presente es momentáneo y leve en nuestra tribulación, nos da un peso de gloria sobremanera alto y eterno" (For what is momentary and light in our affliction at present is giving us an extremely lofty and eternal weight of glory).

43. The critic Charles Morice, quoted in Paul Stapfer, *Des Réputations littéraires*, 55–56, writes that even if flocks did not exist, meadows would flourish, as is their destiny. Poets write to fulfill their destinies. "Émanations de Dieu,

étincelles échappées du foyer de la toute lumière, ils y retournent . . . En pro-
duisant son œuvre, une âme de poète ne fait point autre chose que décrire son
essentielle courbe radieuse et retourner à Dieu" (Emanations of God, sparks
escaped from the fire of total light, they return there . . . When producing its
work, a poet's soul does nothing but describe its essential radiant arc and return
to God). There is also an echo of Maxwell: see note 45 below.

44. In *Welt als Wille und Vorstellung*, 1:32.207, Arthur Schopenhauer considers as follows the relationship between the individual and universal ideas: "Die
Zeit ist bloss die vertheilte und zerstückelte Ansicht, welche ein individuelles
Wesen von den Ideen hat, die ausser der Zeit, mithin ewig sind: daher sagt Platon, die Zeit sei das bewegte Bild der Ewigkeit. αἰῶνος εἰκὼν κινητὴ ὁ χρόνος (Time
is merely the spread-out and piecemeal view that an individual being has of the
Ideas. These are outside time, and consequently eternal. Therefore Plato says
that time is the moving image of eternity: αἰῶνος εἰκὼν κινητὴ ὁ χρόνος [*Timaeus*
37d]): *World as Will and Idea*, tr. E. F. J. Payne, 1:176. With typical plasticity,
Unamuno makes God the filmmaker of eternity. He has read as follows in
Albrecht Ritschl, *Rechtfertigung und Versöhnung*, 262: just as the temporality of
our self-consciousness can be briefly abrogated as we review the past or glimpse
the future, so as a rule this image of time (*Zeitvorstellung*) can be suspended by
God, "welcher als der Urheber der Zusammenhanges der einzelnen Dinge
denselben vollkommen durchschaut" (to Whom, as the Author of the connection of individual things, that connection is perfectly transparent).

45. The great physicist James Clerk Maxwell expressed as follows the Principle of Law of the Conservation of Energy: "The total energy of any body or system of bodies is a quantity which can neither be increased nor diminished by any
mutual action of these bodies, though it may be transformed into any other
forms of which energy is susceptible" (*Theory of Heat*, 93). Unamuno has read of
this law in B. Brunhes, *Dégradation de l'Énergie* (Degradation of Energy), discussed in *Del sentimiento trágico de la vida*, in *Obras Completas*, 7:248–49.

46. With Paul Stapfer (*Des Réputations littéraires*, 81–82) in mind as he writes,
Unamuno doubtlessly recalls a quote from Thomas Carlyle about Catholicism, a
quote he himself applies to his own person: "Une ancienne forme ne meurt
point, aussi longtemps que toute la quantité de bien et de vrai que était en elle
n'a pas encore passé dans la forme qui doit lui succéder" (A bygone form does not
die at all for as long as all the quantity of goodness and truth that was in it has
not passed yet into the form that should succeed it)."

47. In *Theologie und Metaphysik*, 192, Georg Wobbermin writes that within
our consciousness of being identical over the course of time, a segment of our
lives eludes our memory of being ours. To be sure, in that segment different
images and other contents of our consciousness form the bases of the whole
broader development of that consciousness. But either the memory of individual
events of consciousness is fully missing, or else presents itself as being different
from our other memories. These float freely in the air, like memories of dreams
which we are not fully certain belong to us.

48. In ibid., 201, after analyzing ego-awareness in normal human psychic life,
Georg Wobbermin maintains the existence of the ego as a lasting, operating
reality.

49. "Le livre de l'écrivain, c'est lui-même, c'est l'essence la plus subtile et la
plus pure de son être spirituel, c'est, de tout ce qu'il fut, la seule partie que

demeurera quand le reste aura disparu . . . , c'est la forme vivante à jamais de ce qu'il a senti, imaginé, pensé dans sa minute d'existence, c'est son moi profond, c'est son âme" (The writer's book is himself, it is the most subtle and purest essence of his spiritual being, it is, of all that he was, the only part that will last when the rest has disappeared . . . , it is the ever-surviving form of what he has felt, imagined, thought in his minute of his existence, it is his deep ego, it is his soul): P. Stapfer, *Des Réputations littéraires*, 92.

The inspiration for the idea of beauty as essence may stem from Paul Stapfer, ibid. For Stapfer, to be is to be forever. He defines the essence of a person as that part which lasts. He follows the French Encyclopedist Denis Diderot, for whom a beautiful woman, captured on canvas, in bronze, or marble, tries to please wherever she is not and after she ceases to exist. Writes Stapfer (ibid., 10): "La beauté est la qualité essentielle de la femme, sa principale raison d'être" (Beauty is the essential quality of woman, her main reason for being). Prolonging the fleeting years when the male looks lovingly at her should be her greatest effort. Hence she finds nothing more desirable for her vanity than to have the memory of that instant fixed in a "vivante peinture" (living painting). Stapfer's writing has inspired Unamuno's character Helena in the novel *Abel Sánchez*, in which the painter Abel perpetuates her beauty, so that she proudly walks through her city like "un immortal retrato viviente" (immortal living portrait): *Obras Completas*, 2:695.

50. In Plato's *Symposium* 208 e 2, the wise Diotima tells Socrates that human beings are in love with what is immortal (τοῦ γὰρ ἀθανάτου ἐρῶσιν). Hence some die for their beloveds to acquire immortal memory. Others mate with women to obtain immortality through children. Still others engender loftier progeny through government and justice; *Symposium* 208e3–209b1.

51. See ch. 4, note 8, above.

52. This whole paragraph stems from manuscript series B, Unamuno's number (8). I have inserted it into my translation of manuscript series A, precisely where Unamuno has written (8).

53. Cf. Saint Thomas Aquinas, *Summa Theologica*, First Part of the Second Part, Question 65, Article 5, reply to objection 1, defining charity as love of God whereby we love Him as an Object of bliss. Unamuno would substitute compassion for bliss in Aquinas's definition, more in accordance with his Spanish ascetic readings.

54. See ch. 2, note 27 on Ritschl as probable source of this idea.

55. *1 Corinthians* 1:23.

56. *Matthew* 11:27.

57. Up the left-hand margin of [61] Unamuno lightly writes, "Un Dios que sufre y muere y resucita" (A God that suffers and dies and is resurrected).

58. Here Unamuno returns to his critique of the Scholastic doctrine of God for its excessive intellectualism. See ch. 1, note 7, above; ch. 4, note 37, above; and ch. 8, note 29, below.

59. A reference to Tertullian's notion of soul as having a bodily substance. See ch. 2, n. 23.

60. Characterizing the danger of the solitary, inward, religious mode of existence, Kierkegaard writes as follows in *Stadier paa Livets Vei*, in *Samlede Værke*, 6:493: "Paa 70,000 Favne Bands Dyb mange mange Mile fra al menneskelig Hjœlp at være glad: ja det er stort! At fvœme paa Lavden i Selfkab med Badere er ikke det Religieuse" (*Stages on Life's Way*, tr. Hong and Hong, 470: "To be joyful out on 70,000 fathoms of water, many many miles from all human help—yes,

that is something great! To swim in the shallows in the company of waders is not the religious").

61. For Kierkegaard, *Entweller/Oder*, in *Samlede Værke*, 147 (*Either/Or*, pt. 1, tr. Hong and Hong, 1:150), Christ attains absolute suffering. In general, tragic action contains some suffering, tragic suffering some action. But in the life of Christ, absolute suffering becomes identical to absolute action: his suffering is absolute, equal to absolutely free action; his action is absolute suffering in its obedience.

62. On the manuscript page 62 of the *Tratado*, Unamuno writes in the right margin, beside the distinction between anguish (*congoja*) and pain (*dolor*), the notation, "Kierkegaard I 125." In Kierkegaard's *Samlede Værke*, this reference corresponds to a passage in *Entweller/Oder* on page 125 (1st. ed. used by Unamuno: see Mario Valdés, *Unamuno Source Book*, 130) or page 144 (2nd. ed. consulted by me): "Sorg indeholder altid noget mere Substantielt i sig end Smerte" (Sorrow always has something more substantial than pain: *Either/Or*, pt. 1, tr. Hong and Hong, 1:148). Pain is mediated by reflection; sorrow is immediate, hence more intimate.

63. Happiness entails taking the endless risk of believing. In *Stadier paa livets vej* in *Samlede Værke* 6:493, Kierkegaard writes that a religious person is ever joyous because always in danger. Discovery of the danger arouses fear (ibid., 491), yet the continued production of self-torment (ibid., 493).

64. "A mortificação que não acende o amor de Deus, é suspeitosa: e o amor, que não mortifica, não merece tão divino nome" (The torment that does not kindle love of God is suspect; and the love that does not torment does not deserve so divine a name): *Trabalhos de Jesus* (Tribulations of Jesus), 1:39. The ascetic Portuguese writer, Fray Tomé de Jesus (1536?–1582?), of the Order of Hermits of St. Augustine, penned this moralizing treatise while suffering captivity at the hands of North African Moors. The work was based on the idea that Jesus's suffering, evidence of God's boundless love, moves the devout to imitate their beloved Jesus.

65. William James, *Varieties of Religious Experience*, 476, writes that when we lovingly see all things in God, "the deadness with which custom invests the familiar vanishes."

66. The final sentence in this paragraph stems from manuscript series B, Unamuno's number (9), the same number appearing here on [63].

67. "To conquer the world by loving it—to be blest by ceasing the pursuit of happiness, and sacrificing life instead of finding it—to make a hard lot easy by submitting to it: this was [the apostle Paul's] divine philosophy of life" (F. W. Robertson, "God's Revelation of Heaven," in *Sermons Preached at Trinity Chapel*, 1:14.

68. In *Stadien paa Livets Vey*, in *Samlede Værke*, 6:466, Kierkegaard writes that the religious sphere of living is "qvalitativt dialektisk og forsmaaer Qvantiteten" (qualitatively dialectic and disdains quantity: *Stages on Life's Way*, tr. Hong and Hong, 443). For the finite being in the God-relationship, "er den negative Uendelighed det Hoieste, og det Positive en mislig Veroligelse": Kierkegaard, op. cit., 467 ("negative infinity is higher, and the positive a dubious reassurance": Hong and Hong, op. cit., 444); for positive infinity is usually reserved only for God, eternity, and the dead.

This paragraph in my translated text stems from manuscript series B, Unamuno's number (10). I have inserted it precisely where Unamuno has written (10) in manuscript series A.

69. In the *Diario íntimo* (*Intimate Diary*), *Obras Completas*, 8:806, Unamuno writes of his sadness upon awakening at night with his hand asleep. He hastened to move and touch it out of concern that it might be dead and withered, and that death was coming through it.

70. On a page numbered 20, bearing notes to the *Tratado*, Unamuno has scrawled "Fe en Dios" (faith in God), and next to that, "La comprensión, no el conocim[ient]o de Dios por el amor de libertad. v. II Cor. III, sobre todo 6 y 17 y 18. Visión amorosa, ó sea comprensiva, del Universo, compadecer a Dios. No nos dicen que Cristo fué Dios y nos excitan á compadecerle cuando muere en la cruz? La vida toda de Dios, preso del Universo, es, en cierto sentido, una crucifixión cristiana. Libértate, Señor. Pondré de lema del libro II Cor. 3:18?" (Understanding, not knowledge of God through love of freedom. See *2 Corinthians* 3, especially verses 6 and 17 and 18. Loving, that is, understanding vision of the Universe, to pity God. Do they not tell us that Christ was God and move us to pity him when he dies on the cross? The entire life of God, prisoner of the Universe, is, in a certain sense, a Christian crucifixion. Free yourself, Lord. Will I use as a beginning quote for the book [*Tratado*] 2 *Corinthians* 3:18?).

71. Cf. Fray Tomé de Jesus, *Trabalhos de Jesus*, 2:384, deriving consolation from having Jesus as companion of his pains: "Por este respeito, Nosso Senhor, já que determinou acompanhar os atribulados, e consola nossos trabalhos com os seus, não se contentou, senão com tomar sobre si tantos e tão vários, que nenhum atribulado lhe possa apresentar suas queixas, que logo não ache nele outra semelhante aflição, de que possa aprender a tirar proveito da sua" (For that consideration, since Our Lord resolved to accompany the afflicted, and consoles our troubles with his, he was not satisfied except by taking upon himself so many and such varied ones, that no afflicted individual could present him his complaints that he later did not find in him another like affliction from which he could learn to draw some advantage from his own).

72. See ch. 4, note 15.

73. In *Philosophy of Religion*, 283, Harald Høffding writes that for many, religious sympathy goes beyond humanity and embraces cosmic totality to which they feel their fates bound. He quotes *Romans* 8:22–23: "The whole creation groaneth and travaileth in pain together until now. And not only they, but ourselves also, which have the firstfruits of the Spirit, even we groan within ourselves."

74. "For in Him we live and move and are" (*Acts* 17:28).

75. "Now, the Lord is the Spirit, and where the Spirit of the Lord is, there is freedom" (2 *Corinthians* 3:17).

76. On self-pity, see ch. 2, notes 23, 24, and 25, above.

77. See ch. 2, note 25, above.

78. See ch. 2, note 26, above.

79. See ch. 6, note 6, below, on charity as overflow of compassion and life.

Chapter 6. What Is Charity?

1. "If we love one another, God abides in us and his love is perfected in us" (*1 John* 4:12).

2. Unamuno's attitude implies an imitation of Christ as seen by Fray Tomé de

Jesus. Anguished about his inability to manifest all his love while on earth, unable to suffer insofar as he was divine, he employed his humanity as an instrument to show his infinite love through suffering: "todo el tiempo que era necessário esperar, e represar a fúria do amor, que desejaba arrebentar, lhe dava muito grande trabalho" (all the time it was necessary to wait and dam up the fury of love, which wished to burst, it caused him a great deal of tribulation): 1:102.

3. For Georg Simmel, *Einleitung in die Moralwissenschaft*, 1:429, fellow-feeling is suffering, and awareness of another's suffering can arise only by analogy with an intimate sensation, transferred to the subject outside me. Unamuno assumes that such transference produces relief in me. He therefore agrees with Jean-Marie Guyau, *Esquisse d'une morale sans obligation ni sanction*, 101, for whom charity is like a mother needing to give her milk to more than her own children, and also with Frederick W. Robertson, "Worldliness," *Sermons Preached at Trinity Chapel*, 2:157–58, for whom love supposes "pent-up energy," like a steam-engine at the bursting-point.

4. Plato, *Symposium* 205 b 10–c 13.

5. In manuscript series B, on a page numbered 84, bearing note 27, which Unamuno did not insert into the manuscript of the *Tratado*, he refers to William Henry Rolph, *Biologischen Probleme, zugleich als Entwicklung einer rationellen Ethik* (*Biological Problems, an Attempt at the Development of a Rational Ethics*). Unamuno holds that life strives not only to persevere in being, but also to increase itself, to be everything. In chapter 6 of the *Tratado*, he is applying this biological principle to charity. I herewith copy Unamuno's remarks on Rolph, revelant to many doctrines of the *Tratado*:

Cada ser se esfuerza por perseverar en su ser mismo, pero las cosas vivas, los vivientes, no sólo por perseverar sino por aumentar, ser otra cosa, serlo todo. Según Rolph 'Biologischen Probleme' 1884 no es la lucha sino la superfluidad, el cogüelmo, lo que empuja el desarrollo evolutivo. Cada especie crece mientras el animal toma más alimento del que necesita para conservarse, y por ello puede cumplir un más de desarrollo. La necesidad (Noth) y la lucha no hacen sino seleccionar entre las variaciones nacidas. Sólo es posible una variación de una especie por alimentación más rica que la necesaria para mantener la vida, pero esa más rica alimentación sólo puede seguirse si las necesidades del individuo sobrepujan á lo que toca á la Nahrung y Nothdurft de la vida. Según Darwin el crecimiento exige aumento de alimentación, según Rolph es el aumento de alimentación lo que determina el crecim[ien]to. Para él la lucha por la existencia no es una lucha por lo necesario (Nothdurft) que mantiene precisam[ent]e la vida sino una lucha por acrecentar la alimentación, la vida; no una lucha defensiva, sino ofensiva, que sólo en ciertas condiciones toma la forma de defensa.

[Every being strives to persevere in its being, but living things, organisms, not only to persevere but to increase, to be something else, to be everything. According to Rolph, *Biological Problems*, 1884 it is not struggle but superfluity, the overflow, which impels evolutionary development. Each species grows while the animal takes more nourishment than it needs to preserve itself. And therefore it can fulfill a plus of development. Need (*Noth*) and struggle do no more than select among born variations. The variation of a species only is possible through richer nourishment than is necessary to maintain life, but that richer nourishment can follow only if the needs of the individual surpass what concerns the nourishment and need of life. According to Darwin, growth demands increase of nourishment; according to Rolph, it is the increase of growth that determines growth. For him the struggle for existence is not a struggle for what is necessary (*Notdurft*) that precisely maintains life, but a struggle to increase nourishment, life; not a defensive, but an offensive struggle, which only takes the form of defense under certain conditions].

The same theories appear in Unamuno, "La locura del doctor Montarco" (Dr. Montarco's Madness), in *Obras Completas*, 1:1131.

6. See ch. 5, note 73 above, from Høffding.

7. Unamuno here modifies Simmel, *Einleitung der Moralwissenschaft*, 1:427, viewing morality as the growth of the impulse for happiness beyond individual limits. In the strong sense of family we tend to feel the happiness of our next of kin as our own. The naïve human being feels and behaves this way unaware of promoting his own or his neighbor's happiness. A rejected handwritten page (numbered 44) of the *Tratado*, collected in manuscript series C, shows that Unamuno originally had this passage from Simmel in mind, but later introduced the notion of sympathy into it to avoid its eudemonism and to stay consistent with his own pessimism, compatible with Kierkegaard's and Schopenhauer's.

8. See ch. 2, note 26, above.

9. Here Unamuno refers to the famous legend that Saint Francis of Assisi once addressed a fierce wolf attacking men and beasts in Gubbio. Calling him "Brother Wolf," he acknowledged the hunger motivating the beast's attacks, and extracted from the wolf the promise to abstain from attacking in exchange for daily feedings by the townsfolk. As to the wolf's pain on devouring sheep, see ch. 2, note 7, above.

10. See ch. 5, note 73, above, on Høffding.

11. See ch. 2, note 35, above, on A. Sabatier.

12. "N'entrevoyons-nous pas ici le rôle divin de la douleur? Sans elle, il ne semble pas que la vie de l'esprit pût surgir de la vie physique. Tous les enfantements sont douloureux. Comme l'enfant, la conscience naît dans les larmes. Fille de la douleur, elle ne se développera que par elle" (Do we not here catch a glimpse of the divine role of pain? Without it, it does not seem that the life of the spirit can arise out of physical life. All childbirths are painful. Like the infant, consciousness is born in tears. Child of pain, it will develop only through it): Auguste Sabatier, *Esquisse d'une philosophie de la religion*, 15–16.

13. Albrecht Ritschl finds morality rooted in the idea that the moral community of humanity is the purpose (*Endzweck*) of the phenomenal world, dominating all nature: *Rechtfertigung und Versöhnung*, 3:543. If we substitute salvation of the human race after death for Ritschl's moral community, we express Unamuno's thought with precision.

14. See ch. 2, note 34, above, on Antero de Quintal; also Frederick W. Robertson, "Triumph over Hindrances—Zaccheus," in *Sermons Preached in Trinity Chapel*, 1:83: "There is a Spirit pervading Time and Space who seeks the souls of men" (a passage marked in red by Unamuno); also Auguste Sabatier, *Esquisse d'une philosophie de la religion*, 367: "L'esprit ne se dégage des liens de la nature, sa mère, que par une lutte incessante. Qui dit lutte dit opposition et victoire" (Spirit does not disengage itself from the bonds of nature, its mother, except through a ceaseless struggle. To say struggle is to say opposition and victory).

15. An unsettling deformation of 2 *Corinthians* 3:18, wherein we change into the image of the glory of God, contemplated as in a mirror.

16. Here Unamuno makes use of Church Father Origen's doctrine of God, whose omnipotence is limited by His own goodness and wisdom: *Contra Celsus* 3, ch. 70. Unamuno read this doctrine as paraphrased by Friedrich Ueberweg, *Grundriss der Geschichte der Philosophie der patristischen und scholastischen Zeit* (Outline of History of Philosophy of the Patristic and Scholastic Time), p. 97: "Doch ist er nicht ohne Mass und Grenze, sondern sich selbst begrenzend" (Yet he is not without measure and limits, but self-limiting). On the inside back cover of his personal edition of Ueberweg, Unamuno made an exact Spanish translation of the German sentence here quoted: "D[ios] no es sin medida ni límites, sino se auto-limitándose" (God is not without measure or limits, but self-limiting).

17. Here in the text of manuscript series A Unamuno has written the number (11). I insert in my translation of A the material from manuscript series B, numbered (11) by Unamuno. It extends to the end of the paragraph beginning, "Pain, which is an undoing. . . ."

18. "It is a remarkable fact that we know the inward organs chiefly by the pain they have given" (William Ellery Channing, *Complete Works*, 438).

19. Cf. ibid., 439: "It is not enough to say that . . . any outward influences are the sources of suffering. This is to stop at the surface . . . Oh, the great, deep suffering in every human breast!"

20. "Ramené par la sensation douloureuse et l'échec répété de ses efforts, du dehors au-dedans, le moi se prende pour objet de sa propre réflexion; il se dédouble et se connaît" (Brought back by the painful sensation and the repeated repulse of its efforts, from the outside toward the inside, the ego grasps itself as an object of its own reflection; it divides in two and knows itself): Auguste Sabatier, *Esquisse d'une philosophie de la religion*, 15.

21. Cf. Paul Stapfer on Fénelon's doctrine of quietism, or pure love of God (*Des Réputations littéraires*, 53): "Fénelon suppose que Dieu, ayant résolu d'anéantir son âme au moment de sa mort, lui a révélé son dessein. Dans cette hypothèse, il n'y a plus de recompense, ni de béatitude, ni d'espérance de la vie future pour lui" (Fénelon supposes that God, having resolved to annihilate his soul at the moment of his death, revealed to him his plan. In that hypothesis, there is no longer reward, nor bliss, nor hope of future life for him).

22. "Idleness is the mother of all vices" is a universal proverb, whose Spanish version is "La ociosidad es la madre de todos los vicios." Unamuno advocates a morality based on activity. Cf. Jean-Marie Guyau, *Esquisse d'une morale sans sanction ni obligation*, 89: "Agir, c'est vivre; agir davantage, c'est augmenter le foyer de vie intérieure. Le pire des vices sera, à cet point de vue, la paresse, l'inertie" (To act is to live; to act further is to increase the source of inner life. From this viewpoint, the worst of all vices may be laziness, inertia).

23. On this hunger see ch. 4, note 74, concerning Alonso Rodríguez.

24. Albrecht Ritschl, *Rechtfertigung und Versöhnung*, 3:28.182–83, idealizes the moral community of humankind. Therefore, against Feuerbach, who finds egoism a constant of religion, Ritschl thinks this attitude abnormal in religion. Unamuno apparently agrees, assigning society a morally positive value, though subordinated to the desire for individual immortality.

25. See ch. 4, note 27, on Simmel.

26. In "Caiaphas's View of Vicarious Sacrifice," *Sermons Preached at Trinity Chapel*, 1:149, Frederick W. Robertson preaches that Christ's sacrifice of life for

the world's sin has no spatio-temporal limit. Therefore the sins of Robertson's listeners "nailed Him to the cross." Robertson counsels, "Say to yourself, . . . I am crucifying the Son of God afresh" (ibid., 150).

27. Absent here is the doctrine of transubstantiation, holding that the material element of the bread, the body of Christ in potential, becomes the real body of Christ through the operation of the Holy Ghost. Instead, Unamuno treats the Eucharist as if he were worshipping prior to the institution of transubstantiation. For Adolf von Harnack, *Dogmengeschichte*, 2:426, the first Christians, on referring to Christ's body in the Last Supper, did not think of the historical Christ's body, but only of his spirit, his Word. By speaking of the bread as the "symbol," Unamuno identifies himself as a "symbolo-fideist" like Auguste Sabatier. But he shifts opinion in *Del sentimiento trágico*, in *Obras Completas*, 7:148. Here, after the publication of the encyclical *De dominici pascendi*, Unamuno polemicizes with Harnack for his critique of the materialistic realism of transubstantiation. The lyrical version of this polemic appears in Unamuno's greatest poem, *El Cristo de Velázquez* (*The Christ of Velázquez*) in *Obras Completas*, 6:417–93. See my study, "Harnack y la fe del pueblo español en *El Cristo de Velázquez*."

28. Fray Tomé de Jesus, *Trabalhos de Jesus*, 1:66, writes of Jesus that "seu puro amor, sem outra nenhuma obrigação, acabou com ele, que se ofrecesse a padecer" (his pure love, without any other obligation, finished off him who offered himself for suffering).

29. This is the "Golden Rule," expressed in many religions: Judaism, Talmud, Shabbath 31a; Christianity, *Matthew* 7:12; Brahminism, *Mahabarata* 5:1517; Buddhism, *Udana-Varga* 5:18, and others: see "Golden Rules," *Encyclopedia of Religious Quotations*, by J. W. Hughes (ed. Frank S. Mead), http://www.geocities.com/SoHo/8933/GoldRule.htm

30. Along the left margin of manuscript page 71 Unamuno writes, "v. Fray Thomé de Jesus" (see Fray Tomé de Jesus). In Tomé de Jesus's *Trabalhos de Jesus*, 1:384–86, Christ is said never to have rested in little more than his last three years, but to have visited many cities and towns, healing, resurrecting the dead, teaching, suffering, dying, returning to life, and rising to heaven. Endeavoring to save humanity in obedience to his Father, even when weary he found nothing more relieving than doing godly deeds, whether the beneficiaries wished them or no. Fray Tomé infers that God does not wish life to be leisurely, but filled with occupations that bring heavenly glory. Other objectives in life are either fruitless, transitory, or dissatisfying, making life ill-spent. Fray Tomé (ibid., 386) gives the example of the miser (*avarento*) unsatisfied with prosperity acquired all his life and reputedly so uncharitable, that of bread-crumbs eaten by dogs under his table, none remained for the pauper Lázaro. The miser went to hell, Lázaro to heaven. Having wishes as short-sighted in the Afterlife as in life, the miser received no relief. Fray Tomé concludes that to negotiate for our salvation is to satisfy Christ's hunger and to relieve his tribulations.

31. Saint Thomas Aquinas, *Summa Theologica*, Second Part of the Second Part, Question 35, Article 4, Reply to Objection 2, agrees with Pope Gregory I (the Great) that sloth is a capital sin with six "daughters": "malice, spite, faintheartedness, despair, sluggishness in regard to the commandments, wandering of the mind after unlawful things." The kinds of sloth called despair and faintheartedness foster the others. Yet in *Del sentimiento trágico*, in *Obras Completas*, 7:274, Unamuno writes that sloth, mother of all vices, in fact gives birth to greed and envy, source of the others.

32. Unamuno echoes *El Diablo mundo,* canto 1, lines 778–79, by Spanish Romantic poet José de Espronceda (1809–42): "Aquí, para vivir en santa calma, / o sobra la materia o sobre el alma" (Here, trying to live in holy calm or near it, / there's either too much matter or too much spirit): Kerrigan and Nozick, in Unamuno, *Tragic Sense of Life,* 457n262. In Espronceda's "philosophical" digression, the poetic voice holds that matter wishes rest and with its inertia sinks the individual into the mud, while spirit prides itself on deifying all and wandering in the infinite. Cf. Auguste Sabatier, *Esquisse d'une philosophie de la religion,* 367: "L'homme est en train de se faire esprit" (The human being is in the process of becoming spirit).

33. *Matthew* 25:18, 25, 28.

34. Ibid., 29. See my "Introduction," p. xxi on "¡Adentro!," where Unamuno uses this parable to encourage high-minded ambition.

35. *Matthew* 5:48.

36. Cf. Frederick W. Robertson, "God's Revelation of Heaven," *Sermons Preached at Trinity Chapel,* 1:12: "God is Infinite; and to love the boundless, reaching on from grace to grace, adding charity to faith, and rising upward ever to see the ideal still above us, and to die with it unattained, aiming insatiably to be perfect even as the Father is perfect—that is to love God."

37. An ironic variation on the prayer of the possessed child's father in *Mark* 9:24: "I believe, help my unbelief." See ch. 4, note 46.

38. This statement is a condensation of Fray Luis de León's definition of perfection. See my "Introduction," notes 54–55.

39. See ch. 2, note 35, above.

40. On the sphinx, see ch. 4, note 54.

41. George Wade Robinson (1838–77), English pastor of Congregational churches, in *Philosophy of Atonement and Other Sermons,* 209, wrote, "God is a great miller, and He grinds human hearts. He grinds them, and He means us to suffer, and it is all in love. He has a high destiny for us, and to reach that destiny we must be ground." Unamuno has annotated this work (but not the passage here cited). Not all ideas he uses from others receive his markings.

42. After the word "almas" (souls), Unamuno indicates that he wishes to insert the words "quien te quiere amor Fray Tomé" (the one who loves you Fray Tomé). Cf. *Del sentimiento trágico,* in *Obras Completas,* 7:275: "Bien se dijo aquello de 'Quien te quiera, te hará llorar,' y la caridad suele hacer llorar. 'El amor que no mortifica, no merece tan divino nombre,' decía el encendido apóstol portugués fray Thomé de Jesus (*Trabalhos de Jesus,* parte primera)" (What a well-put saying, the one that went, 'Whoever loves you well will make you cry,' and charity tends to cause crying. 'Love that does not torment, does not deserve so divine a name,' said the ardent Portuguese apostle Fray Tomé de Jesus [*Tribulations of Jesus,* Part 1]). On Tomé de Jesus and this quote, see ch. 5, note 64, above. God's love for us is self-imposing love, since according to Fray Tomé (*Trabalhos de Jesus,* 1:70), God loves each of us with the infinite love with which He loves Himself. On the other hand, each of us imposes our love on Him, because each of us can say with the apostle Saint Thomas, "My God and my Lord and my love" (*John* 20:28), "como se não houvesse outra alma cujo fosse, senão meu" (as if there were no other soul to which He belonged but mine): *Trabalhos de Jesus,* 1:70–71.

The number (20) follows the insertion about Fray Tomé on the manuscript page. I have introduced into my translation of manuscript A the passage following the number (20) on manuscript series B. The passage continues to the end of the paragraph beginning, "The great principle of intimate morality is mutual imposition."

43. Titus Maccius Plautus, Roman comedy-writer (245–184 B.C.), used the expression, "Victis, vincimus" (Conquered, we conquer), in *Casina*, act 1, scene 1, about a slave girl who conquered her aged master's affections.

44. According to Kerrigan and Nozick in Unamuno, *Tragic Sense of Life*, 465n309, French Romantic poet and playwright Alfred de Musset (1810–57) composed the line, "Mon verre est petit, mais je bois dans mon verre" (My glass is small, but I drink in my glass), from "Le Coupe et les lèvres" (The Cup and the Lips) in *Premières poésies*.

45. Musset's attitude represents smug small-mindedness for Unamuno, obliviousness to the world around him.

46. *Acts* 17:28.

47. This is the ideal of the apocatastasis for Origen, the final restoration of all thinking creatures to God, realizing Saint Paul's prophecy of the subjection of all things to God and of the Son to Him as well, and with God being everything to everyone. Adolf von Harnack, *Dogmengeschichte*, 1:631, annotated by Unamuno.

48. On an unnumbered page forming part of manuscript series C, Unamuno writes, "El Renacimiento paganizado y el amor á la gloria Burkhart (sic) II 193" (The Renaissance made pagan and the love of glory Burkhardt II 193). In Jakob Burkhardt, *Kultur der Renaissance in Italien* (The Culture of the Renaissance in Italy), 2nd. section, "Der moderne Ruhm" (Modern Fame), Burkhardt notes that fame takes on new significance in the Renaissance. In note 1 he mentions Blondus, *Roma triumphans* (Triumphant Rome), assembling from the ancients definitions of glory and expressly attributing to Christ a desire for fame.

49. On a numbered page 46, forming part of manuscript series C, Unamuno writes, "La parte ascética-rigorística del Evangelio fundada en la proximidad del fin del mundo: Pfleiderer 86 . . . sigue en pié á pesar 90–91 porque para cada uno está cerca el fin del mundo. El mundo un convento" (The ascetic, rigoristic part of the Gospels [is] grounded on the nearness of the end of the world: Pfleiderer 86 . . . [this part] keeps active despite [everything]: ibid. 90–91, because for everyone the end of the world is near. The world is a convent). Otto Pfleiderer, *Entstehung des Christentums* (Origination of Christianity), finds Jesus a self-conscious moralist in temporal history: he focuses on a "rigoristic" demand for renunciation of this world and its social goods, despite the paradox which asceticism presents to a morality of love (p. 86). Jesus's ascetic rigorism arises out of the apocalyptic expectation of the approaching end of the here and now, soon to give way to a new world. On ibid., 90–91, Pfleiderer deems Jesus's rigoristic morality no longer valid in its original sense. What truth it contains appears in *Matthew* 16:25 and *Mark* 10:43. In the first text, salvation depends on self-denial, complete surrender to the highest purpose, the realization of the divine Will, Whose instrument Jesus knew he was. The second text bases the social value of each individual on the measure of his or her service to the total society.

50. Adolf von Harnack, *Dogmengeschichte*, 1:75–77.

51. Here Unamuno applies Pascal's wager (see ch. 4, note 94, above): if God exists, He is merciful and we win; if He does not and it is useless to pray for His mercy, nothing is lost.

52. In George Lord Byron's one-act play *Cain: A Mystery*, Cain asks Lucifer,

"Are you happy?" and Lucifer reluctantly responds, "No. Are you?" Unamuno, *Del sentimiento trágico*, in *Obras Completas*, 7:170.

53. For Kierkegaard, *Afsluttende uvidenskabelig Efterskrift*, in *Samlede Værke* 7:453, the individual living for outer immediacies differs from the essentially existing person, for whom inwardness means suffering. To revoke suffering is to revoke inwardness (hence self-consciousness for Unamuno). Likewise, Richard Hooker, *Of the Laws of Ecclesiastical Polity*, 6 (indicated by Unamuno), decries apparent happiness as incognizant, and inward desolation as spiritually superior. For A. Sabatier, *Esquisse d'une philosophie de la religion*, 17, experience proves that the exclusive pursuit of happiness only leads to a greater capacity for suffering.

54. The maternal cloister is the womb, a metaphor suggested to Unamuno by combining two passages he marked from Henri-Frédéric Amiel, *Journal intime*, 1:135 and 1:177. The first is as follows: "Le cloître, c'est la vie simplifiée, le refuge pendant l'exil, le péristyle du paradis, le port des âmes faibles ou brisées, qui ont besoin . . . du repos, du silence" (The cloister is simplified life, refuge during exile, the peristyle of Paradise, the port of weak or wounded souls needing . . . peace, quiet). The second compares mystic introspection to unbirth, return to the womb: "Le corps a disparu, l'esprit s'est simplifié; passion, souffrances, volontés, idées, se sont résorbés dans l'être . . . L'âme est rentrée en soi, . . . elle remonte dans le sein de sa mere, redevient embryon divin" (The body has disappeared, the mind has simplified; passion, sufferings, wishes, ideas are reabsorbed into being. . . . The soul has reentered into itself . . . It reascends into the bosom of its mother, becomes a divine embryo once again).

55. The last two paragraphs echo Frederick W. Robertson's sermon "Realizing the Second Advent," *Sermons Preached at Trinity Chapel*, 1:166: "Trial brings man face to face with God—God and he touch; and the flimsy veil of bright cloud that hung between him and the sky is blown away."

56. Unamuno puns on the Spanish words for solidarity and for soldering, with the same first few letters (*sol-d*) in Castilian as in English. Cf. Paul Stapfer's "Confession d'un égoïste" in *Des Réputations littéraires*, 101, admitting inability to forget himself and become an anonymous servant of the community: "Je reste extrêmement peu sensible aux grands mots à la mode de religion humaine, de solidarité sociale, de travail collectif" (I remain extremely insensitive to the great words in vogue like religion of humanity, social solidarity, collective labor).

57. This final paragraph of ch. 6 stems from manuscript series B, Unamuno's number (17). I have inserted this paragraph in the text of my translation of manuscript series A, precisely where Unamuno has written (17). On Nietzsche, see ch. 4, notes 112 and 113, above.

Chapter 7: Life in God

1. "God himself, in short, may draw vital strength and increase of very being from our fidelity. For my own part, I do not know what the sweat and blood and tragedy of this life mean, if they mean anything short of this": William James, *Will to Believe*, 61 (marked by Unamuno).

2. See ch. 2, n. 44 and accompanying text from the *Tratado*.

3. Otto Pfleiderer, *Entstehung des Christentums* (Origination of Christianity, 147, marked by Unamuno), tries to explain St. Paul's mystic insight into Christ's death, whereby he substantiates the death and rebirth of Christ in secret ways. Pfleiderer suggests the possible influence on Paul of the then popular images of the dying and reborn deity, as in the Near Eastern cults of Adonis, Attis, or Osiris.

4. In speaking of touching his soul, Unamuno expresses his affinity to the Church Father Tertullian, for whom the soul is bodily; see ch. 2, note 23, above, and Unamuno's praise of Tertullian for this belief in *Del sentimiento trágico, Obras completas*, 7:293.

5. In the 1904 essay "¡Plenitud de plenitudes y todo plenitud!" (Plenitude of Plenitudes and Everything Plenitude!), in *Obras Completas*, 1:1171–82, after beginning with the quote from *Ecclesiastes* 1:2, "Vanity of vanities and all vanity!," rejecting literary fame as a shadow of immortality (cf. Stapfer, *Des Réputations littéraires*, 99), Unamuno recommends reciting, "Plenitude of plenitudes and all plenitude," ascertaining with spiritual touch that one's own soul exists, then basing belief in its immortality in the wish to be immortal (also recommended by Stapfer, ibid., 97).

6. Jean-Marie Guyau, *Esquisse d'une morale sans obligation ni sanction*, 29: "Le désir de l'immortalité n'est que la conséquence du souvenir: la vie, en se saisissant elle-même par la mémoire, se projette instinctivement dans l'avenir. Nous avons besoin de nous retrouver et de retrouver ceux que nous avons perdus, de réparer le temps" (The wish for immortality is only the consequence of memory: life, when laying hold of itself through memory, instinctively projects itself into the future. We have a need to recover ourselves and to recover those that we have lost, to repair time).

7. An individual who remained himself through all eternity would fall short of Unamuno's desire to be oneself and, while ceasing to be it, to be at the same time everyone else. Cf. Søren Kierkegaard, *Afsluttende uvidenskabelig efterskrift* (*Unconcluding Scientific Postscript*), in *Samlede Værker*, 7:161, where dabblers in everything anxiously ask the pastor if they will stay the same in the Afterlife after trying out all kinds of change in this life.

8. Cf. Søren Kierkegaard, *Fear and Trembling*, 54: "Only the lower natures forget themselves and become something new. Thus the butterfly has entirely forgotten that it was a caterpillar, perhaps it may in turn so entirely forget it was a butterfly that it becomes a fish."

9. "A nameless *Unheimlichkeit* comes over us at the thought of there being nothing eternal in our final purposes, in the objects of those loves and aspirations which are our deepest energies." William James, *Will to Believe*, 83. Paul Stapfer, *Des Réputations littéraires*, 52n2, writes that we can no longer conceive immortality as blissful or expiatory with bliss in view, while hell repels reason and modern consciences. Today all terror lies in the idea of the nothingness.

10. Unamuno seems to dialogue with Harald Høffding, *Philosophy of Religion*, 374–75, who suggests that every moment of life has its own (eternal) value irrespective of life to come. Hence, the eternal exists at present, and living eternal life amidst time constitutes the true immortality, whether or not any other exists.

11. Harald Høffding, ibid., 374, informs that humanity soon discovered that the highest phase of life excluding possible development leads to paralysis and

death: ancient Indians saw the joylessness in the persistence of sameness, and held that admittance into heaven implies restlessness and striving toward higher stages; German philosopher Wilhelm Leibniz sought progress (*progressus*) in eternal bliss lest stupor set in. Unamuno's hope in the endless "approach" to God through a "growing" or becoming (*Werden*) responds to Adolf von Harnack. See note 15, below. However, the growth proposed by Unamuno ("crecimiento," "ir acrecentándose") has a more vegetative nuance than in Harnack. Unamuno's notes to the *Tratado* suggest that he has in mind the theory of William Rolph, who holds that the struggle for existence is not one strictly to maintain life, but rather "una lucha por acrecentar la alimentación, la vida" (a struggle to increase nourishment, life): Unpublished notes, page 84n27. See ch. 6, note 5, above, on Rolph in the present book.

12. In *Del sentimiento trágico*, in *Obras Completas*, 7:248, Unamuno criticizes the mechanistic worldview yoked to the formula of the French chemist Antoine-Laurent Lavoisier (1743–94): "Nothing is created, nothing is lost, everything is transformed." He suggests the ambiguity of that principle of the conservation of energy because from the practical standpoint energy means useful energy, continually lost and degraded. To that effect he quotes B. Brunhes, *Dégradation de l'Énergie*, pp. 23–28.

13. In series D of the manuscripts, containing Unamuno's notes, on a page headed "Erostratismo" (Herostratism), he mentions Georg Wobbermin's *Theologie und Metaphysik*, 147 et seq., especially 155–58. Pages 155–58 unveil various theories of impersonal immortality, whereby in the Afterlife human spiritual life is or includes something different from the continuous sequence of conscious acts. For Franz Brentano, whether or not we presume a psychic substance, a certain continuation of our psychic life on earth is undeniable: Wobbermin, op. cit., 156. E. Koch holds that even psychology without a subject does not prejudice the question of immortality: experiences will continue after death as they did in life: ibid. Wobbermin disputes this rationale, for some relationship exists between conscious events and movements in the nervous system; such movements undoubtedly serve as material supports of conscious events. If conscious life is nothing but a sum total of successive conscious events, of which each has its support in the psychic nerve process, to destroy the psychic support is to put an end to individual consciousness: ibid., 157. On the same page of notes, Unamuno has written, "La inmortalidad de Weissmann." He is clearly referring to the 1890 conception of biologist August Weismann, who contrasted immortality (=activity and change of cycle of life) with eternity (of dead, unstructured matter, of lifeless substance).

14. In *Des Réfutations littéraires*, 53–54, Paul Stapfer criticizes the French Quietist bishop Fénelon for supposing that God, determined to annihilate his soul at death, revealed to him His plan; hence Fénelon resolved to expect no reward, to harbor no hope of future life, yet not to renounce God, but to fulfill his duty to give Him pure, disinterested love.

15. Unamuno here dialogues with Adolf von Harnack, *Dogmengeschichte*, 3:375, holding mysticism synonymous with Catholic piety and characterizing it as pointing beyond itself and allowing only "eine unendlich fortschreitende Annäherung an die Gottheit" (a perpetually increasing approach to the Deity). It "lässt aber niemals das stetige Gefühl eines gewissen Besitzes aufkommen. Dass man als Christ immer im Werden sein muss, hat die katholische Frömmigkeit

richtig erkannt; aber es ist nicht hell und friedevoll aufgegangen, dass dieses Werden an der sicheren Zuversicht auf den gnädigen Gott, also an der Seligkeit, seinen festen, unverlierbaren Grund haben kann und soll" ([It] never allows the constant feeling of a sure possession to arise. That, as a Christian, one must always be growing, was rightly discerned by Catholic piety; but it never arrived at a clear and peaceful vision of the truth that this growth can and must have its sure and unalienable basis in firm confidence in the God of grace, that is, in salvation: tr. William M'Gilchrist, *History of Dogma*, 6:68).

16. Unamuno makes use of Søren Kierkegaard's famous image, in *Fear and Trembling* (tr. Walter Lowrie, 47), of the leap of faith, whereby the believer, like Abraham about to sacrifice Isaac while believing that God will not require the sacrifice, loses his reason and all finiteness which reason brokers, in order to pass through faith into infinity. The notion of being absorbed in God after death through loss of self-consciousness and loss of memory of self appears in William Ellery Channing, "Critique of Fénelon," *Complete Works*, 571.

17. This is William James's vision of God as "Producer of Immortality" before all else (*Varieties of Religious Experience*, 524), and it harmonizes with J. H. Leuba's view of God's not being understood, but used: ibid., 506.

18. *Judges* 13:22. In the 1907 article "Ibsen y Kierkegaard," in *Obras Completas*, 3:290, Unamuno associates this biblical passage with Kierkegaard. According to *Afsluttende uvidenskabelig Efterskrift*, in *Samlede Værker*, 7:474, to the individual in the God-relationship, God represents Himself as an Absolute, perceived at every moment. The finite individual suffers a dying away from the immediate sphere. The relativity of his immediate consciousness undergoes annihilation. Kierkegaard supposes that this experience explains the lethal vision of God mentioned in the Scriptures.

19. Unamuno seems to respond to the guilt-ridden Paul Stapfer, author of *Des Réputations littéraires*, who in a chapter titled "Confession d'un égoïste" (p. 102), vis-à-vis society and humanity, asking him to suppress his own person, responds, "C'est mon *moi* que je veux sauver, ô Père de la personne humaine!" (It is my self that I wish to save, Oh Father of the human person!).

20. At this point in the text of manuscript series A Unamuno has written (16), corresponding to a long, seven-paragraph insertion from manuscript series B also numbered (16). I have made the insertion, which includes all the text up to footnote 25 in my translation of series A.

21. In *Rechtfertigung und Versöhnung*, 3:199, Albrecht Ritschl links the conceivability of divine personality to what we so highly esteem in our own species as "independent personality" (*selbständige Persönlichkeit*). The peculiarity of personality consists of the power to accept stimuli from the surroundings to serve as means for the plan of life, not as hindrances. Everything within the person like memories and principles comes to serve the same end: ibid., 200.

22. As against David Strauss, Albrecht Ritschl, ibid., 197–98, argues that differentiation of oneself from everything else is not personality, but merely the precondition for the personality to encompass everything possible within itself. The better developed the personality, the more its knowledge, the richer its feelings, the stronger its will to reshape objects and lead other personalities. The peculiarity of a person denotes its acquired distinctiveness from all other persons, as opposed to the "formal" (*formalen*), originary self-differentiation of the individual from others, to which Strauss refers. The healthy human being always

overshoots that limit when appropriating any matter for spiritual development. An individual staying closed off in himself, self-comprehensive with respect to others, would have no observable spiritual life. Even if predominantly closed off in the spiritual appropriation of objects, he would not usually be appreciated as a personality at all.

23. The contrast between individuality (psychic form) and personality (psychic content) appears at least as early as 1895 in Unamuno's *En torno al casticismo* (On Authentic Tradition), criticizing the excess of individuality and the deficit of personality in the typical Castilian controlling Spanish culture: *Obras Completas*, 1:841, 852. This seems to have preceded Unamuno's reading of Ritschl, who later enriches him. He may, however, have read a theory of personality very similar to Ritschl's in Georg Simmel, *Einleitung in die Moralwissenschaft* (1892–93), 2:370–80, distinguishing the unity of the soul (=empirically normal coexistence of its content) from its personality (=peculiar shading for all its multifarious contents).

Unamuno insists more strongly than either Simmel or Ritschl on the contrast between individuality and personality, form and content. For his basic philosophical intuition is that every being as such is a desire to persist in its own being (corresponding to individuality) and, at the same time, to be all else (coinciding in human beings with personality, or harmonization of multifarious psychic content).

24. For William Ellery Channing, *Complete Works*, 31, the idea of God is likewise the idea of the "Perfect Being," a conception so majestic that "the treasures of the world are poor in contrast."

25. In his sermon "The Trinity," *Sermons Preached at Trinity Chapel*, 3:59, Frederick W. Robertson analyzes the Trinity as evincing the wealth of God as a Personality: "These, then, my Christian brethren, are the three consciousnesses by which He becomes known to us. Three, we said, *known* to us. We do not dare to limit God; we do not presume to say that there are in God only three personalities, only three consciousnesses: all that we dare presume to say is this, that there are three in reference to us, and only three; that a fourth there is not; that, perchance, in the present state a fourth you can not add to these: Creator [=the Father], Redeemer [=the Son], Sanctifier [=the Holy Spirit]." Unamuno's association of God with a society may stem from Albrecht Ritschl, *Rechtfertigung und Versöhnung* 3:18.83: "Das Attribut des Vaters steht in Beziehung auf die relativ sittliche und rechtliche Gemeinschaft der Familie" (The attribute of Father stands in relation to the peculiar moral and legal [community] of the family: Macintosh and Macaulay, 95).

26. Cf. William James, *Will to Believe*, 17 (with Unamuno's marginal marking): "Our great difference from the scholastic lies in the way we face. The strength of his system lies in the principles, the origin, the *terminus a quo* of his thought; for us the strength is in the outcome, the upshot, the *terminus ad quem*. Not where it comes from but what it leads to is to decide." Unamuno apparently finds the origin as enigmatic as the outcome, and here echoes Vinet on Pascal's view of the human being: "Les ténèbres qui enveloppent sa nature s'étendent également sur son avenir" (The darkness that envelops his nature extends equally over his future): *Études sur Blaise Pascal*, 28.

27. Cf. Fray Tomé de Jesús, *Trabalhos de Jesus*, 1:96: "Porque tenho por muito coisa que por vosso amor padeço? Convosco não usais de peso, nem medida, pois

a medida de vosso padecer, é vosso amor" (Why do I make so much of the amount I suffer for love of you? With yourself you use no weight or measure, for in the measure of your suffering is your love). See ch. 6, note ?, above.

28. *1 Corinthians* 15:27–28.

29. Origen (185–253 A.D.), Christian theologian and researcher of the Bible in Alexandria, attracts Unamuno for his idea of the apocatastasis, "universal salvation, the universal restoration of all creation to God in which evil is defeated and the devil . . . repent[s]. . . . He interpreted hell as a temporary purgatory in which impure souls were purified and made ready for heaven": Louis P. Pojman, "Origen," 636. Unamuno was impressed with Adolf von Harnack's exposition of this doctrine in the *Dogmengeschichte*, 1:631, as his annotation reads, "Salvación final universal según Orígenes" (Final universal salvation according to Origen). Harnack notes how Origen broke with precedent in holding that all spirits without exception would be saved and glorified. His system, writes Harnack (ibid., 646), ousted the Gnostics, attractive to Greek philosophers, and gave justification to the Christianity of the clergy.

30. For Harnack, Origen's doctrine of universal salvation was revolutionary, yet went virtually unnoticed as such by posterity (ibid.). The sinner Unamuno, thereby assured of salvation, necessarily regards this as a "strong point" in religion. His disbelief in hell, he has revealed, once did away with his Catholic faith altogether. Origen, however, all but closed hell down.

31. In this profound conception of religion, Unamuno synthesizes at least three authors, A. A. Cournot, Friedrich Schleiermacher, and A. von Harnack. In *Traité de l'enchaînement des idées fondamentales dans les sciences et dans l'histoire*, 450 (marked by Unamuno), Cournot finds religious manifestations the consequence of a human tendency to create an unseen, supernatural world of wonders, conceivable either as a reminiscence of an earlier state or as "le presentiment d'une destinée future" (the foreshadowing of a future destiny). Schleiermacher, we shall note (see ch. 8, note 5, below), regards religion as a relationship of dependence. Finally, for Adolf von Harnack, the Gospels are both "individualistic and socialistic" in the sense of being linked both to Christ's historic singularity, on the one hand, and to God the Father and the communion of brethren, on the other. See ch. 9, note 5, below.

Chapter 8: Religion

1. William James, *Varieties of Religious Experience*, 26–27.

2. In manuscript series D, in a paragraph titled "Proceso de la fe" (Process of the Faith), paraphrasing Harnack, *Dogmengeschichte*, 1:156, Unamuno clarifies this contrast between faith as sentiment (=*pistis*) and faith as doctrine (=*gnosis*): "Unidad de fe de *pistis* en las primitivas comunidades, bajo el entusiasmo, cuando apenas *gnosis*—es unidad de indiferenciación. En el seno de ella la *gnosis*, porque las comunidades compuestas de personas de diferentes procedencias. Marcha la diferenciación, la unidad de fe se pierde en la variedad de creencias, y ahora hace falta la integración de las varias creencias en la unidad de fe, intregración facilitada . . . como toda, por la homogeneidad primitiva, por la comunidad persistente bajo la separación. El cristianismo enriquecido" (Unity of the faith of *pistis* in the primitive communities, under [the influence of their] enthu-

siasm, when [there is] hardly [any] *gnosis:* it is unity of indifferentiation. In the bosom of it [comes] *gnosis*, because the communities [are] composed of persons of different origins. The differentiation progresses, the unity of faith gets lost in the variety of beliefs, and now what is needed is the integration of the several beliefs in the unity of faith, an integration eased—like all—by the primitive homogeneity, by the community persisting beneath the separation. Christianity enriched).

3. Auguste Sabatier, *Esquisse d'une philosophie de la religion*, 24, defines religion as "un commerce, un rapport conscient et voulu, dans lequel l'âme en détresse entre avec la puissance mystérieuse dont elle sent qu' elle dépend et que dépend sa destinée" (an intercourse, a conscious and voluntary relationship, entered into by a soul in distress with the mysterious power upon which it feels itself to depend and upon which its fate is contingent). This definition, directly quoted in English in *Varieties of Religious Experience*, 464–65, receives the author William James's emphatic approval.

4. Unamuno leaves a blank space here about the length of a five- or six-letter word. But because he seems to be following Auguste Sabatier's definition of religion so closely (see note 3, above), he may well have meant to write *deseado* for *voulu* (wished-for) in the blank.

5. Friedrich Schleiermacher (1768–1834), German preacher, philosopher, and theologian, in his major work *Der christliche Glaube nach den Grundsatzen der evangelischen Kirche* (*The Christian Faith*, 1821–22, heavily modified in 1830–31), regarded religious feeling as a "feeling of absolute dependence" on God, conveyed by Christ through the Church, as opposed to dogmas, literal readings of the Bible, or rational theology. From this dependence stem dogmatic theology and its law. Auguste Sabatier, *Esquisse d'une philosophie de la religion*, 25, though criticizing Schleiermacher's conception for overstressing the passivity of piety and neglecting the activity of prayer, in actuality espouses it, in op. cit., 20.

6. For Matthew Arnold (1822–1888), English poet and critical essayist, "The true meaning of religion is thus not simply morality, but morality touched by emotion." Preface to the 1883 edition, *Literature & dogma: an essay towards a better apprehension of the Bible* (New York: Macmillan, 1883), xxviii. This sentence on Arnold stems from manuscript series B, Unamuno's number (22). I have inserted it into my translation of manuscript series A precisely where Unamuno has written (22).

7. This notion, variously stated in multiple Latin works, received one of its earliest and most often quoted formulations in Publius Papinus Statius in the first century: *Primus in orbe timor fecit deos* (First in the world fear created gods), *Thebais* 3.5. Unamuno recognizes his debt to Statius in *Del sentimiento trágico de la vida* (*Obras Completas*, 7:201). Auguste Sabatier, *Esquisse d'une philosophie de la religion*, 12–13, quoting Statius, does not dispute that disorderly natural forces awaken terror in the human heart and arouse religion, but he finds primal terror always accompanied by hope for salvation.

8. According to Ludwig Stein, *Die soziale Frage in Licht der Philosophie* (*The Social Question in the Light of Philosophie*), 159–60 (marked by Unamuno), fear first becomes sublimated into reverence, gods become spirits, and spirit God, in peoples that have learned to value spirit as the loftiest form in which human beings participate. The first souls worshipped in religion were the dead.

9. Ludwig Stein, ibid., 161, holds that the simple hope of winning divine benef-
icence in human affairs produces belief in the supernatural. The content of all
religions evolves with the ability for abstraction. From worship of the dead
human beings pass to the adoration of natural powers, afterwards of moral
forces, the gods of polytheism, the One God, and abstract formulas for natural
laws.

10. Auguste Sabatier, *Esquisse de la philosophie de la religion*, 9, writes that
children and savages animate all surrounding objects with psychic beings. They
see particular wills behind all phenomena exciting their fear or hope. This myth-
making is the beginning of science, whose ultimate aim, writes Sabatier (ibid.,
18), is to bring order and stability into the world.

11. Unamuno means that our consciousness of the law frees us to impose that
law on the world. The inner law of every being is to persevere in being, and this
message deserves universal diffusion. In manuscript series D, in a paragraph
labeled "Libertad Ley" (Freedom Law), Unamuno writes, "Según Kant la ley es la
conc[iencia] de la libertad. Mas bien es la libertad la conc[iencia] de la ley. La ley
íntima del alma es la ley de la persistencia y por tanto la lib[ertad] religiosa es la
conc[iencia] de la ley de persistencia. Para Kant la liber[tad] es la facultad de pro-
ducir un comienzo absoluto. La lib[ertad] es la facultad de ver al porvenir, de persistir, de obrar para siempre *sub specie aeterni.* // Hay derecho á hacer persistir á
otro, á hacerle bueno, á imponerle la dicha" (According to [Immanuel] Kant law
is the consciousness of freedom. Rather freedom is the consciousness of law. The
inner law of the soul is the law of persistence and therefore religious freedom is
the consciousness of the law of persistence. For Kant freedom is the faculty to
produce an absolute beginning. Freedom is the faculty to see the future, to persist, to act forever from the standpoint of eternity. // There is a right to make
one's neighbor persist, to make him good, to impose bliss upon him). German
philosopher Kant (1724–1804), in the foreword to his *Kritik der reinen Vernunft
(Critique of Practical Reason)*, note 1, perceives the moral law as the condition
under which we can first acquire consciousness of freedom. The ideas of immortality and of God are, in turn, only conditions of the object of the will determined
by that law. Unamuno, however, disagrees. He has read in Albrecht Ritschl,
Rechtfertigung und Versöhnung, 3:253, that freedom means self-determination
to pursue the goal with the most universal content, enabling all individual drives
and all less universal aims to be subordinated to it. Hence Unamuno speaks of
freedom as consciousness of the law (Ritschl's goal with the most universal content). For Ritschl the most universal goal is the kingdom of God; for Unamuno,
individual immortality.

12. Readings in Rohde, *Psyche*, determine Unamuno's choice of heroes. In
manuscript series D, on a paper headed merely "Amor de Dios" (Love of God),
next to the word, "Heroismo," Unamuno has written, "Héroe es el hombre
inmortalizado, deificado. Edipo, Aquiles, etc. Desaparece, no muere, es asumido.
La asunción. En Rohde se explica el proceso de heroicización, v. su registro
alfabético. Acabó por hacerse héroes a los de la familia" (Anfiarao, Tr[ofonio],
Rómulo, Henoc, Elías, Eneas, Turno]" (Hero is the immortalized, deified man.
Œdipus, Achilles, etc. He disappears, does not die, is assumed. The assumption.
In [Erwin] Rohde [*Psyche: The Cult of Souls and Belief in Immortality among the
Ancient Greeks*] the process of becoming a hero is explained, see his alphabetical
index. [The hero] ended up by making heroes of his family members [Amphiaraus,

Trophonius, Romulus, Enoch, Elijah, Æneas, Turnus]). Rohde regards heroes as a post-Homeric phenomenon: once living men, they became heroes after death. They are souls that after separating from the body and dying, attain a loftier, imperishable existence: Rohde, op. cit., tr. W. B. Hillis, 117. Rohde, ibid., 123–24, discusses hero-worship as ancestor-worship, especially in royal or aristocratic families. Rohde, ibid., 430, writes of the once ill-starred Œdipus, involuntarily parricidal and incestuous, that according to Sophocles's tragedy Œdipus at *Colonus,* he was unique in being spared annihilation and was elevated death-lessly out of this life by the gods. A like fate awaited Amphiaraus, warrior and seer who participated in the civil war for the Theban throne between Œdipus's sons: while fleeing in battle, according to the Epic Cycle, the earth swallowed him, his charioteer, and chariot, and Zeus immortalized him: ibid., 89–90. Similarly, the epic titled the *Aithiopis* relates that Achilles, hero of the Trojan War, was spirited away from his funeral pyre by his goddess mother Thetis, resurrected, immortalized, and set down in the "White Island" of Leuke: ibid., 65.

13. William James, *Varieties of Religious Experience,* 523–24.

14. Remarks Auguste Sabatier, *Esquisse d'une philosophie de la religion,* 376: "L'objet de la connaissance scientifique est toujours hors du moi et c'est à le connaître comme objet hors du moi que consiste l'objectivité de cette connaisance" (The object of scientific knowledge is always outside the ego, and it is the knowing of it as an object outside the ego that comprises the objectivity of that knowledge). By contrast, the object of religious, moral, divine, or aesthetic knowledge is inapprehensible outside and apart from the ego.

15. Unamuno exposed the same notion, though with a more positive slant, in his 1895 book of essays *En torno al casticismo,* in *Obras Completas,* 1:789. He borrowed the idea of scientific quantification as a sign of cognitive progress from Herbert Spencer's essay "The Genesis of Science." See my article "El horizonte krausopositivista de *En torno al casticismo,*" 34–35.

16. Writes Auguste Sabatier, *Esquisse d'une philosophie de la religion,* 121: "Notre science n'est que la projection de notre conscience au dehors, et . . . à cette condition seulement le monde nous devient intelligible" (Our science is only the projection of our consciousness on the outside, and . . . only on that condition does the world become intelligible for us).

17. See ch. 3, note 24.

18. Ibid.

19. Ludwig Feuerbach held that the human being creates gods in his own likeness. But in a passage marked by Unamuno, Ludwig Stein, *Die soziale Frage in Licht der Philosophie,* 158, notes that long before Feuerbach, Eleatic philosopher Xenophanes of Colophon (570?—475? B.C.) wrote that mortals regard their gods as engendered as the worshippers were, with similar clothes, voices, and forms (Fragment B14). A critic of polytheism, he noted that Ethiopians make their gods black and snub-nosed, while Thracians say that theirs possess red hair and blue eyes (B16). He added that if oxen, horses, and lions could paint, horses would make the gods in the form of horses, and oxen in that of oxen (B15). Hermann Diels and Walter Kranz, *Fragmente der Vorsokratiker.*

20. Cf. Ritschl: see ch 1, note 12, above.

21. Albrecht Ritschl, *Rechtfertigung und Versöhnung,* 3:28.180–82.

22. According to Ritschl, ibid., 3:28, 180, materialism claims to invalidate the Christian worldview, yet engages in reductionism, trying to deduce organic

beings from mechanical laws, and even more complex beings from subordinate ones. Too much falls to the workings of chance without any delving to the supreme law of things. The materialistic theory of the origin of the world displays to Ritschl an expenditure of imagination paralleled only by heathen cosmogonies. Not scientific method, but a misguided religious impulse unclear about itself prevails here.

23. Auguste Sabatier, *Esquisse d'une philosophie de la religion*, 10, remarks that the more science progresses and realizes its true method and limits, the more it distinguishes itself from philosophy and religion. Scientific research merely determines phenomena and their spatio-temporal conditions. Philosophy strives to understand the universe as an intelligible whole (Unamuno's essence of things). Religion displays the instinct of every being to wish to persevere in its being.

24. "I am the Way, the Truth, and the Life," *John* 14:6. Historian Ernest Renan defends to the death erudition, solid fact-gathering, while leaving truth to the future: "Nous consentons à ignorer, afin que l'avenir sache" (We agree to stay ignorant so that the future may have knowledge). Cited in Paul Stapfer, *Des Réputations littéraires*, 24.

25. Auguste Sabatier, *Esquisse d'une philosophie de la religion*, 371, finds physical science concerned with judgments of existence, hence, only with causality, succession, distribution of phenomena, that is, "les rapports des objets entre eux, abstraction faite du sujet" (relationships of objects among them, abstraction made of the subject).

26. Unamuno follows Adolf von Harnack, *Dogmengeschichte*, 3:315: "Scholastik ist Wissenschaft, angewandt auf die Religion und—wenigstens bis zu Zeit, wo sie sich zersetzte—von dem Axiom ausgehend, dass aus der Theologie alle Dinge zu verstehen, . . . desshalb auch auf der Theologie zurückzuführen sind" (Scholastic philosophy is science, applied to religion and—at least until the time it disintegrated—starting from the axiom that all things are to be understood from theology, [hence] . . . to be reduced to theology).

The expression *ancilla theologiae* stems from the Vatican Council of 1869–70, which distinguished between dogmatic theology and philosophy—in their cognitive principles (faith, reason), objects (dogma, rational truth), motives (divine authority, evidence), and ends (beatific vision, natural knowledge of God). When pronouncing philosophy the handmaid of natural theology, the Catholic Church studied the various systems and decided to select the philosophy most harmonious with its own revealed doctrine (acknowledging a personal God, immortality of the soul, and the moral law). The Church aroused opposition among the modernists (of whom Unamuno was one): "Dogmatic Theology," *Catholic Encyclopedia*, http://www.newadvent.org/cathen/14580a.htm.

27. For Harnack's student Georg Wobbermin, *Theologie und Metaphysik* (Theology and Metaphysics), 119–20, the main problem of theological metaphysics lies in the inquiry into the existence of God. In old Scholastic dogmatics, the proofs for divine existence formed the basis for the theological doctrine of God. Yet Wobbermin finds this reasoning a contradiction of Christian faith qua faith, different from knowing or thinking, and leading to a "falsification" (*Verfälschung*) of the Christian concept of God. God's properties were deduced from an "insufficient, sub-Christian concept" of God as *simplicissima essentialis spiritualis infinita* (simplest infinite essential spirit): ibid., 229.

28. According to Adolf von Harnack, *Dogmengeschichte*, 3:441, Medieval Scholastic theologians held that religion and theology had to lead the individual to eternal bliss, signifying *fruitio dei* (enjoyment of God in the intellect or the will). Harnack finds that "this individualistic version of bliss" (*diese individualistische . . . Fassung der Seligkeit*) leaves the Church out of account or else treats it merely as a means to that personal end (ibid., n1).

29. Harnack (ibid., 393) informs that jurisprudence became the favorite science of the clergy in St. Thomas Aquinas's time. Aquinas's *Summa Theologica*, Part 1, Questions 2–27, contains the five proofs of God's existence and the divine essence (which Unamuno finds too intellectualistic). But Part 2, Section 1, begins with the human being's goal (heavenly bliss, God, the beatific vision: Harnack, *Dogmengeschichte*, 3:426n) and ends with external principles of moral conduct, a discussion pervaded with considerations on the law (*Gesetz*): eternal law (of God's conduct and its applications to the creatures), natural law, human law, Old and New Testament law, and law of counsels for special perfection. New Testament law contains the law of grace, assisting the human being in procuring the supernatural good (ibid., 427n). This legalism, facilitating immortality, tempers the Scholastic depersonalization of God for Unamuno.

30. See note 28, above.

31. In fact, this is the motto of Saint Anselm (1033–1109), Archbishop of Canterbury, reputed founder of Scholastic philosophy, summing up in Latin Saint Augustine's reason for conversion to Christianity: faith properly educated in the Bible. Augustine (354–430) had previously tried out Manicheism, Aristotelianism, Epicureanism, and Neoplatonism. Anselm tried to follow in Augustine's footsteps by applying reason to faith.

32. Auguste Sabatier, *Esquisse d'une philosophie de la religion*, 11, reminds that the founder of scientific positivism, Auguste Comte (1798–1857), though predicting the demise of religion, at the end of his career founded a positivist church modeled after Roman Catholicism. British positivist Herbert Spencer (1820–1903) crowned his system with an indeterminate and unconscious force, the Unknowable, the cause explaining the evolution and source of everything—for Sabatier (ibid., 12), the old First Cause of philosophers and theologians under a different name.

33. On religion as an individual science (insofar as it orients the believer toward immortality), cf. note 28, above. In speaking of true science as social, Unamuno may refer either to the cooperative unity of scientists, to the collective nature of their subject matters, or to their beneficiary, society. Paul Stapfer, *Des Réputations littéraires*, 20, finds that in the community of natural and human scientists, leading mankind to the conquest of truth, the scientist is annihilated as an individual. Stapfer, ibid., 68, reflects that at the base of all positive sciences lies the notion that individuals in substance constitute nothing, while societies of which they form part are the only living, lasting realities. Hence science researches species, genera, races, families, nations, social bodies. Finally, Stapfer, ibid., 69–70, remarks that among human sciences, the sociological standpoint prevails, with the vision of the human qua social being taken as the most interesting and worthy of study.

34. In *Die soziale Frage in Licht der Philosophie*, 54n, Ludwig Stein revises Georg Simmel's opinion that the usefulness of knowing produces for us at the same time the objects of knowledge. Stein maintains that not the individual, but

social groups convert what is useful into what is true. The conversion takes place by instinct in a process arising like language, religion, or art.

35. Socrates (469–399 B.C.), Greek philosopher noted for his view that only the rationally or "scientifically" examined life is worth living, wrote nothing but spent his days as the "gadfly of Athens," arousing fellow Athenians out of moral complacency by posing ethical questions to them like the meaning of virtue, so as to improve human life. Daniel Trent Devereux, "Socrates," *Cambridge Dictionary of Philosophy*, 859. Unamuno tries to spark his Spanish readers out of religious complacency.

36. William James, *Varieties of Religious Experience*, 524, writes, "Religion, in fact, for the vast majority of our own [human] race *means* immortality, and nothing else."

37. See Appendix 1, note 9, on Voltaire as source of this idea.

38. Albrecht Ritschl, *Rechtfertigung und Versöhnung*, 3:32.219–20, argues the inadequacy of the analogy of civil law to God's moral order. This analogy compels God to punish violations of His law. The same necessity supposedly governing divine justice forces God to reward human obedience with eternal life. Ritschl reminds that in the State the police force and the penal code regulate like justice. Religion differs in goals and in ways to achieve them.

39. Reinhold Seeberg, "Christliche-protestantische Ethik," in *Systematische christliche Religion*, 191, writes, "Während Kant die Religion von der Sittlichkeit abhängig machte, und neuerdings Religion und Sittlichkeit oft ganz voneinander getrennt werden, ist in Wirklichkeit die Sittlichkeit stets abhängig von der Religion" (Whereas Kant made religion dependent on morality, and once again religion and morality are often wholly divided from one another, in reality morality is always dependent on religion). For in Christianity, religion requires experiencing the redeeming God's governance, morally pointing our souls toward attainment of the Kingdom of God. Unamuno cites from another passage of Seeberg's article in *Del sentimiento trágico de la vida*, 7:220n.

40. See ch. 7, notes 29 and 30, above, on this notion in Origen.

41. The idea of wishing immortality into existence is what Paul Stapfer has called "immortalité facultative" (facultative immortality): *Des Réputations littéraires*, 97. Cf. *Matthew* 11:12: "The kingdom of heaven suffers violence, and the violent take it by force."

42. For Søren Kierkegaard, *Afsluttende uviderskabelig efterskrift*, in *Samlede Værker*, 7:159, the question "Do I become immortal or am I immortal?" rightly belongs only to the existing subject, who wishes to live for religious inwardness. The question resists systematic, abstract demonstration.

43. The previous two paragraphs in the text stem from manuscript series B, Unamuno's number (24). I insert them into my translation of manuscript series A precisely where Unamuno has written (24).

44. In manuscript series D appears an unnumbered page with the words, "Ciencia-filosofía-poesía-religión" (Science-philosophy-poetry-religion), and underneath, the words, "Practicismo: la religión, que es lo teleológico, para la vida; es sabiduría, no ciencia" (Practicism: religion, which is the teleological, for life; it is wisdom, not science). Cf. *Del sentimiento trágico de la vida*, in *Obras Completas*, 7:226: "La fe religiosa . . . no es ya tan sólo irracional, es contra-racional. 'La poesía es la ilusión antes del conocimiento; la religiosidad, la ilusión después del conocimiento. La poesía y la religiosidad suprimen el vaude-

ville de la mundana sabiduría de vivir. Todo individuo que no vive o poética o religiosamente, es tonto.' Así nos dice Kierkegaard (*Afsluttende uvidenskabelig Efterskrift*, capítulo IV, sect. II A, párr. 2)" (Religious faith . . . is not only irrational, it is counter-rational. 'Poetry is illusion before understanding, religiousness illusion after understanding. Poetry and religiousness suppress the vaudeville of the worldly wisdom about life. Every individual who does not live either poetically or religiously is obtuse.' Thus Kierkegaard tells us [*Concluding Unscientific Postscript*, ch. 4, sec. 2 A, paragraph 2]). If we follow the Hong translation (S. Kierkegaard, *Concluding Unscientific Postscript*, 1:457), Unamuno's word "suprime" (suppress) mistranslates Danish *opfører* (*Samlede Vaerker*, 7:446), meaning "performs." The word that Unamuno inserts on his own stresses his irrationalism.

45. Cf. Søren Kierkegaard, *Afsluttende uvidenskabelig Efterskrift*, in *Samlede Værker*, 7:610: "Det at være Christen bestemmes ikke ved Christendommens Hvad, men ved den Christens Hvorledes" (Tr. Hong and Hong, *Concluding Unscientific Postscript*, 1:610: "Being a Christian is defined not by the 'what' of Christianity but by the 'how' of the Christian"). This "how" is a specific experience of inwardness.

Chapter 9: Christianity

1. "We live surrounded by Christian institutions; breathe an atmosphere saturated by Christianity. It is exceedingly difficult even to imagine another state of things" (Frederick W. Robertson, "First Advent Lecture—The Grecians," *Sermons Preached at Trinity Chapel*, 1:167).

2. In *Will to Believe*, 44, William James mentions ex-Calvinists, exultant at ridding themselves of the "sophistication" of reverence towards their ancestral God, while worshipping nature as an idol in rites also leading to sophistication.

3. "At tænke Existents . . . i Abstraktion, er væsentligen at ophæve den": Søren Kierkegaard, *Afsluttende uvidenskabelig Efterskrift*, in *Samlede Værker*, 7:295 (To think existence . . . in abstraction is essentially to annul it: tr. Hong and Hong, *Concluding Unscientific Postscript*, 1:308).

4. Søren Kierkegaard, *Afsluttende uvidenskabelig efterskrift*, in *Samlede Værker*, 7:360: "Derimod maa jo den Christen tillige vide hvad Christendom er, og kunne sige os det—jorsaavidt han selv er blevet det" (On the other hand, the Christian must indeed also know what Christianity is and be able to tell us—provided he himself has become one: tr. Hong and Hong, *Concluding Unscientific Postscript*, 1:372).

5. Frederick W. Robertson contrasts pagan (here, Greek) worship of humanness in general with Christian worship of the human being qua divine: "First Advent Lecture—The Grecian," *Sermons Preached at Trinity Chapel*, 1:205–6. Richard Hooker, *Of the Laws of Ecclesiastical Polity*, 221n1, footnotes a quote from Tertullian, emphatically noted by Unamuno and insisting on fleshly concreteness: "How is it true of Christ that he died, was buried, and rose again, if Christ had not that very flesh the nature whereof is capable of these things, flesh mingled with blood, supported with bones, woven with sinews, embroidered with veins?" Finally, Adolf von Harnack, *Dogmengeschichte*, 1:68n, insists on the historic singularity of Jesus's person as the basis of Christianity, explaining its

founding, propagation, and maintenance. The inestimable intrinsic value of each individual human soul—an idea dispersed throughout some psalms and Greek philosophical works—receives stress in Jesus's preaching. Linked to the notion of God the Father and to the loving communion of brethren, it makes the Gospel "individualistic and socialistic" (ibid., 68) in Harnack's words. Everywhere Unamuno insists on the social aspect of religion as such, and links his own desire for self-immortalization to a loving communion with the universe.

6. In Kierkegaard's *Afsluttende uvidenskabelig efterskrift*, in *Samlede Værker*, 7:152, the first-person speaker contrasts himself with the deceased bookseller Soldin, for whom dying was merely "Roget i Almindelighed" (something in general). Yet he himself maintains the following: "Er for mig slet ikke saadan Roget i Almindelighed; for Andre er det, at jeg døer, saadan Noget. Jeg er heller ikke for mig saadan Roget i Almindelighed" (But for me, *my* dying is by no means something in general; for others, my dying is some such thing. Nor am *I* for myself some such thing in general): tr. Hong and Hong, *Concluding Unscientific Postscript*, 1:167.

7. Unamuno incorporates into his text the phrase of Saint Athanasius, "Hence, not for being human did he afterwards become God, but for being God he afterwards became a man so that he might better make us divine." A literal Spanish translation of Athanasius's Greek appears in *Del sentimiento trágico de la vida* (*Obras Completas*, 7:147): "No, pues, . . . siendo hombre se hizo después Dios, sino que, siendo Dios, se hizo después hombre para que mejor nos deificara." Saint Athanasius's phrase, derived from his First Prayer against Arius, appears quoted in the original Greek by Adolf von Harnack, *Dogmengeschichte*, 2:204n (a source also cited by Unamuno): "Οὐκ ἄρα ἄνθρωπος ὢν ὕστερον γέγονεν θεός, ἀλλὰ θεὸς ὢν ὕστερον γέγονεν ἄνθρωπος, ἵνα μᾶλλον ἡμᾶς θεοποιήσῃ."

8. Søren Kierkegaard, *Afsluttende uvidenskabelig efterskrift*, in *Samlede Værker*, 7:393: "I den evige Salighed er der ingen Lidelse, men naar en Existerende forholder sig til den, udtrykkes Forholdet ganste rigtigt ved Lidelsen." (There is no suffering in the eternal happiness, but when an existing person relates himself to it, the relation is quite properly expressed by suffering): *Concluding Unscientific Postscript*, 1:452.

9. Unamuno agrees with Saint Athanasius's doctrine that God the Son and God the Father have the same substance. See note 10, paragraph 2, below.

10. According to Adolf von Harnack, *Dogmengeschichte*, 1:193–97, Emperor Constantine convoked the Synod of Nicæa in 325 to settle the controversy between the Bishop of Alexandria and the priest Arius. Arius (250?—336?) had taught that God alone is increate, eternal, inexpressible, inconceivable, and unequalled. He had not always been the Father. Otherwise His creatures would have been increate and eternal too. God created an independent being as a worktool, called by the Scriptures Wisdom, the Son, divine image, or Word. The Son's wisdom was creaturely and derivative, with an essence different from the Father's. Like all rational creatures, the Son had the capacity for change and free will, freely chose to be good and remained so. Not eternal like his Father, he lacks divine characteristics, has only relative knowledge of God and of his own essence, and deserves less reverence than his Father. He stands in a special relationship to God by participating in His grace and through him was everything created. In reference to his becoming and being human, Arius agrees with everything written and handed down about the Son.

The majority of bishops gathered at Nicæa, among them Athanasius, anathematized Arius. They held that the Son was of the same substance or essence as the Father, and that through that substance everything had been created. This same substance, ὁμοούσιος, was the symbol of Nicæa to which Unamuno refers. The bishops maintained that the Son came down for humankind, became incarnate and human, suffered, was resurrected the third day, and returns to judge living and dead. Harnack finds Arius more or less coherent, but Athanasius confused, confusing, and absurd. Unamuno sides with Athanasius against the rationalist Harnack for favoring the deification of the human being through Christ.

11. For Harnack, ibid., 2:218n2, those adhering like Arius to the self-developing and struggling Christ cannot grasp him as savior, but only as teacher and model.

12. The Unitarian William Ellery Channing, "Jesus Christ the Brother, Friend, and Saviour," *Complete Works*, 40, holds that Jesus's humble birth, human wants and trials, and sensibility to pain made him "one of us." At the same time, Channing preaches that his moral perfection made him an imitable example: "The Great Purpose of Christianity," ibid., 178, and "The Imitableness of Christ's Character," ibid., 243–46.

13. On Arius, see note 10, above. The stress in Arianism on Jesus's humanity over his divinity makes that doctrine comparable for Unamuno to Unitarianism (notes 11 and 12, above).

14. See quote from Reinhold Seeberg, ch. 8, note 39, above.

15. Here Unamuno disputes Adolf von Harnack's preference for the historical Jesus (the virtuous teacher favored by the clear and more or less rational Arius) over the eschatological Christ (the God-Man, made of conceptual contradictions by Athanasius). See note 10 above. Eschatology (concern for the Afterlife) prevails in Unamuno over ethics (concern for right living, here and now).

16. God the Producer of immortality is William James's formula, several times cited by Unamuno, to mean that the imparting of immortality to the believer is God's primary function: see ch. 4, n. 53. God as the *product* of immortality seems to allude to Unamuno's doctrine that to believe is to create: see ch. 3, note 10. Hence, the believer in a certain sense "creates" or produces the God that gives him immortality (although God is within him, enabling this process).

17. Unamuno again employs the notion of Saint Athanasius, quoted above in footnote 7.

18. Unamuno, *Del sentimiento trágico*, in *Obras Completas*, 7:148: "En Nicea vencieron . . . los idiotas—tomada esta palabra en su recto sentido primitivo y etimológico—, los ingenuos, los obispos cerriles y voluntariosos, representantes del genuino espíritu humano, del popular, del que no quiere morirse, diga lo que quiera la razón" (In Nicæa triumphed the idiots, to take this word in its correct original, etymological meaning—the naive, closed-minded, willful bishops, representative of the genuine human spirit, the popular one, of the one that does not wish to pass on, whatever reason may say). Unamuno's irony reflects Harnack's disapproval of the bishops (although he himself concurs with them for reasons explained above in note 10).

19. On Unamuno's (and Harnack's) opposition to concern with the *filioque* (substantial relationship between the Father and the Son) as mere formalism that helped produced the schism between the Eastern and Western churches, see Appendix, note 16, below.

20. Adolf von Harnack, *Dogmengeschichte*, 2:44, finds the essence of Christianity in the salvation it offers through redemption from perishableness and sin. The religion offers divine life (contemplation of God), already consummated in the Incarnation and conferred by the bonding of human beings with the Son of God. The conferral achieves completion in the "Vergöttung des Menschen durch die Gabe der Unsterblichkeit" (deification of the human being through the gift of immortality). In a note (ibid., 44–45n2), Harnack adds that this idea of human deification recurs after the third century in all (Greek) Fathers of the ancient Church. Among them, deification did not mean "Werden wie Gott" (becoming like God), but in keeping with their characteristic way of thinking, neither did the notion go beyond imperishableness (Unvergänglichkeit).

21. Non-believers in Christ's immortality would include Arians and Socinians, among others. In *Del sentimiento trágico* (*Obras Completas*, 7:147), a work more sympathetic to eschatological dogmas than is the *Tratado*, Unamuno also adds Unitarians to this list.

22. William Ellery Channing, "Love to Christ," *Complete Works*, 251–53, distinguishes between love of Christ based on a just view of him and love of Christ of doubtful worth. Just love of Christ perceives the virtues preferred by the faith come alive in his character. Lowly affection towards him simply in order to weep for his sufferings and nothing more, or else to exaggerate the worshipper's own guilt, seems depraved to Channing. Rather, Christ's mission is to suit worshippers for heaven, according to Channing: ibid., 234.

23. Karl Heinrich von Weizsäcker, *Das apostolische Zeitalter der christlichen Kirche* (*The Apostolic Age of the Christian Church*, 102), read by Unamuno, and marked with pencil, is literally translated from German to Spanish in *Del sentimiento trágico* (*Obras Completas*, 7:146): "Se puede decir que es, en general, la teología del Apóstol la primera teología cristiana. Es para él una necesidad: sustituíale, en cierto modo, la falta de conocimiento personal de Jesús" [It can be said that in general the theology of the Apostle [Paul] was the first Christian theology. It is for him a necessity: in a certain sense it replaced for him the lack of personal acquaintance with Jesus]. In Unamuno's words, "Pablo no había conocido personalmente a Jesús, y por eso le descubrió como Cristo" [Paul had not known Jesus personally, and therefore discovered him as Christ]: ibid.

Appendix: What Is Truth?

1. *John* 18:38. Albert Réville, *Jesus de Nazareth*, 2:395.1, treats this dialogue between Pilate and Jesus as a literary composition with Pilate as the skeptical type. The notions of the kingdom of the other world and of the witness to truth are alien to a Roman magistrate's mind.

2. In his personal edition of González's *Filosofía elemental*, Unamuno delighted in noting down errors. For instance, according to González, *op. cit.*, 1:1, St. Thomas Aquinas traces the word "philosophy" back to Pythagoras; Unamuno crosses out St. Thomas and substitutes Cicero. González, ibid., 2:6, classifies the wolf and the lion in the same biological species, the canine; Unamuno corrects this error with a marginal pencil note to the effect that the lion is a feline. On the same page, González classifies geometry and optics as mathematical sciences; Unamuno disagrees in the margin, categorizing optics as a physical

science instead. The marginal discrepancies abound and would constitute an amusing study.

3. Zeferino González, *Filosofía elemental*, ch. II, art. I, 1, 2nd., pág. 126.

4. Ibid., ch. II, art. I, 1, 3rd., pág. 128.

5. *Summa Theologica*, First Part, Question 16, Art. 1, Response to Objection 3. Zeferino González, *Filosofía elemental*, cap. II, art. I, I, 5.¶, pág. 129, quotes the definition in Latin and translates it to Spanish.

6 Ibid., ch. II, art. I, 1, 4th., pág. 128.

7. In Shakespeare's *Hamlet*, act 2, scene 2, talkative old Polonius asks the protagonist, "What do you read, Lord?" An ironic Hamlet, with a veiled allusion to that loquacity, responds, "Words, words, words."

8. Cf. "The Faith of the Centurion," *Sermons Preached in Trinity Chapel*, 2:119, where Frederick W. Robertson explains *Matthew 8:10*, showing Jesus's wonderment at the centurion's faith. The centurion, according to Robertson, displays his "belief in an invisible, living Will. 'Speak the word only.' Remark how different this is from a reliance on the influence of the senses. He asked not the presence of Christ, but simply an exertion of His will."

9. "Si Dieu n'existait pas, il faudrait l'inventer" (*Epître sur Les trois Imposteurs*, 1768, line 22, cited in *Œuvres complètes de Voltaire*, 10:402). In this letter in verse, vis-à-vis a text that denies the existence of God, Voltaire develops his idea that belief in God helps to maintain order in society.

10. Here Unamuno is distinguishing faith conceived as sentiment or *pistis* from faith as *gnosis*, or adherence to doctrine, and expressing his preference for the first. See "Translator's Introduction," note 83, above.

11. *1 Corinthians* 1:22.

12. *Matthew* 5:8.

13. In *The Varieties of Religious Experience*, 350, William James offers Saint Louis of Gonzaga as an example of an individual who carries self-purification to a point "which we cannot unreservedly admire." In his zeal to eliminate externals and discords, he neglects what James calls "social righteousness." James finds it better by far to sacrifice cleanliness and to "contract many a dirt-mark" than to "forfeit usefulness" in the endeavor to "remain unspotted": ibid., 354.

14. William James quotes from the personal memoirs of Finney (1792–1875), American evangelist, extensively in ibid., 207n1.

15. Ibid., 354.

16. *Filioque* (literally, "and the Son") expresses the procession of the Holy Spirit both from the Father and from the Son. Father and Son are taken as a single Principle. In the ninth century, the Greek clergy began to deny the double procession of the Holy Spirit. This denial contributed to the rupture between Western and Eastern Christianity. In the Western Church, the Fourth Lateran Council (1215) pronounced the *filioque* a dogma of faith. Yet Adolf von Harnack, *Dogmengeschichte*, 3:341, deems the *filioque* a dogma of second order for Catholicism, as compared with the doctrines of Christ, the Trinity, and certain sacraments. Unamuno agrees and attacks the formalism of the *filioque* as early as 1900 in his essay "La fe" (Faith), *Obras Completas*, 1:968–69.

BIBLIOGRAPHY

Amiel, Henri-Frédéric. *Fragments d'un journal intime*. 2 vols. Geneva: Georg et Co., 1908.

Aquinas, St. Thomas. *On Being and Essence*. Edited by Armand Maurer. Toronto: Pontifical Institute of Mediæval Studies, 1968.

———. *Summa theologica*. Edited by the Ottawa Institute of Medieval Studies. 5 vols. Ottawa, Ontario: Comissio Plana, 1955.

Aristotle. *Metaphysics: Books 1–9*. Translated by Hugh Tredennick. 10th ed. Cambridge, MA: Harvard University Press, 1996.

———. *Metaphysics: Books 10–14. Oeconomica. Magna Moralia*. Translated by Hugh Tredennick. 9th ed. Cambridge, MA: Harvard University Press, 1997.

Arnobius. *The Seven Books of Arnobius against the Heathen (Adversus Gentes)*. Translated by Archibald Hamilton Brice and Hugh Campbell. Edinburgh: T. & T. Clark, 1871. http://www.ccel.org/fathers2/ANF-06/anf06-134.htm#TopOfPage.

Arnold, Matthew. *Literature & dogma: An essay towards a better apprehension of the Bible*. New York: Macmillan, 1883.

Arouet, François Marie (Voltaire). *Epître à l'auteur du livre des Trois imposteurs*, in *Œuvres complètes de Voltaire*, 10:402–405. Edited by Louis Moland. Paris: Garnier, 1877–85.

Augustine. *Confessions*. Edited by James J. O'Donnell. 3 vols. Oxford: Oxford University Press, 1992.

———. *The Confessions of Saint Augustine: Books 1–10*. Translated by F. J. Sheed. New York: Sheed and Ward, 1942.

———. *On the Trinity: Books 8–15*. Edited by Gareth B. Matthews. Translated by Stephen McKenna. Cambridge: Cambridge University Press, 2002.

Balfour, Arthur James. *The Foundations of Belief*. London: Longmans Green, 1901.

Bell, Robert E. "Sphinx." In *Women of Classical Mythology: A Biographical Dictionary*, 402–3. New York: Oxford University Press, 1993.

Bien, Joseph. "Rousseau, Jean-Jacques." *Cambridge Dictionary of Philosophy*, 800–801.

Boccaccio, Giovanni. *Opere minori in volgari*. Edited by Mario Marti. Milan: Rizzoli, 1969–72.

Brenan, Gerald. *The Spanish Labyrinth: An Account of the Social and Political Background of the Civil War*. 17th ed. Cambridge: Cambridge University Press, 1990.

Bretz, Mary Lou. "Unamuno, Miguel de." *Dictionary of the Literature of the*

Iberian Peninsula, 2:1631–34. Edited by Germán Bleiberg, Maureen Ihrie, and Janet Pérez. Westport, CT: Greenwood Press, 1993.

Brooks, Phillips. *The Mystery of Iniquity and Other Sermons*. London: Macmillan, 1900.

Brunhes, Antoine Joseph Bernard. *La Dégradation de l'énergie*. Paris: Flammarion, 1912.

Burkhardt, Jacob. *Die Kultur der Renaissance in Italien*. 2 vols. Leipzig: Seeman, 1899. http://gutenberg.spiegel.de/burckhar/renaiss/rena203.htm#Anm8.

———. *Die Kultur der Renaissance in Italien*. 2nd edition. Vienna: Phaidon, 1934.

Butts, Robert E. "Spencer, Herbert." *Cambridge Dictionary of Philosophy*, 869–70.

Calderón de la Barca, Pedro. *El gran teatro del mundo*. Edited by John J. Allen and Domingo Ynduráin. Barcelona: Crítica, 1997.

———. *La vida es sueño*. Edited by Ciriaco Morón Arroyo. 3rd ed. Madrid: Cátedra, 1978.

Cambridge Dictionary of Philosophy. Edited by Robert Audi. 2nd edition. Cambridge: Cambridge University Press, 1999.

Carlen, Claudia. *The Papal Encyclicals: 1903–1939*. Raleigh, NC: Pierian Press, 1981.

Carlyle, Thomas. *The French revolution: A history*. 3 vols. Leipzig: Tauchnitz, 1851.

———. *Sartor resartus; On heroes, hero-worship, and the heroic in history; Past and present*. London: Routledge, 1888.

Castro, Guillén de. *Las mocedades del Cid*. Edited by José García Nieto and José Hierro. Madrid: Editora Nacional, 1969.

Cerezo Galán, Pedro. *Las máscaras de lo trágico: Filosofía y tragedia en Miguel de Unamuno*. Madrid: Trotta, 1996.

Cervantes, Miguel de. *Novelas ejemplares*. In *Obras completas*, 769–1026. Edited by Angel Valbuena Prat. Madrid: Aguilar, 1960.

Chabrán, H. Rafael. "Young Unamuno: His Intellectual Development in Positivism and Darwinism, 1880–1884." PhD diss., University of California, San Diego, 1983.

Channing, William Ellery. *The Complete Works of W. E. Channing, Including the Perfect Life*. London: Christian Life, 1884.

Clavería, Carlos. "Sobre el tema de Caín en la obra de Unamuno." In *Temas de Unamuno*, 97–129. Madrid: Gredos, 1970.

Comellas, José Luis. *Historia de España moderna y contemporánea, 1474–1965*. Madrid: Ediciones Rialp, 1967.

Conerly, Porter. "Giner de los Ríos, Francisco." *Dictionary of the Literature of the Iberian Peninsula*, 1:733–35.

Cottingham, John. "Descartes, René." *Cambridge Dictionary of Philosophy*, 223–27.

Cowper, William. *The Poetical Works of William Cowper*. Edited by William Benham. London: Macmillan, 1889.

Crozals, J. de. "Jules Michelet: l'homme et l'œuvre." *L'Encyclopédie de L'Agora*. http://agora.qc.ca/reftext.nsf/Documents/.

Dante Alighieri. *The De Monarchia of Dante Alighieri*. Edited and translated by Aurelia Henry. Boston: Houghton Mifflin, 1904.

————. *La Divina Commedia.* Paris: Didot, 1853.

Darío, Rubén. *Semblanzas.* In *Obras completas,* vol. 2. Madrid: Afrodisio Aguado, 1950.

Devereux, Trent. "Socrates." *Cambridge Dictionary of Philosophy,* 859–60.

Díaz Díaz, Gonzalo. "Balmes, Jaime." *Hombres y documentos de la filosofía española.* Madrid: Consejo Superior de Investigaciones Científicas, Instituto de Filosofía «Luis Vives», 1980, 1:469–87.

————. "Castro y Quesada, Américo." *Hombres y documentos de la filosofía española,* 2:270–78. Madrid, 1983.

————. "Costa y Martínez, Joaquín." *Hombre y documentos de la filosofía española,* 2:432–41.

————. "Donoso Cortés, Juan." *Hombres y documentos de la filosofía española,* 2:602–13.

————. "Sanz del Río, Julián." *Hombres y documentos de la filosofía española,* Madrid, 2003, 7:193–201.

Dictionary of the Literature of the Iberian Peninsula. Edited by Germán Bleiberg, Maureen Ihrie, and Janet Pérez. 2 vols. Westport, CT: Greenwood Press, 1993.

Diehls, Hermann, and Walter Kranz, eds. *Die Fragmente der Vorsokratiker, griechisch und deutsch.* 6th. ed. 3 vols. Dublin and Zurich: Weidmann, 1952.

"Dogmatic Theology." *Catholic Encyclopedia.* http://www.newadvent.org/cathen/14580a.htm.

Espronceda, José de. *Obras poéticas completas.* Madrid: Aguilar, 1951.

————. *Poesías líricas y fragmentos épicos.* Edited by Robert Marrast. Madrid: Castalia, 1970.

Evans, C. Stephan. "Kierkegaard, Søren Aabye." *Cambridge Dictionary of Philosophy,* 468–70.

Forster, Wolfgang. *Karl Christian Friedrich Krauses frühe Rechtsphilosophie und ihr geistesgeschichtlicher Hintergrund.* Ebelsbach: Aktiv Druck & Verlag GMBH, 2000.

Franz, Thomas. "Nietzsche and the Theme of Self-Surpassing in *Abel Sánchez.*" In *Perspectivas de la novela: Ensayos sobre la novela española de los siglos XI y XX de distinto autores,* 59–81. Valencia: Albatros/Hispanófila, 1979.

————. *Parallel but Unequal: The Contemporizing of "Paradise Lost" in Unamuno's "Abel Sánchez."* Valencia: Albatros Ediciones, 1990.

————. "The Painting of the Banquet Scene in Abel Sánchez." *Hispanic Review* 72.1 (Winter 2004): 65–76.

Gamache, Lawrence B. "Toward a Definition of Modernism." In *The Modernists: Studies in a Literary Phenomenon; Essays in Honor of Harry T. More,* edited by Lawrence B. Gamache and Ian S. Macniven, 32–54. Rutherford, NJ: Fairleigh Dickinson University Press, 1987.

García Blanco, Manuel. "Introducción." In Miguel de Unamuno, *Obras Completas,* 1:7–36. Madrid: Escelicer, 1966.

————. "Introducción." In Miguel de Unamuno, *Obras Completas,* 7:7–104. Madrid: Escelicer, 1966.

Gómez Molleda, María Dolores. *Unamuno "agitador de espiritus" y Giner de los Ríos.* Salamanca: Universidad de Salamanca, 1976.

González, Zeferino. *Filosofía elemental.* 2 vols. Madrid: Policarpo López, 1876.

Grisebach, Eduard. *Schopenhauer's Briefe.* Leipzig: P. Reclam jun., 1898.

Guyau, Jean-Marie. *Esquisse d'une morale sans obligation ni sanction.* Paris: Alcan, 1885.

——. *La morale anglaise contemporaine: Morale de l'utilité et de l'évolution.* Paris: Alcan, 1885.

Halliday, David, and Robert Resnick. *Fundamentals of Physics.* 3rd ed. New York: Wiley, 1988.

Harnack, Carl Gustav Adolf von. *Lehrbuch der Dogmengeschichte.* 3 vols. Freiburg i. B.: Mohr, 1890–94.

Hegel, Georg Wilhelm Friedrich. *Grundlinien der Philosophie des Rechts: oder Naturrecht und Staatswissenschaft im Grundrisse.* Edited by Helmut Reichelt. Frankfurt am Main, Berlin: Ullstein, 1972.

——. *Wissenschaft der Logik.* Edited by Leopold von Henning. 3 vols. Berlin: Duncker und Humblot, 1841.

——. *Wissenschaft der Logik.* 1st. Pt. *Die objective Logik.* In *Sämtliche Werke,* edited by Hermann Glockner. *Dritte Auflage der Jubiläumsausgabe.* Stuttgart: Fr. Frommans Verlag, Günther Holzboog, 1958.

Henríquez Ureña, Pedro. *Breve historia del modernismo.* 2nd ed. Mexico City, Buenos Aires: Fondo de Cultural Económica, 1962.

Herrmann, Wilhelm. *Der Verkehr des Christen mit Gott.* Stuttgart: Cotta'schen Buchhandlung, 1896.

Higgins, Kathleen Marie. "Schopenhauer, Arthur." *Cambridge Dictionary of Philosophy,* 820.

Høffding, Harald. *The Philosophy of Religion.* Translated by B. E. Meyer. London: Macmillan, 1914.

Hombres y documentos de la filosofía española. Edited by Gonzalo Díaz Díaz. 7 vols. Madrid: Consejo Superior de Investigaciones Científicas, 1980–2003.

Homer. *Odyssée.* Paris: Hachette, 1904.

Hooker, Richard. *Of the Laws of Ecclesiastical Polity: Books 1–5.* 2 vols. London: Dent, 1907.

Howe, Elizabeth T. "Juan de la Cruz, San." *Dictionary of the Literature of the Iberian Peninsula,* 1:890–94.

——. "Teresa de Jesús, Santa." *Dictionary of the Literature of the Iberian Peninsula,* 2:1561–64.

Hull, David L. "Darwinism." *Cambridge Dictionary of Philosophy,* 204–6.

Irizarry, Estelle. "Generation of 1898." *Dictionary of the Literature of the Iberian Peninsula,* 1:707–15.

James, William. *The Varieties of Religious Experience: A Study in Human Nature.* London: Longmans, Green, 1902.

——. *The Will to Believe and Other Essays in Popular Philosophy.* New York: Longmans, Green, 1902.

Jiménez, Juan Ramón. *El modernismo: Notas de un curso (1953).* Madrid: Aguilar, 1962.

Jiménez García, Antonio. *El krausismo y la Institución Libre de Enseñanza.* Madrid: Cincel, 1985.

——. "Urbano González Serrano y la fundamentación del krauso-positivismo," *Letras Peninsulares* 4.1 (Spring 1991): 185–206.

Jiménez Moreno, Luis. *Nietzsche, 1844–1900.* Madrid: Ediciones del Orto, 1995.

Jordan, Mark D. "Augustine." *Cambridge Dictionary of Philosophy,* 60.

——. "Eckhart, Johannes." *Cambridge Dictionary of Philosophy,* 252.

Juan de los Àngeles, Fray. *Diálogos de la conquista del espiritual y secreto reino de Dios.* In *Obras místicas del P. Fr. Juan de los Àngeles.* In *Nueva Biblioteca de Autores Españoles,* edited by Fr. Jaime Sala, 20:33–153. Madrid: Casa Editorial Baillo/Bailliére, 1912.

Jurkevich, Gayana. *The Elusive Self: Archetypal Approaches to the Novels of Miguel de Unamuno.* Columbia: University of Missouri Press, 1991.

Kant, Immanuel. *Kritik der praktischen Vernunft.* Edited by Otfried Höffe. Berlin: Akademie Verlag, 2002.

———. *Kritik der Urteilskraft.* Edited by Heiner F. Klemme. Hamburg: Meiner, 2001.

Kerrigan, Anthony, and Martin Nozick. "Notes." In Miguel de Unamuno, *The Tragic Sense of Life in Men and Nations,* translated by Anthony Kerrigan, 377–487. Princeton, NJ: Princeton University Press, 1972.

Kierkegaard, Søren. *Afsluttende uvidenskabelig Efterskrift.* In *Samlede Værker,* vol. 7. Copenhagen: Gyldendal, 1925.

———. *Concluding Unscientific Postscript to Philosophical Fragments.* Vol. 1. Edited and translated by Howard V. Hong and Edna H. Hong. Princeton, NJ: Princeton University Press, 1992.

———. *Entweller/Oder.* Vol. 1. In *Samlede Værker,* vol. 1. Copenhagen: Gyldendal, 1920.

———. *Fear and Trembling and Sickness unto Death.* Edited by Walter Lowrie. 2nd ed. New York: Princeton University Press, 1968.

———. *Søren Kierkegaard's samlede værker.* Edited by A. B. Drachmann, J. L. Heiberg, and H. O. Lange. 2nd edition. 14 vols. Copenhagen: Glydendal, 1920–1931.

———. *Stadier paa Livets Vei.* In *Samlede Værker,* vol. 6. Copenhagen: Gyldendal, 1924.

Kohlenberger, John R., and James A. Swanson. *The Hebrew—English Concordance to the Old Testament.* Grand Rapids, MI: Zondervan, 1998.

Krause, Karl Christian Friedrich. *Ideal de la humanidad para la vida.* Translated by Julián Sanz del Río. Madrid: F. Martinez Garcia, 1871.

"Lamentabili Sane": The Syllabus of Errors (Condemning the Errors of the Modernists). Sacred Congregation of the Holy Office, July 3, 1907. http://www.newadvent.org/docs/df07ls.htm.

Lenz, Maximilian. *Martin Luther.* Berlin: Gaertner, 1897.

León, Fray Luis de. *De los nombres de Cristo.* In *Obras completas castellanas,* edited by Félix García, 1:403–825. Madrid: Biblioteca de Autores Cristianos, 1991.

———. *Names of Christ.* Translated by Manuel Durán and William Kluback. New York: Paulist Press, 1984.

Leopardi, Giacomo. *Canti.* Florence: Felice Le Monnier, 1960.

———. *Poems of Leopardi.* Translated by Geoffrey L. Bickersteth. Cambridge: University Press, 1923.

Lewis, Alan E. "Athanasius." *Cambridge Dictionary of Philosophy,* 59.

———. "Tertullian." *The Cambridge Dictionary of Philosophy,* 908.

Longeway, John. "Boehme, Jakob." *Cambridge Dictionary of Philosophy,* 91.

López-Morillas, Juan. *Racionalismo pragmático: El pensamiento de Francisco Giner de los Ríos.* Madrid: Alianza, 1988.

Machiavelli, Niccolò. *Il principe.* Torino: G. Einaudi, 1972.

Malón de Chaide, Fr. Pedro. *Tratado de la conversión de la gloriosa Magdalena.* In *Biblioteca de Autores Españoles,* 27:275–417. Madrid: Librería y Casa Editorial Hernando, 1926.

Mautinband, James H. "Pindar," *Dictionary of Greek Literature,* 321. Paterson, NJ: Littlefield, Adams, 1963.

Martín Buezas, Fernando. *Teología de Sanz del Río y del krausismo español.* Madrid: Gredos, 1977.

McDermott, John J. "James, William." *Cambridge Dictionary of Philosophy,* 446–48.

Miller, Stephen. "Krausism." *Dictionary of the Literature of the Iberian Peninsula,* 1:901–3.

———. "Menéndez Pidal, Ramón." *Dictionary of Literature of the Iberian Peninsula,* 2:1071–72.

———. "Menéndez y Pelayo, Marcelino." *Dictionary of the Literature of the Iberian Peninsula,* 2:1072–75.

———. "Modernism." *Dictionary of the Literature of the Iberian Peninsula,* 2:1104–7.

Nietzsche, Friedrich. *Der Antichrist: Versuch einer Kritik des Christentums.* In *Werke in zwei Bänden,* 2:211–42. Leipzig: Alfred Kroner Verlag, 1930.

Nozick, Martin. *Miguel de Unamuno.* New York: Twayne, 1971.

Origen. *Origen Against Celsus.* In *The Ante-Nicene Fathers,* edited by Alexander Roberts and James Donaldson, vol. 4. Grand Rapids, MI: Eerdmans, 1978–81.

Orringer, Nelson R. "Harnack y la fe del pueblo español en *El Cristo de Velázquez.*" In *Historia, literatura, pensamiento,* 2: *Estudios en homenaje a María Dolores Gómez Molleda,* edited by M. Samaniego Boneu and V. del Arce López, 223–239. Salamanca: Narcea, 1990.

———. *Hermann Cohen, 1842–1918: Filosofar como fundamentar.* Madrid: Ediciones del Orto, 2000.

———. "El horizonte krausopositivista de *En torno al casticismo.*" In *El joven Unamuno en su época,* edited by Theodor Berchem and Hugo Laitenberger, 31–43. Salamanca: Junta de Castilla y León, 1997.

———. "Ortega y Gasset, José." *Dictionary of the Literature of the Iberian Peninsula,* 2:1192–99.

———. *Ortega y sus fuentes germánicas.* Madrid: Gredos, 1979.

———. "Unamuno and Plato: A Study of Marginalia and Influence." *Revista Canadiense de Estudios Hispánicos* 11 (1987): 331–53.

———. *Unamuno y los protestantes liberales: Sobre las fuentes de Del sentimiento trágico de la vida, 1912.* Madrid: Gredos, 1985.

Ortega y Gasset, José. *España invertebrada.* In *Obras Completas,* 3:49–128. Madrid: Alianza Editorial/Revista de Occidente, 1983.

———. "Fiesta de Aranjuez en honor de Azorín." In *Obras Completas,* 1:261–63.

———. *El tema de nuestro tiempo.* In *Obras Completas,* 3:143–242.

———. "Unamuno y Europa, fábula." In *Obras Completas,* 1:128–32.

———. "Los versos de Antonio Machado." In *Obras Completas,* 1:570–74.

———. *Obras Completas.* 12 vols. Madrid: Alianza Editorial/Revista de Occidente, 1983.

Ortega y Gasset, José, and Miguel de Unamuno. *Epistolario completo Ortega –*

Unamuno. Edited by Laureano Robles. Madrid: Ediciones el Arquero/ Fundación José Ortega y Gasset, 1987.

Otto, Rudolf. *Lo santo*. Translated by Fernando Vela. Madrid: Revista de Occidente, 1925.

Ouimette, Victor. *José Ortega y Gasset*. Boston: Twayne, 1982.

Pascal, Blaise. *Pensées et opuscules*. Edited by Léon Brunschvicg. Paris: Hachette, 1951.

Pfleiderer, Otto. *Die Entstehung des Christentums*. Munich: Lehmann, 1905.

———. *Religionsphilosophie auf geschichtlicher Grundlage*. Berlin: Reimer, 1896.

Pindar. *The Odes of Pindar*. Translated by Sir John Sandys. London: John Heinemann, 1930.

Pippin, Robert B. "Hegel, Georg Wilhelm Friedrich." *Cambridge Dictionary of Philosophy*, 365–70.

Pius X. "Encyclical on the Doctrines of the Modernists." http://www. vatican.va/holy_father/pius_x/encyclicals/documents/hf_p-x_enc_ 19070908_pascendi-dominici-gregis_en.html.

Plato. *Cratylus. Parmenides. Greater Hippias. Lesser Hippias*. Translated by H. N. Fowler. 8th ed. Cambridge, MA: Harvard University Press, 1996.

———. *Euthyphro. Apology. Crito. Phaedo. Phaedrus*. Translated by Harold North Fowler. 18th ed. Cambridge, MA: Harvard University Press, 1995.

———. *Lysis. Symposium. Gorgias*. Translated by W. R. M. Lamb. 10th ed. Cambridge, MA: Harvard University Press, 1991.

Plautus, Titus Maccius. *Casina*. Edited by W. T. MacCary and M. M. Willcock. Cambridge: Cambridge University Press, 1976.

Pojman, Luis B. "Origen." *Cambridge Dictionary of Philosophy*, 636.

Quental, Antero de. "Redención." Translated by Miguel de Unamuno, in his *Obras Completas*, 6:926–27.

———. *Os sonetos completos de Anthero de Quental*. Edited by J. P. Oliveira Martins. Porto: Liv. Portuense de Lopes, 1890.

Quevedo, Francisco de. *Virtud militante: contra las quatro pestes del mundo, invidia, ingratitud, soberbia, avaricia*. Edited by Alfonso Rey. Santiago de Compostela: Universidad de Santiago de Compostela, 1985.

Ritschl, Albrecht. *The Christian Doctrine of Justification and Reconciliation*. Translated by John S. Black. Edited by H. R. Macintosh and A. B. Macaulay. Clifton, NJ: Reference Book Publishers, 1966.

———. *Die christliche Lehre von der Rechtfertigung und Versöhnung*. 3 vols. Bonn: Adolph Marcus, 1870–74.

———. *Geschichte des Pietismus*. 3 vols. Bonn: Marcus, 1880–86.

Rivera de Ventosa, Enrique. *Unamuno y Dios*. Madrid: Encuentro, 1985.

Robertson, Frederick W. *Sermons Preached at Trinity Chapel*. 4 vols. Leipzig: Bernhard Tauchnitz, 1866.

Robinson, Wade. *The Philosophy of Atonement and Other Sermons*. London: Dent, n.d.

Rodríguez, Alonso. *Ejercicio de perfección y virtudes cristianas*. 8th ed. Madrid: Editorial Apostolado de la Prensa, 1954.

Rohde, Erwin. *Psyche: The Cult of Souls and Belief in Immortality among the Ancient Greeks*. Translated by W. B. Hillis. Chicago: Ares, 1987.

Rolph, William Henry. *Biologische Probleme: zugleich als Versuch einer rationelle Ethik*. Leipzig: Wilhelm Engelmann, 1882.

R. S. "Stapfer, Paul." *La Grande Encyclopédie*, vol. *30*, p. 443. Paris: Larousse, 1971–76.

Rousseau, Jean Jacques. *Émile ou l'éducation.* 3 vols. Paris: Didot, 1817.

Sabatier, Louis Auguste. *Esquisse d'une philosophie de la religión d'après la psychologie et l'histoire.* Paris: Fischbacher, 1897.

Sabatier, Paul. *Vie de S. François d'Assise.* Paris: Fischbacher, 1894.

Sánchez Barbudo, Antonio. "El misterio de la personalidad en Unamuno. *Cómo se hace una novela.*" In *Estudios sobre Galdós, Unamuno y Machado*, 175–232. Madrid: Guadarrama, 1968.

Schleiermacher, Friedrich. *Der christliche Glaube nach den Grundsätzen der evangelischen Kirche.* Ed. Martin Redeker. 7th ed. 2 vols. Berlin: Walter de Gruyter, 1960.

Schmidt, Johann Kaspar [Max Stirner, pseud.]. *Der Einzige und sein Eigentum.* Leipzig: Otto Wigand, 1845.

Schopenhauer, Arthur. *Parerga und Paralipomena.* 4th ed. 2 vols. Leipzig: F. A. Brockhaus, 1878.

———. *Über den Willen in der Natur.* In *Sämtliche Werke*, 1–147. Wiesbaden: Eberhard Brockhaus, 1950.

———. *Die Welt als Wille und Vorstellung.* 2 vols. Leipzig: F. A. Brockhaus, 1887.

———. *The World as Will and Representation.* 2 vols. Translated by E. F. J. Payne. New York: Dover, 1969.

Seban, Jean-Loup. "Swedenborgianism." *Cambridge Dictionary of Philosophy*, 893.

Seeberg, Reinhold. "Christliche-protestantische Ethik." In Ernest Troeltsche, Joseph Pohle, Joseph Mausbach, Cornelius Krieg, Wilhelm Herrmann, Reinhold Seeberg, Wilhelm Faber, Heinrich Julius Holtzmann, *Systematische Christliche Religion*, 181–225. Berlin and Leipzig: B. G. Teubner, 1909.

Sénancour, Étienne Jean Baptiste Pierre Ignace Pivert de. *Obermann.* Paris: Charpentier, n.d. [1844?].

Shakespeare, William. *The Works of William Shakespeare.* 4 vols. Edited by Howard Staunton. London: Routledge, Warne, 1864.

Shipley, George. "León, Luis de." *Dictionary of the Literature of the Iberian Peninsula*, 2:930–36.

Silva, José Asunción. *Poesías.* Buenos Aires: Espasa-Calpe, 1948.

Simmel, Georg. *Einleitung in die Moralwissenschaft: Eine Kritik der ethischen Grundbegriff.* 2 vols. Stuttgart-Berlin: Cotta, 1904.

Spencer, Herbert. *First Principles.* New York: Appleton, 1882.

Spinoza, Baruch. *Benedicti de Spinoza opera quae supersunt omnia.* Edited by Karl Hermann Bruder. 3 vols. Leipzig: Tauchnitz, 1843–46.

———. *Ethics.* Translated by W. H. White and A. H. Stirling. In *Great Books of the Western World*, edited by Robert Maynard, 31:355–463. Chicago: Encyclopedia Britannica, 1952.

Stanley, Arthur Penrhyn. *Lectures on the History of the Eastern Church.* London: Dent, 1907.

Stein, Ludwig. *Die soziale Frage im Lichte der Philosophie.* Stuttgart: Enke, 1897.

Stapfer, Paul. *Des Réputations littéraires. Essais de morale et d'histoire.* Paris: Hachette, 1893.

Statius, Publius Papinus. *Thebais*. Tr. J. B. Poynton. 3 vols. Oxford: Shakespeare Head Press, 1971–75.

Strauss, David Friedrich. *Vie de Jésus ou examen critique de son histoire*. Translated by E. Littré. 2 vols. Paris: Ladrange, 1864.

Surber, Jere Paul. "Krause, Karl Christian Friedrich." *Cambridge Dictionary of Philosophy*, 476.

Suso (Seuse), Heinrich. *Schriften*. Edited by H. S. Denifle. Munich: Literarisches Institut v. Dr. M. Zuttler, 1876.

Tennemann, Wilhelm Gottlieb. *Geschichte der Philosophie*. 11 vols. Leipzig: J. A. Barth, 1798–1819.

Tertullian. *Tertulliani adversus Praxean liber*. Edited by Roger Pearse. The *Tertullian Project*. http://www.tertullian.org/

Theologica Deutsch. Edited by Franz Pfeiffer. Gütersloh: Bertelsmann, 1900.

Thomé de Jesús, Fr. *Trabalhos de Jesus*. 3 vols. Lisbon: Lello & Irmão, 1951.

Thoreau, Henry David. *Walden*. Boston: Houghton Mifflin, 1902.

Ueberweg, Friedrich. *Grundriss der Geschichte der Philosophie*. Edited by Max Heinze. Berlin: Mittler, 1905.

Unamuno, Miguel de. *Abel Sánchez. Una historia de pasión*. In *Obras Completas*, 2:685–759. Madrid: Escelicer, 1966.

———. "¡Adentro!" In *Obras Completas*, 1:947–53. Madrid: Escelicer, 1966.

———. *La agonía del cristianismo*. In *Obras Completas*, 7:305–64. Madrid: Escelicer, 1966.

———. "Aldebarán." In *Obras Completas*, 6:545–48. Madrid: Escelicer, 1969.

———. *Americanidad*. Edited by Nelson R. Orringer. Caracas: Biblioteca Ayacucho, 2002.

———. *Amor y pedagogía*. In *Obras Completas*, 2:305–430.

———. "Ciudad y campo: De mis impresiones de Madrid." In *Obras Completas*, 1:1030–42.

———. "Comentarios quevedianos." In *Obras Completas*, 3:1060–64.

———. *Del sentimiento trágico de la vida en los hombres y en los pueblos*. Madrid: Renacimiento, 1912.

———. *Del sentimiento trágico de la vida en los hombres y en los pueblos*. In *Obras Completas*, 7:109–302.

———. *Diario íntimo*. In *Obras Completas*, 8:775–880.

———. *En torno al casticismo*. In *Obras Completas*, 1:775–869.

———. "Examen de conciencia." In *Obras Completas*, 7:416–20.

———. "La fe." In *Obras Completas*, 1:962–70.

———. "La locura del Dr. Montarco." In *Obras Completas*, 1:1127–36.

———. *Niebla (nivola)*. In *Obras Completas*, 2:543–682.

———. *Obras Completas*. 9 vols. Madrid: Escelicer, 1966–71.

———. "¡Pistis y no gnosis!" In *Obras Completas*, 3:681–85.

———. "¡Plenitud de plenitudes y todo plenitud!" In *Obras Completas*, 3:1171–82.

———. "Principales influencias extranjeras en mi obra." In *Obras Completas*, 9:816–18. Madrid: Escelicer, 1971.

———. *The Private World: Selections from the Diario íntimo and Selected Letters, 1890–1936*. Translated by Anthony Kerrigan, Allen Lacy, and Martin Nozick. Princeton, NJ: Princeton University Press, 1984.

———. "¿Qué es verdad?" *La España Moderna*, 18th. Yr., no. 207 (Madrid· March 1, 1906): 5–20. In *Obras Completas*, 3:854–64.

———. *Recuerdos de niñez y de mocedad*. In *Obras Completas*, 8:97–169.

— —. *The Tragic Sense of Life in Men and Nations*. 2nd edition. Translated by Anthony Kerrigan. Princeton, NJ: Princeton University Press, 1977.

———. "Tratado del amor de Dios." Unpublished manuscript. 92 folios + 14 folios of unpublished supplementary passages to be inserted. 1905–8. Casa-Museo Unamuno, Universidad de Salamanca.

———. *Tres novelas ejemplares y un prólogo*. In *Obras Completas*, 2:971–1036.

———. *Vida de Don Quijote y Sancho*. In *Obras Completas*, 3:51–256.

Unamuno, Miguel de, and Francisco Giner de los Ríos. "Epistolario entre Unamuno y Giner de los Ríos." *Revista de Occidente*, 2a. época, 25, no. 73 (April 1969): 11.

Valdés, Mario, and Valdés, María Elena. *An Unamuno Source Book*. Toronto: University of Toronto Press, 1973.

Vermeersch, A. "Modernism." *Catholic Encyclopedia*, vol. 10. http://www. newadvent.org/cathen/10415a.htm.

Vinet, Alexandre-Rodolphe. *Études sur Blaise Pascal*. Paris: Fischbacher, 1904.

Weizsäcker, Carl von. *Das apostolische Zeitalter der christlichen Kirche*. Freiburg: Mohr, 1892.

Wilde, Oscar. *De profundis*. Edited by Robert Ross. 2nd ed. New York: Modern Library, 1929.

Wobbermin, Georg. *Theologie und Metaphysik*. Berlin: Duncker, 1901.

Wordsworth, William. *The Poetical Works of William Wordsworth*. London: Warne, n.d.

Xenophon. *Memorabilia*. Translated by Amy L. Bonnette. Ithaca: Cornell University Press, 1994.

Zubizarreta, Armando F. "Una desconocida 'Filosofía Lógica' de Unamuno." In *Tras las huellas de Unamuno*, 15–32. Madrid: Taurus, 1960.

INDEX

MIGUEL DE UNAMUNO (1846–1936) was one of Spain's most accomplished authors. Novelist, essayist, playwright, and philosopher, Unamuno was the undisputed intellectual leader of the Generation of 1898 that ushered in a second golden age of Spanish culture. His works include *The Tragic Sense of Life in Men and Peoples, Abel Sanchez, Mist,* and *Love and Pedagogy.*

NELSON R. ORRINGER is Professor Emeritus of Spanish and Comparative Literature at the University of Connecticut. Twice a Fulbright scholar, he has authored *Unamuno and the Liberal Protestants, Ortega and His Germanic Sources,* and *Angel Ganivet (1865–1898): Divided Mind,* among other works.